Built to Change

How to Achieve Sustained Organizational Effectiveness

Edward E. Lawler III

Christopher G. Worley

FOREWORD BY JERRY PORRAS

JOSSEY-BASS
A Wiley Imprint
www.josseybass.com

Published by Jossey-Bass
A Wiley Imprint
989 Market Street, San Francisco, CA 94103-1741   www.josseybass.com

Jossey-Bass books and products are available through most bookstores. To contact
Jossey-Bass directly call our Customer Care Department within the U.S. at
800-956-7739, outside the U.S. at 317-572-3986, or fax 317-572-4002.

Jossey-Bass also publishes its books in a variety of electronic formats. Some content
that appears in print may not be available in electronic books.

Library of Congress Cataloging-in-Publication Data

Lawler, Edward E.
  Built to change : how to achieve sustained organizational effectiveness / by
Edward E. Lawler III, Christopher G. Worley ; foreword by Jerry Porras.—1st ed.
     p. cm.
  Includes bibliographical references and index.
  ISBN-13: 978-0-7879-8061-0 (cloth)
  ISBN-10: 0-7879-8061-7 (cloth)
  1. Organizational change. 2. Organizational effectiveness. I. Worley, Christopher
G. II. Title.
  HD58.8.L379 2006
  658.4'06—dc22   2005031021

Printed in the United States of America
FIRST EDITION

HB Printing   10 9 8 7 6 5 4

Contents

Foreword *by Jerry Porras*   v

Preface   xiii

Chapter 1 Why Build Organizations to Change   1

Chapter 2 A Dynamic View of   23
             Organizational Effectiveness

Chapter 3 Strategizing   54

Chapter 4 Structuring for Effectiveness and Change   88

Chapter 5 Developing the Right Information,   118
             Measurement, and Decision-Making
             Processes

Chapter 6 Acquiring the Right Talent   153

Chapter 7 Managing Human Capital   179

Chapter 8 Meeting the Leadership Challenge   213

Chapter 9 Designing Reward Systems   236

Chapter 10 Rewarding Performance and Change   256

Chapter 11 Creating a Built-to-Change Organization   283

Contents

Notes   313

Acknowledgments   319

About the Authors   321

Index   323

Foreword

During the past decade, scandals at Enron, Tyco, WorldCom, and others brought into sharp relief difficulties in governing organizations in a world fraught with unbounded greed and abundant opportunity to satisfy it. Driven by technological innovation, new industries sprouted with few rules or norms to guide the behavior of their leaders. As we face the next decade, organizations will become even more global, with flatter hierarchies, faster information flows, and increased interdependence. New competitors from exploding economies such as China and India will change the economic landscape, causing some U.S. industries to fight for their lives while others face limitless opportunity.

What might organizations do differently to respond more quickly and effectively to this increasingly chaotic environment? What might leaders do differently to build their organizations for change?

I will explore two themes as the basis for dealing with these questions. First, leaders must understand their organization's values, and work to shape them in such a way that those values guide and sustain needed changes rather than undermine them. Second, leaders must architect their organizations to embrace rather than resist change. In *Built to Last,* Jim Collins and I found that the enduringly great (visionary) companies we studied held a small set—between three and five—of values so fundamental and long-lasting that they could be thought of as *core*. These core values helped to guide behavior in the company over the very long term and kept it from engaging in practices detrimental to its essence. As such, core values can play a positive role in change by defining what's "in play" and what's not, that is, change everything in the organization except the core values. Ed Lawler and Chris Worley agree, and use the concept of identity to recognize the importance of stability.

The notion of values is a tricky one, especially when we think about the ways values become imbedded in an organization or, more important, changed. Increasingly, leaders attempt to define new values for their organizations and then go about "selling" them to employees, only to find out that the selling doesn't always work as well as expected. Often, the breakdown occurs when leaders attempt to convince their employees to accept and internalize the new values as core. I don't think anyone can convince adults to adopt a core value not previously held. Core values exist deep in a person's belief system and generally develop as a result of early childhood experiences and learning. Once embraced, changing them just doesn't happen. Here, too, Lawler and Worley agree, and build their changeable organization approach around the idea of stability.

So, what are leaders to do? Well, first and most obvious, leaders must seek to discover those values truly core for the organization. Unfortunately, in my experience, few organizations succeed in this search because the vast majority of them don't have core values. For a value to be core it must pass three tests: it should (1) have existed in the organization since its earliest days; (2) still be around 100 years from now; and (3) have evidence of events in which the organization lived the value and paid some cost or suffered in some meaningful way for doing so. Most organizational values come and go as CEOs change or strategies change, or fall by the wayside when a significant benefit can be gained by ignoring them. Bottom line, all organizations have values, but few have any that meet the *core* standard.

So, if no core values exist for the organization, an alternative for a leader is to identify a set of values that the organization aspires to make core. (Important to note: when communicated, these values must be clearly labeled as aspirational. Failing to refer to them as such risks cynical reactions from organization members who may well possess numerous examples of their leaders not living them.) As aspirational, these values provide a future to strive for, and hopefully, in ten to twenty years, the organization can provide concrete evidence of actually having lived them. People won't follow leaders who espouse core values but don't live them. More likely, they will follow leaders who aspire to live a new set of values they wish to make core and who want to be held accountable when they don't.

Once identified, core or aspirational core values must guide hiring and firing decisions ("If you fit, join us!" "If you don't fit, leave."), reward and promotion decisions, and generally the architecture of the organization. I'll speak more about this point later, but for now, let's turn to a second recommendation on how leaders can use values to enhance the organization's ability to effectively change.

Leaders must understand the difference between core values and all the other values floating around in an organization. Not all organizational values are core or aspirationally core, and those that aren't can be thought of as "strategic," that is, values that the organization adopts to help it successfully implement a specific strategy developed for a specific external environment. Not deeply anchored in the belief system of either the individual or the organization (that is, not core), these values can and should change—should change because, if they don't, they inhibit the implementation of any new strategy. Often strategic values that played a significant role in making execution of the previous strategy successful simply don't fit a new strategy. Helping organizational members see and accept the difference between core and strategic values makes change in the latter easier.

Finally, some values promote change while others inhibit it. Inculcating core values such as customer focus, risk taking, innovation, open communication, collaboration, or participation can help an organization to continually change. Other values such as loyalty, consistency, individuality, profit maximization, or engineering excellence may—especially when taken to their extreme—block or inhibit effective change. The lesson here points to the necessity of being careful about the core values a leader wishes to instill in his or her organization. *Built to Last* taught us that enduringly great companies have a passion for change, and the core values guiding these organizations support their ability to do that.

Earlier I surfaced the idea of organizational architecture. Let me now be more specific about what I mean. Architecting an organization for change means designing its key work-setting components such that they promote change while at the same time are themselves readily changeable. In agreement with the main theme of this book, the *Built to Last* findings showed that for an organization to be enduringly great it must be incredibly skilled at changing itself. And, in these companies, organizational change began with change in their senior leaders.

Since the top leader must change first before change in others can be expected, leaders must develop their ability to change themselves before they attempt to change the organizations they manage. Yet, it has been my experience that most leaders do not possess the skills to change themselves. They focus so much on managing others and getting others to do their bidding that self-awareness tends to fall by the wayside. Increased coaching and exposure to group process skills training will go a long way toward developing this skill.

Leaders also must begin to see themselves as organizational architects instead of rock star, charismatic, visionary types. They must see themselves as builders of their organization rather than as traditional leaders. They must understand the key principles of organizational architecture before they can begin to design work settings that promote change. They must value the role of architect and have as their passion building an enduringly great organization rather than striving to have their picture on the cover of *Fortune* or *Business Week*.

When something is built it must have architecture—architecture guided by a set of principles that provide the basis for design. In the case of organizations, the design principles would need to explain how and why people change their behaviors and the role the work setting plays in precipitating desired change. I'd like to focus on the work setting because I adhere to the body of psychological theory that emphasizes the role of environment in precipitating individual behavior change. In the case of organizations, the relevant environment for individuals is the work setting.

Let's turn then to some examples of work-setting dimensions to consider when thinking about how to design organizations for change.

Audacious goals—bold, exciting, compelling, highly stretching, deadline based—drive change in the organization. When setting truly audacious goals leaders don't know exactly how to achieve them. They have confidence that they will figure out what it will take, but at this point in the process they aren't sure of the exact steps. New capabilities must be developed, new skills evolved—the organization and its people must change.

Highly audacious goals also drive change because employees who must execute on the goals can't achieve them by just working harder, faster, or longer hours. They must, in addition, do new and different things. Without change in the organization and the behavior of its people, this type of goal can't be attained. Our research showed that when organizations set and truly committed themselves to highly audacious goals, they changed their ways of operating and, almost all of the time, successfully achieved them.

Not so surprisingly, organizations that achieve truly audacious goals also perform at a superior level while doing so—witness NASA when it pursued the audacious goal of getting a man on the moon and back by the end of the decade.

Cultural norms that support rather than resist change also play a key role in how well an organization alters its functioning. Charles O'Reilly identifies social control as the most powerful type of control in organizations. Guided by norms, people pressure each other to adhere to them or risk negative reactions from their colleagues. Since norms can either block or encourage change, organizational architects must support norms that promote behaviors facilitative of change.

Evaluation and reward systems that measure and reward needed changes in behavior provide an obvious work-setting dimension to design appropriately. Often organizations talk change but, in fact, don't measure or reward it—then they wonder why people resist so much. Clearly many reasons exist for individual resistance, but the evaluation and reward system—perhaps the most easily accessible change lever—should be pulled first and often.

Another important change lever—control and information systems—presents a significant opportunity for designing change friendly work settings. The more expensive a system design and implementation, the less inclined leaders will be to subsequently change it. Designing systems with an eye toward their future change makes the expense of subsequent alterations much lower and their change more likely.

Job design also plays a key role in the group of work-setting dimensions that either facilitate or block change. Jobs can be rigid or flexible, tightly controlled or autonomous, highly specified or end-results focused, and on and on. Jobs that sit more at one end of these continua than the other facilitate change. Designing changeability into the way work gets done either helps needed future change or blocks it.

Typically, physical settings impede change rather than assist it. Office walls can't be removed or moved easily. Expanding to adequate office space costs more than the company wants to spend. Moving people's offices to match new organizational structures seems too expensive. Yet, all of these physical setting issues impact changes in other organizational dimensions and often make needed behavior change quite difficult. Designing facilities to support existing organizational configurations and work processes—and then to be easily changeable—provides advantages for any organization attempting to change itself.

These are but a few examples of architecting an organization for change. Many more exist, and leaders must continually experiment with different forms to discover the ones that most facilitate change in their own companies. *Built to Change* is about just such an architecture; it describes ways to think about strategizing, creating value, and designing organizations that are changing all the time. Organizations differ, and architectures must also differ to fit specific needs. However, in any case, great companies that endure need to be guided by meaningful, unchanging core values while at the same time be architected to change. This paradox of no change and change helps leaders create superior organizations that last.

Palo Alto, California   *Jerry Porras*
November 2005

Preface

Excellence is about change. We would not have said this in the 1980s or perhaps even in the 1990s. Today it almost goes without saying. Most organizations simply cannot sustain excellent performance unless they are capable of changing.

In the 1980s, the best-known management book was *In Search of Excellence*. It identified a number of companies that were excellent performers. By the late 1980s many of them had ceased to be excellent performers. It was not that they had lost the ability to do what they had done; it was simply that what they had done no longer fit the demands of the business environment.

In the 1990s, the leading book on organizational excellence was *Built to Last*. Contrary to many people's perceptions, *Built to Last* was not about high-performing organizations, although the authors report that their visionary companies outperformed the market. Their purpose was to identify the principles that allow firms to endure.

Foster and Kaplan, in their book *Creative Destruction*, make a strong case that surviving is not the same thing as performing. They note that only 29 of the firms in the original 1917

Forbes 100 list made it to 1987. The survivors earned a long-term return during the period that was 20 percent less than the market. Similarly, they note that of the firms in the 1957 S&P 500—a list that contains both *Built to Last* visionary companies and their paired counterparts—only 74 remained on the list in 1997 and only 12 of them outperformed the S&P 500 index over the same period. Foster and Kaplan's analysis shows that many of the *Built to Last* visionary organizations were never consistently high performers, just really good survivors.

It is interesting to note that over the last decade about half of the *Built to Last* companies have not been able to sustain a high performance level. It is about the same percentage of *In Search of Excellence* companies that struggled in the decade following the publication of Peters and Waterman's best-selling book.

The frequent decline of high-performing organizations makes a sobering point: successful management approaches and business strategies often have an expiration date. As a result, we have not written a book about patterns and principles we found in studying companies that have been highly successful. Nor have we created a list of high-performing companies to emulate. Instead we have written a book about a useful and internally consistent vision of how organizations should be designed so that they can be successful *and* change. Our belief is that by looking forward we have identified what organizations can do to achieve and maintain excellence.

As the rate of change in the business environment continues to increase, the premium on organizations' being able to change is growing ever more significant. Senior managers in particular need to constantly ask themselves whether they are providing the kind of leadership and direction to their corporation that will allow it to change when needed.

For several decades, we have been interested in why organizational change efforts so often fail. Like many others, we have been intrigued by the various change models that have been offered. Most of them suggest that with the right interventions, most, if not all, organizations can make significant changes. We are not at all sure that this is true. If it were, more of the *Built to Last* companies would still be excellent performers. Many of them tried to change and had the resources to change but still fell short.

We believe that some, maybe even most, organization change projects are doomed to failure from the beginning. The type and amount of change that is being attempted is simply beyond the ability of most organizations to adopt successfully. Admittedly, some organizations have made amazing transformations. Nokia, for example, has become a successful global electronics company, even though its roots were in a different technology and a local market. But the reality is that most change efforts in established organizations fail to meet expectations because the internal barriers to change are so strong. We believe that the only way to ensure that organizations will be able to change is to *design* them to change, to create organizations that love to change.

There is a great deal of research today on organization effectiveness and organization design that provides invaluable information about how to build an organization that is ready to change. We also can identify a number of examples of companies that have successfully managed to change time and time again. In many respects this is a book about those organizations, one driven by them and based on their successful change efforts. It is about how Procter & Gamble, Johnson & Johnson, Limited Brands, and Toyota have managed to respond to a changing business environment. The contrast between them and companies that have failed to change is dramatic. GM continues to lose market share; Toyota gains it. Sears has struggled while the Limited has grown. Proctor & Gamble and Johnson & Johnson have both shown that they can nimbly adapt to a notoriously changeable world.

This book is not focused on the kind of transformation that AT&T needed to make, and failed to make, when it was suddenly faced with deregulation. Even if AT&T had been designed to change, it is doubtful that it could have successfully made the transition from a regulated monopoly environment to today's crazily competitive telecommunications world. In short, the company was probably doomed to fail; it was just a matter of time before it did. Enron is a high-profile example of just what can happen when a transformation fails. It was transformed from a regulated public utility to a financial trading organization. In some respects, this was actually a successful transformation, but it ended in disaster because Enron moved too far away from its core identity and lost touch with reality.

Although we are pessimistic about organizational transformations of the kind that AT&T needed to make and the kind that Enron tried to make, we are optimistic that organizations can be built to change. Our optimism is based on the ability of some companies to do this and on research that suggests the right policies, practices, and organization designs can make a company "change ready."

In many respects, the ultimate competitive advantage in today's business environment is the ability to change. *Built to Change* focuses on how organizations can develop this advantage. We have chosen to focus on identifying practices and designs that organizations can adopt in order to be able to change. Through examples, we show how some organizations have successfully used pieces of a built-to-change approach. We have chosen not to identify a set of built-to-change (b2change) organizations—in part because an organization's past success, the usual criterion for identifying excellent companies, is not a sufficient basis for identifying companies that are likely to be successful in the future.

We recognize that it is increasingly difficult for senior executives to think very far into the future because of the tremendous pressure placed on current operating results. Thus, as we look at practices and designs that make an organization ready to change, we also consider whether they contribute to current organizational effectiveness. The optimal practices and designs are those that create high-performance organizations that are ready and able to change. There are enough of these practices available that organizations can—with only a little additional investment in change readiness—be both high performance and built to change.

A word about our title is in order. It plays off the mistaken notion that *Built to Last* was about organizing for stability. Collins and Porras clearly suggest that the study was not about stability but about the principles of survival over long periods resulting in truly iconic companies. Collins suggests, in his Preface to the 2004 edition, that *Built to Last* is the sequel to his 2001 book *Good to Great*. We see *Built to Change* as the sequel to *Built to Last*; it represents what organizations need to do once they have developed the foundation for survival and want to increase their effectiveness over time.

We begin our discussion of b2change organizations by identifying the determinants of organization effectiveness and providing a way to think about these determinants. We then look at the various required elements in the design of a b2change organization. These include the strategy and the ability to change the strategy, as well as the processes, structure, leadership behaviors, human capital, and reward system of the organization. In each case, we focus on practices that both support current high levels of performance and facilitate an organization's ability to change.

We conclude by discussing the challenges involved in creating a b2change organization—a difficult journey and one that not all organizations are likely to be able to measure up to. We believe that those companies that do make the transition will thrive, because they will be able to respond effectively to an uncertain and often unpredictable future.

Los Angeles, California
November 2005

Edward E. Lawler III
Christopher G. Worley

Chapter 1

Why Build Organizations to Change

Built-to-Change Strategy:
Seek Temporary Advantages

All organizations are experiencing a business environment characterized by rapid change. This is not news to most people—their lives have changed because of it. What may be news is just how much the speed of change has increased. An analysis of Fortune 1000 corporations shows that between 1973 and 1983, 35 percent of the companies in the top twenty were new. The number of new companies increases to 45 percent when the comparison is between 1983 and 1993. It increases even further, to 60 percent, when the comparison is between 1993 and 2003. Any bets as to where it will be between 2003 and 2013? An early indicator is that the 2004 list shows a 10 percent change in comparison to the 2003 list.

Wal-Mart is now seen as an unstoppable giant (in 2004, it was once again at the top of the Fortune 1000), but in 1993 it was not even on the top twenty list. Back then, Wal-Mart ranked twenty-sixth—behind Sears! In the ten years from 1993 to 2003, Sears, JCPenney, Kmart, and Montgomery Ward all lost market share to Wal-Mart and to newcomer Costco.

Montgomery Ward ended up in bankruptcy; Kmart and Sears merged to try to compete with Wal-Mart and Costco. In their heyday, Kmart and Sears probably felt safe—and were safe. Retail was a traditional, unattractive industry, and they were well-established incumbents. But feeling safe and being safe are two different things. The growth of Wal-Mart demonstrates how a changing environment can rapidly dethrone existing leaders. Will Wal-Mart still be at the top in 2013? Given the rate of change, it is far from a sure thing, particularly when you consider that in 2005 Wal-Mart's same-store growth in sales slowed for the second consecutive year.

The lesson from the changing of the guard in the Fortune 1000 is clear: change is all around us and is occurring more and more rapidly. It demands the attention of every executive and every organization that wants to survive.

Not surprisingly, the number of books and articles on organization change has skyrocketed. There are books on how to implement Six Sigma programs, organize work teams, create customer-focused organizations, go global, deploy large-scale information systems, manage change, and lead change. For all that is written about organizational change, companies ought to be getting better and better at it, but they aren't.

We believe that a major reason why organizations are not getting better at executing change is that existing theory and practice in organization design explicitly encourage organizations to seek alignment, stability, and equilibrium. Little mention is made of creating changeable organizations.

Organizations are encouraged to institutionalize best practices, freeze them into place, focus on execution, stick to their knitting, increase predictability, and get processes under control. These ideas establish stability as the key to performance. As a result, organizations are built to support enduring values, stable strategies, and bureaucratic structures, not to change.

Change is viewed as a necessary evil. It is costly, undignified, annoying, hard, and, more often than not, ineffective. Organizations must be disrupted, unfrozen, shocked, and changed; a crisis must be created, a case for change articulated and sold. It is no wonder that people resist it and organizations avoid it. This view of change fails to reflect the reality of today's business environment and needs to go the way of black-and-white TVs, 8mm home movie cameras, and Oldsmobiles.

But what about creating organizations that don't resist change, that are built to change? We believe that instead of pursuing strategies, structures, and cultures that are designed to create long-term competitive advantages, companies should seek a string of temporary competitive advantages through an approach to organization design that assumes change is normal. Instead of having to create change efforts, disrupt the status quo, or adapt to change, organizations should be built to change. Further, we believe that many current organization practices and designs actually prevent leaders from successfully implementing necessary changes. Organizations need to be built around practices that encourage change, not hinder it.

WHY ORGANIZATIONS NEED TO CHANGE

The environment in which most organizations operate today is continuously changing, and the rate of change is accelerating. Looking back only ten or fifteen years, one can see tremendous change. There are new countries, such as Slovenia, Namibia, Slovakia, and Kazakhstan. The Deutschmark and French Franc have disappeared. China has joined the WTO and become a leading force in Western economies. A decade ago, American computer programmers hadn't even heard of Bangalore; now it's the place they go to visit their old jobs.

We are experiencing a massive increase in international trade, partly due to the enthusiastic entry of India and China into the global market, but also stimulated by the opening up of Eastern Europe and the economic growth of such countries as Korea, Singapore, Malaysia, Vietnam, Cambodia, and Thailand.

The globalization of business has had two profound effects. First, it has raised the level of competition in most industries. Singapore is making a play to take a leadership role in bio-tech; Korea's Samsung and LG have become respected international brands; Malaysia is a leader in chip manufacturing. These new competitors have advantages that range from geography to high-skill, relatively low-wage workforces. Second, international trade and information technology have opened new markets and challenged firms to deal with global consumers. Overall, international trade has created a world in which the bar that marks "good enough" keeps moving higher and higher.

Perhaps the most dramatic changes in the last decade have been in the area of telecommunications. The Internet, satellite TV, and cell phones have connected most of the world. Perhaps the most striking example of the rapid evolution of technology is the Internet. The number of unique websites grew an average of 53 percent per year between 1998 and 2002 and continues to grow at a rapid rate. In just a few years, the Internet has created a host of new businesses that serve customers in new and different ways. It also has facilitated the movement of work to India, Russia, and a host of other countries.

Human Capital Is Critical

In this new world of global competition and technological change, the era of human and social capital has arrived. There is no single reason why it has finally happened, but it is possible to identify some key changes. Combined, they have made human capital a critical and nearly universally acknowledged element in the effectiveness of organizations and a key source of competitive advantage.

The rapid growth in scientific and technological knowledge is one driver that has contributed to the growing importance of human capital. Second, the information technology boom of the 1990s and the accompanying talent shortage got firms thinking about human capital as never before. Finally, there is a growing recognition that more and more of the market value of firms rests in their human capital.

Knowledge Is Central

The centrality of knowledge to organizational effectiveness has changed the very essence of organizations, what they do, and how they do it. Because of the growth in knowledge and the ways it is used by organizations, the nature of individual work has changed. Increasingly, work in developed countries is knowledge work in which people manage information, deal in abstract concepts, and are valued for their ability to think, analyze, and problem-solve. Fewer and fewer people are doing the mind-numbing, repetitive manual tasks that used to dominate the work scene. It is being done by machines or transferred to low-wage economies.

Organization Makes a Difference

There is growing evidence that the way corporations are organized can in fact provide a competitive advantage. Research focusing on the performance impact of total quality management programs, knowledge management, employee involvement programs, and various organization designs and structures has shown that getting management and organization right can, in fact, produce superior financial returns for organizations.[1]

Similarly, research on the impact of companies' human capital management practices, such as their training programs, efforts to create a desirable place to work, and reward systems, has found that there are practices that produce superior financial results.[2] Other research suggests that one of the factors that increasingly determines the market value of corporations is the quality of their management talent. When surveyed, stock analysts and investors say that it is a very important intangible feature of a company's assets.

Investors appear to be very aware that a shift in the source of competitive advantage has occurred. A growing body of research shows quite clearly that the stock price of an organization less and less reflects its book value. In other words, investors no longer primarily price a stock based on its tangible assets: cash in hand, equipment, and buildings. Tangible assets accounted for 62 percent of the typical New York Stock Exchange company's value in 1982, whereas in 2000 it had decreased to 15 percent of the company's market value.[3]

Of course, an organization's human capital and management systems are not the only intangibles that make a difference. The company's brands and intellectual property are among its other key assets, although even these cannot be completely separated from its human capital, and certainly not from its management practices. Knowledge is not only generated by individuals but also carried in their minds; it therefore walks out the door every day and may or may not return the next. The return of employees, like their performance, depends on how they are organized and managed.

Perhaps less related to human capital is a company's brand or brands, but they too are definitely related to its organization and people. One slip-up by an employee can quickly destroy the reputation of a major brand in such areas as health care, food, and transportation. A clear example is Krispy Kreme donuts, which seriously tarnished its formerly enviable reputation by stuffing the distribution channel (sending more donuts to stores than could be sold) to meet short-term revenue targets.

When competitive advantage rests in a company's people and its ability to organize its human capital, the situation is dramatically different than when organizations compete on the basis of tangible assets. Organizations are now competing based on their ability to organize. Thus innovations in management and organizational change need to be much more frequent and effective, and survival much more a function of possessing the ability to change. When the development of new approaches to organizing is combined with the rapid changes taking place in the environment and the new competitors that have appeared on the global scene, it is clear that performance levels that were good enough a few years ago are almost never good enough today.

Types of Change

Many of the changes that occurred in the last decade were unpredictable, or at least unpredicted. The rise of the Euro as a potential alternative to the U.S. dollar as a global reserve currency, for example, although discussed at times, certainly was not predicted. The implication of the unpredictable nature of change for organizations is clear: although in many cases they may not be able to anticipate change, they *can* always be fast adapters.

The world of human resources (HR) consulting provides an interesting case of change and product obsolescence. Younger HR managers cannot believe the time and energy that went into job evaluation in the 1970s and 1980s. The major benefactor of this passion for job evaluation was Hay Management Consultants.

In the 1960s, Hay's CEO, Milton Rock, took the pioneering work of Ed Hay and turned it into a finely tuned consulting process. Rock opened Hay offices around the world. Hay raked in the cash. But as the 1980s wound down, the environment started to change.

Big, stable bureaucracies were ripped apart by downsizing. Constant reorganization meant that this week's job evaluation might be obsolete next week. Managers were suddenly saying,

"I don't want to spend two hours in a committee deciding what grade a job is in!" Hay needed to change to survive—it almost didn't. What saved Hay was the acquisition of the McBer consulting firm and the launching of a new area of consulting: competency modeling. The rise of a new consulting practice upset power relationships within Hay, changed the type of consulting Hay did, and required a different image for the firm. Hay was hardly a poster child for smooth transition to a new product area, but it got it done. Hay managed to survive an environmental change that took away a big part of its core business; many firms do not, and this is understandable.

In uncertain and rapidly changing environments, organizations are challenged to accomplish two often conflicting objectives: performing well against a current set of environmental demands and changing themselves to face future business environments. To meet these objectives, organizations must manage at least two types of change: the natural process of evolution, or what we will call strategic adjustments, and strategic reorientations. In some cases they also have to manage a third type of change, transformational change.

Strategic adjustments involve the day-to-day tactical changes required to bring in new customers, make incremental improvements in products and services, and comply with regulatory requirements. This type of change helps fine-tune current strategies and structures to achieve short-term results. It should be incremental, constant, and natural; it should not be an option or a nice thing to do. Like the continuous improvement capability that many organizations focused on in the 1980s, this basic capability to evolve is essential if an organization is to survive.

The second kind of change, strategic reorientation, involves altering an existing strategy and, in some cases, adopting a new strategy. When the environment evolves or changes sufficiently, an organization must significantly adjust some elements of its strategy and the way it executes that strategy. It needs to develop new competencies and capabilities. In the Hay example, the Milton Rock years were a time of strategic reorientation. For example, introducing Hay's existing products and services to foreign markets required hiring new staff, opening new offices, creating new policies regarding worldwide pricing, and developing mechanisms to deliver consistent services in different countries. Hay's shift away from job evaluation toward competency consulting is an example of a strategic reorientation.

More and more often, organizations have to face a transformational change. It involves not just a new strategy but a transformation of the business model that leads to new products, services, and customers, and requires new competencies and capabilities. It is often stimulated by the appearance of what Clayton Christensen calls a disruptive technology.[4] Enron's conversion from a regulated pipeline company to a multibusiness energy financial trader is an extreme example of this type of change. A possible example of this kind of change is under way at BP. Recognizing the finite limits of oil and gas supplies, BP has committed itself to a "green strategy" built on a fundamentally different economic logic, one that will rely more on revenue from solar, fuel cells, and other sources of energy that are currently viewed as "alternative."

Transformational change is something very special. Successful cases of it occur relatively infrequently. Unlike strategic reorientations, during which the strategy can remain relatively stable but the organization's design undergoes substantial revision, transformational change is associated with fundamental shifts in the organization's strategy, organization design, and processes. Unisys is now known as a supplier of IT services, but some readers will recall that it was once a major mainframe manufacturer. This dramatic shift from manufacturing to services is an example of successfully mastering transformational change.

Unfortunately, the execution of transformational change is particularly likely to be inadequate, too late, or poorly managed. To us this is not surprising, considering that despite all the talk about change, organizations are in fact designed for stability. But even if an organization is not designed for stability, it may not be able to execute a strategic transformation quickly enough to be successful. All too often a new organization that doesn't have to change wins out because it gets the new business model right first. Fortunately for existing organizations, the need for transformational change is relatively rare.

ORGANIZATIONS ARE BUILT TO BE STABLE

Most of the writing and consulting done on change management offer suggestions and remedial actions that an organization can take when it is not designed to change. Unfortunately, remedial actions are often desperate efforts to enable an organization to do something that is very much counter to what it is designed to do—change! As a result, most efforts at designing and managing organization change are dismal failures. Scarce resources are wasted, organizational cultures destroyed, and lives disrupted for little or no gain.

Human Nature Is Not the Problem

A major barrier to change is how individuals react to it. There is a great deal of writing on the reactions of individuals to change that emphasizes their resistance to it. Many discussions of change picture this resistance as irrational and perhaps a part of "human nature." We don't think this is true. We know of no evidence that there is a resistance-to-change gene!

It is true that when people have been successful at doing something over and over, and have been rewarded for doing it, they may take a great deal of pride and comfort in doing it. Change is particularly difficult in these situations not because people are inherently resistant—after all, they learned to perform this way in the first place—but because they have not been told to expect change, don't see any advantages to change, continue to be rewarded for doing what they have always done in the past, and are understandably confused by the suggestion that doing what they were trained to do is no longer valued. Further, change often requires learning and developing new skills, forming new relationships, and disrupting one's personal life. Although learning and establishing new relationships can be rewarding, it also can be hard work, uncomfortable, and stressful.

When email was new, many executives would have their assistants print out incoming emails, then write out their replies by hand, which the assistant would then email out. The IT folks tore their hair out! They despaired at this "irrational resistance to change." They said things that we sincerely hope the executives never heard. Yet to the executives, resistance to email was rational. Why take time away from running the business to learn about electronic communication when paper communication had always worked just fine?

The bottom line is that organizational change is difficult because management systems are designed, and people are rewarded, for stability. For people to change, there needs to be a reason for them to change. There may be a few people who irrationally resist change, but given a strong case for change, and appropriate rewards and support, people will change the way they work and the way they operate. We will talk specifically about how to handle rewards in Chapters Nine and Ten.

Traditional Design Is a Problem

In many respects, traditional organizations are built to resist change. Their numerous rules, regulations, and provisions limit experimentation, program in traditional behaviors, and reward consistent performance. They have many checks and balances in place to ensure that the organization operates in the prescribed manner.

Teleworking wasn't widely adopted until long after it was technically possible, simply because organizational rules required people to be physically at their desks. An innovative manager favoring telework had to go up against the bureaucracy in allowing an employee to work at home.

There is good reason why organizations are built to operate in a stable, predictable manner. Behaving this way is often critical to an organization's ability to perform well in the short term. It is perfectly consistent with the objective of achieving success under current business conditions, but it is inconsistent with achieving continuing success when change is needed.

The traditional approach to change management assumes resistance and reinforces stability. It identifies three phases: unfreezing, moving, and refreezing.[5] Unfreezing involves creating dissatisfaction with the current state so that an organization will abandon its traditional ways of operating. The whole notion of unfreezing implies that an organization exists in some form of equilibrium that needs to be disrupted. Once the status quo is considered obsolete or ineffective, the organization is expected to go through a period of change, during which a new set of behaviors and systems is implemented. Refreezing involves institutionalizing the change and returning to a period of stability. As is true of unfreezing, refreezing implies that the organization should seek stability following a period of change.

As a general rule, the more radical or disruptive the changes that an organization tries to implement, the more likely that it will be unable to successfully change. Indeed, the more radical the change, the more likely that new organizations, often start-ups, will ultimately emerge as the winners. There is clearly not just a first-mover advantage when disruptive changes are involved; there is a *new organization* advantage.

Not surprisingly, many major innovations, such as copiers and low-cost air transportation, were developed by start-up companies. Xerox developed and commercialized the copier; Southwest created the low-cost air carrier market. In essence, the new entrant's advantage comes from not having to unlearn old habits and creatively destroy old ways of doing things. It is often easier to start with a blank sheet of paper and to create "from scratch" an organization designed to perform in the way that will best serve the new market.[6]

Even when organizations develop a new technology that leads to a new business, they are often unable to exploit it. The computer industry provides many examples of existing organizations that have ended up as nonplayers even though they pioneered much of the technology. For example, Bell Labs developed transistors, but its parent, AT&T, never became a major player in either semiconductor manufacturing or in the many other products that it has led to.

Xerox developed an early PC and much of the user-friendly software that currently dominates the industry, but it failed to build a computer business. Why? Despite the fact that Xerox had a clear technological lead and a first-mover advantage, it simply was unable to develop the kind of focus and internal organizational capabilities needed to be successful in this new business. In contrast, over the years numerous start-up companies have been able to develop the ability to make quick decisions and stay on the technological edge. Today the PC market is dominated by Dell and Hewlett-Packard, neither of which was in the PC business when it was created.

Consulting work we did with Honeywell years ago helped us understand why existing organizations have problems in businesses that require new kinds of organization designs. Honeywell was an early mover in the computing business. It developed its own product line and also bought General Electric's computer business. There was one glaring difference between the successful start-up firms and Honeywell: the start-ups were more nimble in their decision making. Why was this?

Basically, Honeywell's decision processes were designed to support its major businesses (thermostats, airplane guidance systems) at that time. Most of these businesses were relatively slow moving and did not require high-speed decision making and agile behavior. In contrast, the computer business was changing almost daily and needed to be able to respond quickly to competitors' moves, technology developments, and environmental changes. The required speed of decision making simply did not fit with Honeywell's kind of internal decision processes or with the elaborate justifications that were required for capital investment and product development.

Leadership Is Not the Answer

The implicit, and at times explicit, message of many management and leadership books is that if an organization can find the right leaders, it can successfully change in response to almost any challenge.[7] According to them, the "right" leader is someone who can establish a vision compelling enough to motivate change. The right leader also has the personal drive to get things implemented by challenging the status quo as unacceptable.

The importance of leadership is conveyed by the case studies MBA students are given that feature the leadership behavior of senior executives, and by the popular business press, which profiles leaders who have "successfully changed their organizations despite overwhelming difficulties." One indirect measure of the star status of senior executives is the number of *Business Week* covers featuring CEOs from the Fortune 1000. It went from almost zero in 1981 to twenty in 2000.

The reality is that most heroic leaders fail in their attempts to change organizations. Study after study has shown that most would-be saviors are unsuccessful in producing significant organization change.[8] This is true whether the leaders are from the outside or from the inside. Regardless of their leaders' skills and best efforts, many organizations are so change resistant that it is virtually impossible for a heroic leader or leaders to effect significant change.

Organization Design Is the Issue

Models of strategy and organization design that encourage companies to maintain and fine-tune the status quo work well when organizations face stable environments. For example, making big investments in developing job descriptions makes sense if (but only if) the jobs will not change for many years. When advantage derives from geographical location, financial capital, or legislation, the important thing for an organization is to use these assets effectively, and often this is possible only with stable processes. However, when organizations face uncertain environments, organization designs that capitalize on only these sources of competitive advantage are often not sustainable.

The automobile industry provides a clear example of the changing nature of competitive advantage. Japanese manufacturers have consistently gained market share in the U.S. market, despite the fact that they face a significant location disadvantage and well-established competitors.

Initially, the Japanese manufacturers gained market share by charging lower prices, but that did not prove to be a sustainable competitive advantage, so they began to focus on quality. Until recently, they had a clear-cut quality lead over their American competitors.

Beginning in the early 2000s, U.S. auto manufacturers began to equal Japanese quality; as a result, quality has ceased to be a significant competitive advantage. Consumers now take quality for granted. As a result, the competition has shifted to intangibles, such as design, customer experience, service, and image. There is also growing evidence that customers want a car company to exhibit a sense of social responsibility by producing energy-efficient, low-pollution cars. Perhaps the best way to summarize this is that customers want to make a purchase that not only provides reliable, high-quality transportation but also makes a statement.

The Japanese manufacturers once again have adjusted their strategies. They now lead in service, design, and social responsibility. Once again, the U.S. manufacturers appear to be behind. Some have been able to make creative cars like the Humvee, which makes a statement, but how many people want to make a Humvee-type statement?

Indian call centers appear to be repeating the automotive change experience. They are winning business from U.S. competitors despite being many thousands of miles from their clients and living in a different time zone. One leading outsourcer commented, "We were attracted by cost but stayed because of the superior quality of the Indian call centers"—a replay of the Japanese auto story.

The main lesson from the past thirty years is that as industries, technologies, and environments change, so too do the definitions of advantage. Organizational change, whether planned or by accident, is essential for continued success. Simply stated, the law of competition is that an organization must change or become extinct.

Creating a stable organization to perform in a complex and rapidly changing environment is following a recipe for failure. The primary drivers of organizational effectiveness are fluid and dynamic; so too must be the primary elements and processes of strategy and organization.

We can no longer think of structure as a static concept, we can no longer view strategy as a "thing," and we can no longer accept that people are resistant to change. We need to embrace the view that the ability to change is an organization's best sustainable source of competitive advantage. It is the only way an organization can capitalize on new sources of competitive advantage as they emerge or are anticipated. Organizations must have the ability to quickly reconfigure their work processes, technical knowledge, and human capital in ways that provide new sources of temporary competitive advantage—over and over again.

Simply stated, the challenge for organizations is to perform so well and change so fast that they string together a series of temporary competitive advantages. This is easy to say but very difficult to do. It is hard enough to organize effectively when you can spend years perfecting your organization's strategy and design. It is extremely difficult to do it in a situation where your organization has to adapt to a rapidly changing environment.

It is precisely because it is so difficult to create effective change-friendly organizations in today's business environment that being one provides a competitive advantage. If it were easy to do, the process could quickly be copied, just as most of the traditional sources of competitive advantage can be.

Companies need to devise new ways of organizing that support change, not just pour old wine in new bottles or encourage managers to execute better. These new ways of organizing must be built on different assumptions. We believe that the central assumption should be that organizations always need to be changing and must be able to perform well while changing. Thus, in today's business environment, organizations have to be built to change, not merely changed as a result of a special change program or effort. Change, not stability, must become the coin of the realm.

The *Built to Change* Logic

Strategic management research and practice have struggled with whether organizations designed for flexibility can outperform those designed for stability. We believe that today the rate of environmental change and the economic opportunities provided by change are sufficient to justify adopting a built-to-change (b2change) approach regardless of answer. Even if the operating costs of a b2change organization are slightly higher (and we aren't sure that they necessarily are), they will be more than offset by the organization's ability to capture profits from change and the temporary advantages it creates.

The central thesis of this book, then, is to challenge the "stability equals effectiveness" assumption and propose a model of organization in which change is expected and normal. It is not the same as being good at change management. In change management, the assumption is that organizations, structures, and systems exist in a current state that must be changed and shaped into a future state. In change management, people must be coaxed and motivated, the old way modified, and the new way institutionalized. According to the b2change logic, organizations are always changing, in sometimes fast and sometimes slow ways.

The key issue for the b2change organization is orchestration, or keeping the multiple systems that are changing coordinated to produce high levels of current performance. With the right organizational policies and practices in place, strategic adjustment and reorientation do not require special programs and initiatives; rather, they should and can be natural processes of adaptation to a changing environment. Transformational change is a different matter. It may require special programs even in a b2change organization. It is difficult to execute, even with a lot of design features that support it.

CONCLUSION

Creating a b2change organization calls for a special mind-set with respect to its structure and process. Instead of striving to produce a fine Swiss watch with all the movements aligned so that it consistently produces the same behavior, an organization needs to be designed in ways that stimulate change. This means creating an organization that encourages experimentation, learns about new practices and technologies, monitors the environment, assesses performance, and is committed to continuously improving performance. The organization's strategies, structures, reward system, communication processes, and HR management practices must be designed to change and to encourage the organization to continuously and rapidly change.

Maintaining a changeable organization is not a matter of searching for *the* strategy but continuously strategizing, not a matter of specifying *an* organization design but committing to a process of organizing. It is a search for a series of temporary designs that create short-term advantages. In turbulent environments, organizations that string together a series of temporary but adequate advantages will outperform organizations that stick with one advantage for a long period of time.

Organizations that are built to change must view people as open and willing to learn and as eager to try new things. They must have structures that are constantly refocusing attention and resources on both current and future problems and opportunities. They must have reward systems that encourage learning and growth as well as current value-added activities. Finally, they must have financial processes and other systems that support innovation and the start-up of new products and services.

The challenge, and it is a big one, is to create organizations that have elements and processes that lead to current high performance and that lead to change. What kind of elements and processes can be counted on to do this? That, of course, is the $64,000 question.

For us to answer the question, we need to look first at the key characteristics of an effective organization and then look at specific organizational practices. Creating the right kind of organization is not simply a matter of designing one part, such as the reward system, effectively. It requires an integrated approach that considers all of the parts together and is targeted at producing an organization that is ready, willing, and able to change.

Chapter 2

A Dynamic View of Organizational Effectiveness

Built-to-Change Strategy:
Sustained Effectiveness Requires Continuous Change

Al Egan was born in Sioux City, Iowa, in the early 1940s and was raised as a typical middle-class midwesterner. He went to Morningside Junior College, served in the Marines, and did a tour of duty in the Korean conflict. After he completed his military service, good fortune came his way as he met and married the daughter of an entrepreneur. His new father-in-law founded a company that processed, packaged, and distributed peanut butter and snack foods. Al joined the company and steadily rose through the ranks. Eventually he became VP of operations, responsible for purchasing, manufacturing, and logistics. He was known in the vernacular of the time as a "people person" who was able to work with employees, keep the manufacturing lines operating efficiently, and acquire commodities at good prices. He lived his midwestern values by being a devoted employee who worked for the good of the company.

By the time he was forty, Al and his wife had four children and a five-bedroom house on a golf course. But Al's life was about to hit a wall. His marriage soured, divorce ensued, and Al found himself on the outside of the family business in need of a job. This was a tough time for Al, but trading on his industry knowledge, his reputation for devotedness, and the positive working relationships he had developed, Al found a senior position in a southern California company that processed nuts and chocolates. This allowed him to expand his expertise—he could smell a block of chocolate and tell you where it was made. He thrived for almost ten years in this job. But when his company was acquired by a large multinational, the new parent summarily replaced the top management team with its own people. Al was on the street again.

At fifty years of age, Al was depressed. Although he believed he had many years of productive work left in him, there were few companies that needed his particular mix of skills.

After six months of reflection—he called it hell—Al tapped his unused GI Bill funds to go back to school. He studied accounting, but more important, he got hooked on computers and learned to use CAD-CAM software. Developing a new competency was a breakthrough. Through a temporary agency, Al found a job with an aerospace firm and turned that job into a permanent position. However, Al's career adventures were not

quite over. His organization merged with another defense con-
tractor, and he was laid off. Fortunately, this time it was only a
minor blip. He was quickly rehired because of his performance
and good relationship with management. His rehiring at age
sixty-three allowed him to qualify for retirement benefits.

Al retired at sixty-seven. The transitions in his life did not
leave him with a particularly healthy retirement account, but
he is able to live a good life. He still feels restless about not
doing anything "productive," but enjoys his grandchildren and
spends time at Dodger games, the theater, and concerts.

ORGANIZATIONS ARE LIKE CAREERS

Organizations that are built to change are a lot like today's
careers—both need to be guided by a "dynamic view" of effectiveness. Firms need to not only focus on how well they are
doing today, but also to be especially concerned with how well
they can respond to the changing environment. Depending on
when you look at Al's career, you would say that he was wildly,
moderately, or barely successful. But only by knowing Al's history would you have any real sense of why his effectiveness was
high or low. Similarly, the media's glib attempts to blame current leaders for poor corporate performance (or laud them for
outstanding effectiveness) are misleading. The truth is much
more complicated, as any careful study of organizational effectiveness will reveal.

The story of Nabisco in France is a great example of how
change and time must be accounted for in assessments of an
organization's performance. Increases in before-tax income
between 1970 and 1973 were followed by losses in 1974 as

investments for future growth were made. The losses were unacceptable to the parent firm, and the leader of the organization was replaced by a financially oriented executive.

The new CEO squeezed costs and led a reengineering initiative. Between 1975 and 1982, income before taxes grew at a healthy rate, and the new CEO was applauded. But almost everyone inside the organization agreed that the most important reason for the improved performance was the investment that had taken place during 1973 and 1974.

The financial restructurings of the new CEO mortgaged the future by reducing new product development and throttling innovation. Not surprisingly, performance began to decline, and the once very "successful" CEO was moved out. He had failed to build an organization that fit the changing business environment.

The Built-to-Change Model

To explain the complexities of organization effectiveness over time, we have created the Built-to-Change Model. The model, depicted in Figure 2.1, consists of *Environmental Scenarios* and three primary organizational processes—*Strategizing, Creating Value*, and *Designing*—spinning around the organization's *Identity*.

Environmental Scenarios describe a range of possible future business conditions. Most models of strategy and organization only address the "current environment," but that is not enough when the environment is changing. Looking only at the current environment leads to building a static organization matched to the present but not to possible futures. The

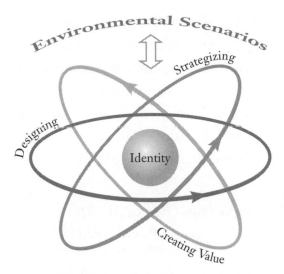

FIGURE 2.1.   The B2Change Model

B2Change Model explicitly addresses ongoing environmental changes and argues that they should be the key *determinants* of strategy, organization design, and effectiveness.

Strategizing, Creating Value, and Designing are the primary *contributors* to organization effectiveness. These organizational processes are how an organization figures out its response to the demands of a changing environment. For example, the strategizing process includes crafting a strategic intent that describes, among other things, the breadth of the firm's product lines, how the firm differentiates itself, and the way profit is generated.

At the center of the model is Identity. It consists of an organization's relatively stable set of core values, behaviors, and beliefs.

The Built-to-Change Model shows the key elements that influence organizational effectiveness in motion. Strategizing, Creating Value, and Designing are each viewed as dynamic processes changing in response to or in anticipation of environmental change. The next four sections of this chapter provide an overview of the four elements of the model. Subsequent chapters will describe them in more detail.

Environmental Scenarios Drive Strategizing and Effectiveness

Al's career spanned several different environments—from nut and candy companies to educational environments to aerospace—and each environment afforded different opportunities. As a VP he had much more upside financial potential than as a CAD/CAM operator. Like a career, an organization's performance is determined in a major way by the current and future environments it operates in.

An organization's external environment includes general business conditions and industry structures. Unfortunately, most traditional strategy analysis techniques are driven by assumptions about congruence and alignment that are the enemy of change. The often-used strengths, weaknesses, opportunities, and threats (SWOT) analysis, for example, encourages the firm to leverage opportunities while avoiding weaknesses and threats. This alignment among positive and negative forces is implicitly assumed to remain constant, and there is no built-in assumption of change.

B2change organizations take a very different view of the environment. First, b2change organizations look at both the current environment and the potential environments that might emerge in the future. Anticipating what the environment will be like is critical to effective change, but knowing what it will be is not possible. However, broad trends and demands can be used to generate a range of scenarios that capture some of the most likely future environments an organization will face. Electronic Arts, the game company, does just this. It spends a lot of time and resources understanding how technologies, user interests, and social trends will play out over the next three to five years and then creates scenarios that allow it to see future demands and opportunities.

Second, b2change organizations recognize that their future performance depends on how effectively they respond to the environment. The calculus of how to operate today and how to operate in the future is an obsession in b2change firms and a clear focus for the strategizing process. Ideally, what the organization offers over time will correspond to what the environment demands. We label this dynamic relationship *proximity* and hypothesize that organizational performance over time is a function of the extent to which an organization's design and the demands of the environment are in proximity.

Since anticipating the exact nature of the environment is difficult, designing a b2change organization to respond quickly to unexpected environments is an important part of the designing process that will be discussed below. That said, a b2change organization spends as much time thinking about what the environment will be as it does thinking about its strategy and design.

Imagine being a provider of mobile Internet services—a business of treacherous, complex, and uncertain proportions.

How should you make decisions on strategy when you are faced with declining bandwidth costs to mobile customers; converging PDA, cell phone, and notebook computer technologies; increasingly sophisticated virus programs; improved voice-based interfaces; global markets developing at different rates; and new competitors entering from a variety of industries? A b2change organization addresses these kinds of factors by generating a variety of possible scenarios.

For example, one could visualize a "Fragmented Hardware" future where the mobility market remains largely uncoordinated. Phone companies, cell phone and PDA manufacturers, and even watch companies compete to be at the center of mobile access. Competing technology standards and price wars between regional providers keep users confused and force them to choose between devices that connect to their personal, corporate, and Internet-based data only through proprietary and slow layers of communication. Customers, confused beyond tolerance, tend to buy one hard-sell approach and minimize their switching to save time. Cell phones and handheld sales stagnate in developed markets, and different technologies barely interoperate.

Another potential scenario could be the "Services Future" where the average individual business user spends $100 per month on mobility services, and the devices themselves are automatically updated by the service provider. PDAs, cell phones, and laptops are interchangeable for most business operations. Directory services that allow you to keep your phone number and email address when you change hardware proliferate. "Home" phones disappear, upgraded to wireless at no cost to the user. Phone and cable companies lose out to more nimble wireless providers.

Finally, a third scenario might be described as "Large Provider–Dominated," where several security software providers team up with a large service provider like IBM or Oracle to provide end-to-end spam- and virus-free connectivity. "Lightweight" email, instant messaging, and data access prove compelling to users who have become fed up with spam voice mail, email, and faxes as well as constant viruses and hoaxes. Original equipment manufacturers (OEMs) partner with a preferred proprietary solution, and it becomes the must-buy add-on for connectivity. Increasing mobile usage and the preference for simple and effective renders the high-end features and integration of the more sophisticated software developers less and less valuable, thereby decreasing upgrades.

Strategizing for a b2change mobile provider would involve crafting a robust strategic intent by looking at the implications of the Fragmented Hardware, Services Future, and Large Provider–Dominated scenarios. This is very different from a SWOT analysis, which is fixated on the current environment.

The mobility business might, for example, choose between focusing on corporate customers or going for the "lowest common denominator." A focus on corporate customers would allow the firm to gain large contracts and experience while avoiding the vagaries of individual customers. Going for the lowest common denominator would allow the firm to develop a reputation for quality first and then move up the value chain as the technology converges. In both cases, the strategic intent doesn't presume a particular future, but it can lead to a successful path through any of the three environmental scenarios. Viewing environments as consisting of unfolding demands and using scenarios to anticipate them can help organizations identify their best strategic options.

In the 1990s, a number of companies believed there was going to be worldwide explosive growth in the market for fiber-optic and broadband communication technology. They were not wrong, but their miscalculations about the timing of the explosion and how the technology would develop nearly wiped out the industry.

Corning, for one, changed its technical core from its wide variety of traditional glass products to fiber optics. Nortel and Lucent projected dramatic growth in the sales of Internet communications equipment. When the expected growth did not materialize, the performance of these companies suffered tremendously. In a very short period of time, they went from market leaders to financial wrecks.

Other examples of environmental change abound, making the point clear: an organization has little choice but to anticipate its future environments and position itself to succeed in those environments. Organizations must deal with uncertainty by making reasoned guesses about the future—and, where possible, hedging their bets by being able to change when the environment changes.

If Nortel and Lucent had been b2change organizations, they would have viewed a range of industry scenarios—including scenarios favorable and unfavorable to them as well as scenarios projecting both slower and faster demand growth. In response, they would have crafted strategic intents that were robust in addressing the alternatives and that identified early warning signals that certain scenarios were more likely to play out than others. The early warning signals would have been used to slow the pace of the organization's transition from older to newer technologies and services and to maintain a tighter proximity with the rate of environmental change.

IDENTITY IS CENTRAL TO GOOD STRATEGIZING

Al's career was anchored by who he was, just as organizations are anchored by who they are. Even though Al couldn't predict the future, his midwestern values guided how he added value in his work. Al was a people person—he got hooked on Dale Carnegie courses—and he believed that success would result from the way he worked with others. Ultimately, it didn't matter whether he was making peanut butter, candy, or aircraft drawings—it was always about people and the importance of loyalty. He never wavered from his identity. It guided him into new situations. Even in the case of the wrenching move from candy to CAD-CAM, he learned new skills but maintained his identity. Organizations, like people, rarely change their identities.

An organization's identity is an overarching and relatively enduring statement of how it will achieve its long-term mission. Identity contributes to effectiveness by specifying the organization's dominant approach to doing business. Costco's fundamental identity is that of being a low-cost provider; Budweiser sees itself as the "king of beers"; Southwest is about low cost, freedom, and customer service; and Exxon is an energy company run by engineers.

Identity derives from the organization's culture—what employees think they should do and what they think they will be rewarded for. It also derives from images of the organization held by competitors and customers. When employees know that their organization's identity is understood and protected, they feel free to innovate, experiment, and push the boundaries of what is possible.

Strategizing is not just about describing a robust intent for a variety of environmental scenarios. It is also about picking an environmental path that allows the organization to remain true to its identity.

Microsoft's enduring identity is one of persistence. The organization often produces imperfect products that are not the first to market. Over time, however, Microsoft works on improving a product's performance until it yields a winning solution.

The importance of Microsoft's identity to its performance was amply demonstrated during the Department of Justice's (DOJ's) antitrust proceedings. Despite the real threat to the organization's identity, Microsoft never abandoned who it was. During that period, Bill Gates and Steve Ballmer said to employees, "You do what you do best. Don't worry about DOJ; that's our problem." Microsoft stayed focused on the real issue of being persistent. During that period, the company's .Net strategy was born, its mobility strategy was taking shape, MSN continued to grow, and the Xbox was being developed.

The importance of identity to performance should not be underestimated. When an organization tries to be something that betrays its identity, successful execution of an intended strategy can be thwarted by turnover, sabotage, incompetence, and reduced productivity and quality.

Many organizations have failed to perform effectively because their strategic intentions did not fit their identity. This was clearly the case when Exxon decided to go into the office equipment business in the 1970s. As one of the original "seven sisters" in the oil and gas business, Exxon (previously Standard Oil of New Jersey) grew up thinking of itself as an exploration and refining organization. Although the logic of diversifying may have been sound, entry into a different industry with completely different technologies and business models was too far beyond Exxon's view of itself, and the effort failed. Enron's transformation from being a gas pipeline company to being a financial trading company ended with even more disastrous results.

STRATEGIZING IS A PIVOTAL CONVERSATION

Strategizing is about describing how an organization's products will remain proximate with an unfolding environmental path. It is a bit like a football quarterback throwing a pass. He must throw the ball to a particular point on the field with the hope that the receiver will be there when the ball comes down. There is a certain amount of faith involved—that the receiver will run the right route and won't trip, and that the defense won't get in the way. The closer the ball is thrown to where the receiver ends up, the greater the chance of a successful catch.

Strategizing is the process an organization uses to decide which products, services, and markets to focus on and how to compete. It results in a *strategic intent* that guides choices about how an organization creates value and designs itself.

Research shows that an organization's current performance depends on the extent to which the intended strategy is proximate with the demands of the environment.[1] Being in a particular business determines performance to some extent. American, United, Delta, Southwest, and Jet Blue are all in the airline transportation business. As a group, their performance over time will more likely mirror each other's than it will the performance of companies in the consumer products industry. But their relative performance reflects the degree to which their strategy is proximate to the environment and how well they execute it.

To be effective, an organization's strategy must address current and future environmental demands. Strategies must also reflect an understanding of the organization's identity. When an organization's strategic intent describes a path that is proximate to both its environment and its identity, the organization achieves *critical configuration*.

We chose the term *critical configuration* to convey the importance of specifying the relationships among environment, identity, and intent. It is critical because it represents, without question, the most important responsibility of a firm's senior management. It is a critical configuration because it represents the set of relationships that most determines performance.

Coors achieved critical configuration in the 1980s when it chose to invest in developing aluminum cans to replace steel cans (steel tainted the beer's taste). That intention honored its identity as a maker of beer of unsurpassed quality and recognized the opportunity to grab margins in that segment of the value chain. If Coors had decided to begin working with an inferior but cheaper type of can, that decision would have collided with the organization's identity. Similarly, if at fifty Al had said, "I've had it with people; I'm just going to put my head down and crank out technical drawings," he may have been responsive to the environment but would have been out of alignment with his identity and would not have been as effective in shifting careers.

Strategizing involves disciplined and continuous conversations about the organization's long-term identity and strategic intent. It achieves its status as the pivotal process in the B2Change Model because it represents a dynamic response to an unfolding and mostly unknowable future. Strategizing is the primary context for making decisions about how the organization will create value and organize in the future.

When it comes to strategizing, b2change organizations need to be different from traditional firms in important ways. In traditional firms, strategic reviews are at best an annual phenomenon, and the conversation is dominated by tones of "Is there any reason to change?" B2change firms are nervous. They agree with Andy Grove that "only the paranoid survive." They continuously examine their strategy and recognize that some things rarely change (for example, identity) and that other things may need to change relatively frequently (for example, intent, structure, and systems). They strategize continually to test whether their identity and intent are still appropriate for current and potential future environments.

B2change firms make a large investment in conversations and reflection, particularly among the senior management. The conversation is focused around the question "What's the next thing that needs changing?" This is an explicit trade-off of some short-term efficiency for greater future effectiveness, a trade-off that makes increasing sense in a rapidly changing world.

CREATING VALUE THROUGH COMPETENCIES AND CAPABILITIES

The specification of strategic intent is important, but it is only part of the strategy story—implementation is the other part. No matter how brilliant a strategy is, its ultimate impact is determined by how well it is implemented. Many more strategies fail because of poor implementation than because they are conceptually flawed.

A strategic intent is just that—a description of a desired set of activities. It describes what the organization *should* do. To do it, an organization must identify and develop its competencies and capabilities.

Competencies

What exactly are organizational competencies? In their influential 1990 *Harvard Business Review* article, Gary Hamel and C. K. Prahalad defined core competencies as a combination of technology and production skills that underlie the product lines and services of an organization.[2] Often parts or all of an organization's competencies can be protected by patents and licensing agreements.

Sony's core competency lies in the miniaturization of technology. It allows the company to make the Walkman, video cameras, notebook computers, and a host of other products. Similarly, Honda's ability to design gasoline engines is critical to the company's success in selling motorcycles, generators, lawn mowers, outboard motors, trucks, and automobiles. 3M's core competency in chemical processes and materials has helped the company develop a wide range of products, from ordinary tape to exotic bonding materials for the aerospace industry.

Capabilities

If competencies are about technologies and knowledge, then what are capabilities? Capabilities are the clearly identifiable and measurable value-adding activities that describe what the organization can do.[3] Usually they cannot be patented but often are hard to copy. Capabilities include the ability to create quality products, operate on a global basis, be a low-cost producer, manage knowledge, develop new products, respond quickly to the business environment, speed products to market, serve customers—and do many other things that have the potential to provide an organization with a competitive advantage.

Organizational success today frequently requires not just a single world-class organizational capability but a combination of several. It may take two or three that are exceptional and a number of others that are at least at a world-class level.

Consider 3M, which for decades has been a prime example of a company with an innovation capability. Much of the company's success and growth over the years has had to do with their organizational capability to create, develop, and market new products, such as Scotch tape, Post-it notes, and thousands of others. The reason for 3M's innovation capability goes far beyond the company's technical competencies in the chemical properties of materials. It results from a variety of company-wide systems, practices, and structures that support innovation. One very specific behavior that 3M has fostered is experimentation. The company has developed a number of policies and practices that give employees time to experiment, and its reward system recognizes innovative work.

An important point about capabilities is that they require ongoing attention and maintenance. Motorola, for one, learned this the hard way. During the late 1990s, the company decreased its focus on its Six Sigma quality program and as a result fell behind the competition in several of its key businesses, including cell phones and semiconductors.

Ford Motor Company also mismanaged its quality capability. Starting in the 1970s, it invested heavily in building a quality capability and enjoyed some success. Do you remember "Quality Is Job One"? When Ford acquired Jaguar, it successfully transferred its quality knowledge to Jaguar, with impressive gains. Jaguar's quality improved so much that during the 1980s and early 1990s it went from being just ahead of the Yugo, considered the world's lowest-quality car, to being one of the top cars in the world in manufacturing quality.

However, while Ford was successfully transferring its quality capability to its newly acquired Jaguar subsidiary, it lost much of its quality capability in its U.S. manufacturing operations. What happened in the United States? Essentially, Ford took its eye off the ball. Like Motorola, it failed to maintain a focus on its quality capability, and as a result, quality deteriorated in its U.S. manufacturing and design facilities.

The most important capability a b2change organization can have is a change capability. And it's the one capability that most organizations lack today. Forward-looking organizations are building and investing in their capability to manage change, but most are not. The incredible growth of the change management practices of many consulting firms is ample evidence that many organizations want but do not have this capability. Moreover, it suggests that most organizations would rather buy the capability to change than invest in it. In our opinion, this is a short-sighted, misguided, and expensive approach, given that change will be even more important in the future.

Competitive Advantage

A competency or capability is valuable to the degree that it produces revenue, reduces costs, or contributes to the real or perceived benefit of a product or service. Competencies and capabilities can be a source of competitive advantage when they are valuable, rare, difficult or costly to imitate, and leveraged. A competency or capability that is valuable but not rare is a commodity.

Some common capabilities are important because they are needed, but they do not produce a competitive advantage. For example, most organizations need to and are able to comply with safety, compensation, and other regulatory requirements. The few that cannot are at a significant disadvantage.

Traditional approaches to strategy seek a single sustainable competitive advantage. The b2change approach seeks a series of temporary advantages. It identifies those advantages through an ongoing investment in strategizing. It capitalizes on opportunities by continually building the appropriate capabilities and competencies. There is never the sense that "once we get this capability into place we will have a sustainable advantage and can relax." Instead there is a constant focus on harvesting the new opportunities that arise.

Because they are embedded in a complex matrix of practices and systems, capabilities are harder to develop, duplicate, and copy than are most competencies. Most people who visit 3M to study how it maintains such an outstanding record of innovation have the same reaction: what 3M does cannot be duplicated in most other companies. They correctly recognize that 3M's organizational capability to innovate does not rest in a single set of skills or a limited set of practices that other organizations can easily copy.

Similarly, a Six Sigma quality capability is not easily developed because it involves a number of organization design features, including the employee selection process, training programs, corporate vision statement, and senior management's behavior. It is not based on any one system or practice; rather it permeates the organization. A capability is more difficult and costly to imitate when it is based on multiple systems and practices that mutually reinforce one another.

Once Motorola recognized the value of its Six Sigma capability, the company began selling it. It offered training programs through Motorola University and sold written materials. It found a number of buyers, including General Electric (GE), which ended up developing a successful Six Sigma capability of its own. Not surprisingly, a number of the buyers were unable to develop a quality capability that led to a competitive advantage.

One of the important points to remember about organizational capabilities is that they do not exist in only one group or function, in the heads of a few technology gurus, or in a small set of functions or patents. In reality, they reside in the many systems and relationships that exist in an organization. They lie in a synergistic combination of individuals and systems that forms the organization's way of operating.

Competencies are different; as characteristics of the organization's technical core they can reside in particular functions, groups, or even individuals. For example, in the late 1980s, the military avionics division of Honeywell received almost 100 percent of the contracts related to human-technical interfaces in helicopters because of the skills and knowledge of one engineer who was the acknowledged leader in the field.

How long an organization can derive a competitive advantage from its core competencies depends on where these competencies are and how easy they are to copy. In general, competencies are easier and less costly to imitate than capabilities. For example, many organizations can duplicate core competencies that are contained in the minds and skills of a small number of employees. These core competencies walk out the door every night, and when they are not treated right, they might not come back.

One of the most dramatic examples of how competencies can spread is Fairchild Electronics, which in the 1970s pioneered the development and production of semiconductors. Fairchild had a high level of technological competency, but a well-deserved bad reputation when it came to the way it managed and treated employees. This made it difficult for Fairchild to maintain its technological advantage. Rather quickly, the pioneering development work it did on semiconductors was lost. When they left, employees simply took with them the knowledge that was part of Fairchild's core competency in semiconductors and used it to start competing businesses that were better managed. The new companies—Intel, AMD, and others—are now among the most successful semiconductor firms in the world today. Fairchild is out of business.

Finally, to result in a competitive advantage and make a durable contribution to performance, competencies and capabilities must be leveraged by the organization. Amazon's "single store" strategy transformed the organization from an Internet retailer to a platform for commerce. Its long-term agreement with Toys "R" Us, for example, allows Amazon to leverage its competencies and capabilities in customer experience, customer filtering, order fulfillment, transaction processing, and customer assistance.

In sum, competencies and capabilities have several similarities but also some important differences. Both competencies and capabilities are dynamic and can change, sometimes rapidly. They both add value, can be sources of competitive advantage, and can be very complex routines of behavior, skill, and knowledge. At the same time, they are different: competencies are more like assets in that they can reside in people and can be acquired quickly if they are not legally protected, whereas capabilities are truly an organizational characteristic. Competencies are based in science, technology, and engineering, whereas capabilities are based in processes, routines, behavior, and systems. Finally, competencies are related to the technical core of an organization, whereas capabilities can be related to any part of the organization's operations.

Designing Integrates the Organization

The third process in the Built-to-Change Model involves designing the structures and processes that enable an organization to perform effectively. It and creating value are the two processes that contribute to effectiveness by determining how and how well a strategy is implemented. To deliver on the promise of its identity and intent and create the right competencies and capabilities, an organization must be designed correctly. It must design and implement supporting structures, attract and retain key human capital, develop and deploy appropriate information systems, develop effective leaders, and craft motivating reward systems. Designing is a dynamic process of modifying and constantly adjusting an organization's structure, systems, people, and rewards so that they provide the called-for performance.

Dynamic alignment exists when all of the pieces in the designing and creating value process are evolving in the same direction and in support of the strategic intent. Dynamic alignment is created when the strategic intent drives the nature and quality of an organization's competencies, capabilities, and design.

Both Dell and Gateway have the same strategic intent: to be affordable PC manufacturers. In both cases there is good alignment with their respective environments and identities. In other words, they both have done a good job of identifying who they are and the requirements of success. However, Dell has done a better job of designing itself, and as a result it has consistently performed better than Gateway.

Designing is the nitty-gritty work of creating a b2change organization, and we look at it in detail in Chapters Four through Ten. There we focus on how to structure organizations, develop measurement systems, manage talent, develop leadership, and build reward systems.

CONFIGURATION AND ALIGNMENT DRIVE PERFORMANCE

Earlier, we suggested that effective organizational performance over time involves two primary and time-based relationships: the one among the environment, a company's identity, and its intent, which we called the critical configuration, and the one among identity, intent, capabilities, competencies, and design, which we called dynamic alignment.

Virtuous Performance Spirals

There are times in an organization's life, decades long in the most extreme cases, when what the organization does and how it does it remain in close proximity with environmental demands. This is the Holy Grail of organization performance—when both critical configuration and dynamic alignment exist for long periods of time. It results in what is called a virtuous spiral, because "everything comes together."[4]

Structure and capabilities that support a good strategic intent generate revenue that boosts the rewards for employees, and increases their motivation and commitment. The more challenging and rewarding work environment that results creates innovative ideas and further reinforces the organization's ability to attract, retain, and develop effective employees, who further positively affect performance. Thus a virtuous spiral forms and expands, matching the expanding environmental potential, and carrying the organization and its members to greater levels of performance. Virtuous spirals thus represent a potentially powerful competitive advantage that is valuable, rare, and hard-to-duplicate.

Nike represents a good example of critical configuration and dynamic alignment that has created a virtuous spiral. Phil Knight's idea to source the manufacturing of athletic wear from low-cost Asian manufacturing sites was a brilliant idea at a time when fitness and health were increasingly important parts of the social environment. This manufacturing strategy allowed the organization to develop a set of competencies and capabilities that created value for its manufacturers, sales and distribution channels, employees, and customers. The company fostered a "just do it" identity that was reflected in its structure, the people it hired, the lack of formal systems, and the way it rewarded people for contributing to the organization. It became one of the most successful organizations of the 1980s and 1990s.

Microsoft's virtuous spiral began with a strong critical configuration. Bill Gates's licensing of MS-DOS to IBM and the subsequent growth of the PC industry created an enormous economic opportunity. But that critical configuration alone is not enough to explain Microsoft's continued success. The company has also enjoyed a virtuous spiral relationship with its people for decades. Since the early 1980s, Microsoft has had an internal environment in which its employees have done well and the company has done well. The employees have had challenging work and, of course, one of the most highly rewarding stock plans around. Microsoft is routinely ranked as one of the best places to work, especially for high performers, and has thereby attracted some of the country's top software engineers and marketing geniuses.

Because of its relationship with its human capital, Microsoft has been able to generate a powerful dynamic alignment in which success begets success, which in turn begets more success. The company's seemingly unstoppable growth began to slow down only in the late 1990s, when it faced a rapidly changing competitive environment along with government challenges to its growing power. But even in the market downturn of the early years of the new century, Microsoft largely continued on a virtuous spiral of increasing growth and success.

Procter & Gamble (P&G) is a great example of an organization that has a strong dynamic alignment. Though the company is over one hundred years old, the past forty years of its existence have been marked by many forward-thinking efforts to establish a virtuous spiral relationship with its employees based on employee involvement and the development of leaders throughout the company. P&G was an early adopter of employee involvement practices in its manufacturing plants. It also has a stock ownership plan that has placed over 30 percent of its stock in the hands of its employees.

Another organization that has clearly enjoyed a virtuous spiral of success for decades is GE. Even before Jack Welch became CEO in the early 1980s, GE established an environment where highly talented individuals wanted to work because of the opportunities the company offered for career development and financial rewards. Able to attract and retain highly talented individuals, GE has enjoyed decades of enviable growth in profits and as a result has attracted highly talented individuals. GE is a clear example of successful performance leading to successful recruitment and motivation of individuals, which in turn produces even more successful performance.

Environmental Change Shatters
Configurations and Alignments

Environmental change is the single biggest threat to virtuous spirals and sustained effectiveness. Because it is largely out of the control of most organizations, environmental change often threatens what once was an excellent response to the demands of the environment. It can render obsolete the competencies and capabilities that created value, and can disrupt dynamic alignment by altering what people need to do and how they should work together. It is precisely because change is such a threat that virtuous spiral organizations need to be sure they can change when they need to.

IBM is illustrative of an organization that has been able to respond to environmental change. It started as a timecard company, but environmental changes (technology) ruined that business. It was able to transform itself into a computer manufacturing company. As a computer company, IBM developed a long-term virtuous spiral relationship with its employees, but its business model began to fail in the 1980s when major environmental changes again occurred. IBM reacted to the decreased profitability of its computer hardware products by breaking the loyalty-based employment relationship it had established over many decades. The company ordered extensive layoffs and broke commitments to employees in the areas of retirement and careers. In some important respects, it changed parts of its identity but still maintained others.

Only in the late 1990s, when IBM established a credible new strategic intent that emphasized services and consulting, was it able to improve its performance and reestablish a virtuous spiral. For the past few years it has done an impressive job of creating a virtuous spiral that relies on an employment relationship based more on skills and performance than on loyalty, a relationship that fits its strategic intent.

There is no hard-and-fast rule concerning how often companies need to make major changes in their strategy. It depends on the type and pace of change in the environment. Some virtuous spiral companies have never needed to alter their strategy. Southwest Airlines has essentially executed the same strategy for over thirty years. That strategy has continued to be a successful one and enabled Southwest to sustain a virtuous spiral relationship with its employees without making major changes in its organization design. Can Southwest continue forever without changing? Probably not! Eventually it will have to change its strategy because of the appearance of new competitors, regulatory changes, or some other environmental change.

Other virtuous spiral organizations have successfully made strategy changes by reinventing themselves in ways that improved their competencies and added new capabilities. A great example is Dayton Hudson Corporation. It recognized that traditional department stores were not necessarily the best place to be in the retail market. They followed up on this conclusion by creating Target, which today is among the most successful retail businesses in the world. Indeed, Target may end up as the only major competitor for Wal-Mart. It has been so successful that Dayton Hudson has adopted Target as its corporate name.

Changing its strategy in the retail business required Dayton Hudson to become more focused on costs and the way it managed its inventory and purchasing. However, the company stayed true to an important aspect of its identity: its approach to corporate governance and human capital management. It had and still has a very strong emphasis on building a virtuous spiral relationship with its employees. As a result, the organization has been honored both for its excellence in corporate governance and for its human capital management practices.

Intel is another virtuous spiral company that was forced by environmental change to make a major strategic shift. Once very successful in the DRAM chip business, Intel realized in 1985 that it needed to exit that business because it could not win against its Asian competitors on the basis of cost. It switched to microprocessors, and the rest is history. As we all know from its memorable marketing campaigns, Intel has now become the major supplier of microprocessors to PC manufacturers. It is one of the few Silicon Valley start-ups from the 1960s and 1970s that is still thriving.

Unfortunately, most organizations are unable to make one, much less two, major transformations in their business models. They typically enter a fast or slow death spiral and eventually go out of business. Major change is extremely difficult because it often requires the development of new core competencies and organizational capabilities, and changes in structures and systems that were built for stability. Indeed, economists have come to refer to corporate failures caused by dramatic changes in the political, economic, or technological environment as *creative destruction*. The term was first coined by the late economist Joseph Schumpter and has since been widely adopted.

Death spirals can be avoided and reversed. Creative destruction is not inevitable. Organizations can be successfully changed. It is not easy, but it can be done if the design of the organization is one that facilitates change.

Dynamic Model

The b2change approach reflects a philosophy of building an organization that is able to maintain critical configuration and dynamic alignment even in the midst of environmental change. Figure 2.2 presents a dynamic virtuous spiral model of what needs to happen for an organization to maintain configuration and alignment. It shows that maintaining an upward spiral of higher and higher performance requires cycles of strategizing, creating value, and designing. To maintain configurations over time, organizations need to be created "change ready." They need to be able to change elements of their strategy, competencies, capabilities, and design whenever the environment calls for it.

The IBM and Microsoft examples are important because they clearly show that environmental change is the single biggest threat to virtuous spirals. It can disrupt any configuration or alignment of identity, intent, capability, and design in very short order. Organizations that rigidly stick to a strategy, capability, or design are bound to fail; it is only a matter of time.

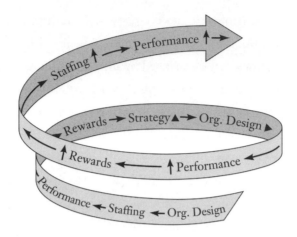

FIGURE 2.2.   **Dynamic Virtuous Spiral**

Conclusion

Most traditional bureaucratic organizations are unable to reinvent themselves in timely ways when faced with major technological, political, or economic change. They are built on the logic that stability is more profitable than change. The b2change approach reflects a different philosophy. It suggests that an organization can be built to dynamically match its strategizing, creating value, and designing processes to the rhythm and substance of environmental change.

To change rapidly and maintain critical configuration and dynamic alignment, organizations need to be designed to change and be capable of high-velocity change. They need to be able to change elements of their strategy, competencies and capabilities, and organization design when the environment calls for it.

In the chapters that follow, we will describe the building blocks of virtuous spirals—the key features and principles of strategizing, creating value, and designing. We describe how each process can be built to change and can be configured and aligned with the others over time. We will show how, by using the right processes and designs, it is possible to build an organization that both performs effectively and changes when needed. We begin with the process used to create and change an organization's strategic intent.

Chapter 3

Strategizing

Built-to-Change Strategy:
Craft a Series of Temporary Advantages

You may have seen the exercise in which a speaker stands in front of a group with a large glass jar that is filled with three or four big rocks. The speaker asks the audience, "Is the jar full?" The answer, of course, is yes. The speaker then adds a cup of smaller rocks that tumble down and fill in the spaces between the big rocks, and repeats the question. A little wiser, the audience usually offers a range of opinions. The cycle is repeated with small pebbles, then sand, then water. Each time the audience is more and more wary about saying yes to the question, "Is the jar full?" The "big rocks" exercise is a great metaphor for thinking about strategy and strategizing in a b2change organization.

STRATEGY IN B2CHANGE ORGANIZATIONS

Strategy is composed of *identity* and *intent*. The big rocks in the jar represent the organization's identity, and the pebbles, sand, and water represent the organization's strategic intent. Identity—the organization's relatively enduring purpose, culture, core values, image, and perspective—is a central concept in the b2change approach. It is an important foundation of future performance. Because the people at Southwest Airlines know that its identity is connected to costs, freedom, and customer service, we can predict what the company will focus on in the future in order to win customers. It is similar to how a person's personality is a good predictor of how he or she will fare in life, come what may.

Strategic intent is a constellation of organizational choices about breadth, aggressiveness, differentiation, orchestration, and logic. For example, in Southwest's case, the choices are about the number of cities flown to and who to serve (breadth), how quickly to expand and how to deal with competitors (aggressiveness), the characteristics of the flying experience that might give people reasons for choosing Southwest over other airlines (differentiators), how to generate revenues and profits (economic logic), and how to coordinate all these moves and strategic choices (orchestration).

The most important feature of strategic intent in a b2change organization is robustness—the ability to succeed under a range of possible environmental scenarios. A robust intent should be relatively stable but much more changeable than identity. The elements of intent may need to be reconfigured relatively quickly in a b2change organization.

We must acknowledge here that good strategy functions under a bit of dynamic tension. On the one hand, a b2change organization needs to make strategic choices that will work out under any of the most likely scenarios it foresees. This implies that intent will not change frequently or radically. On the other hand, the individual elements of intent may need to change and therefore must be relatively easy to change. This approach is more prudent than betting on one scenario and counting on being able to alter intent if that prediction proves inaccurate.

It is possible to change elements of an intent without changing the essence of the intent. For example, just because Nike alters its policies concerning foreign manufacturing plants in response to public pressures about sweatshop conditions doesn't mean that the company's basic intent has changed.

Figure 3.1 illustrates how the key components of strategy relate to environmental scenarios and to the creating value process (competencies and capabilities). At the top of the model, *Environmental Scenarios* provide the context for formulating strategy. *Identity* bridges scenarios and the five elements of strategic intent. These are the relationships within critical configuration that must be specified. Like environmental scenarios, identity guides the specification of strategic intent shown in the middle of the model. Ultimately, intentions guide the process of *Creating Value*, which sits at the bottom of our model.

Although every organization is concerned about its external environment, b2change firms are much more concerned about possible *future* environments. Scenarios provide important contextual information for determining and formulating strategic intent. The relationship goes the other way as well, however, as indicated by the double-headed arrows in Figure

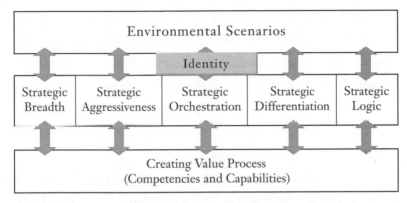

FIGURE 3.1.   The Role of Strategy in the B2Change Model

3.1. Although environmental scenarios of the future guide strategic intent, the cumulative actions of organizations can affect the nature and scope of future scenarios.

The deregulation of the airline industry in 1984 lowered the cost and increased the ease of entry and shifted the industry's requirements for success. Legacy airlines, such as American and Delta, responded to these environmental changes by adjusting their planes, routes, information systems, and other elements of strategic intent. They created hubs and developed Web-based information systems. Entrepreneurial firms, such as People Express and Southwest Airlines, brought new and different strategies to the industry. Over time, the actions of the legacy and entrepreneurial airlines have shifted the environment, and it has become more and more difficult for the legacy airlines to make a profit.

A firm's competencies and capabilities (bottom row of the model) also have a reciprocal relationship with strategic intent. On the one hand, the choice of a strategy should depend greatly on the capabilities available. Southwest's low-cost performance is made possible by its ability to turn planes around quickly. United tried to develop its own low-cost airline (remember the Shuttle and its younger sibling, Ted?) but has never been able to develop the needed capabilities. In retrospect, United shouldn't have tried this strategy because it did not have an identity conducive to efficiency or an organization that was able to develop the needed capabilities.

On the other hand, an evolving strategy often creates the need to develop capabilities and competencies. For example, when AOL broadened its intent from a simple Internet service provider to a media company, it had to acquire the ability to develop and distribute content.

IDENTITY

As we mentioned earlier, identity comprises the big rocks in the jar and creates the spaces for pebbles, sand, and water—the company's strategic intent. Although an organization's identity can usually be described in relatively simple terms, its development is almost always complex and difficult to explain. It is the result of a series of decisions, events, crises, wins, losses, and change efforts that occurred in the past, and is thus unlikely to change quickly or easily. Nevertheless, understanding identity is a key to successful organizational change.

Clarifying Identity

In a traditional firm, culture is seen as a constraint to change and an enemy of strategic adjustments. Executives lament that their true problem is not technology or customer demands but rather an intractable "culture" that thwarts their ability to implement new strategies. In b2change firms, culture is a part of identity and promoted to the status of strategy.

Rather than being a barrier to change, identity needs to be the foundation of performance and the ability to change. This idea may be a bit counterintuitive to some—and downright contradictory to others—but it is critical to our thinking, so we'll say it again in a different way. We think of an organization's identity as something very stable. It is an important source of effectiveness and is potentially a primary reason why a b2change organization can reorient itself easily.

A stable organization identity makes it easier for employees to embrace changes in strategic intent, capabilities, and organization design in the same way that a stable family makes it easier for family members to take on a foreign assignment. It gives them something they can count on while the world around them changes.

Identity is reflected in an organization's culture—a set of values and beliefs about how to view the world, solve problems, and succeed—and image—how the outside world views the firm.[1] A simple way to think about identity is to ask how an organization prioritizes and addresses the often conflicting demands of the environment and its key stakeholders. The answers communicate its identity.

Investors' preferences for higher dividends can conflict with customers' demands for new products, employees' demands for higher wages, and the community's demands for corporate social responsibility. How a company resolves these conflicts is the key part of its identity. If a company's strategy doesn't at least provide neutral to positive results for all of these groups or if employees cannot find ways to produce goods and services in the face of these conflicts, the organization is not likely to survive.

When strategies and value-adding processes work well, they are taught to others and become embedded in the informal, unconscious assumptions of the organization. Ultimately these ways of viewing the world influence the identity of the organization. The following are examples of possible identities that answer the question, "What kind of a company are we?":[2]

- A product- or service-driven company
- A customer- or market-driven company
- A production- or technology-driven company
- A sales- and marketing-driven company
- A results-driven company
- An employee-driven company
- A sustainability company
- A company that welcomes change and innovation

Bancroft-Whitney (BW), a former subsidiary of Lawyers Cooperative Publishing and now part of Thomson Publishing, provides an interesting case study of how simple and complex the identity conversation can be. In support of a strategic change effort to address mediocre performance, the senior management team at BW met to understand the values and assumptions that might help or hinder that effort. The discussion of "What is our identity?" or "What really drives our organization?" created a heated debate.

One camp argued that because the parent company set sales and profit targets for BW, they were really a results-driven company. Managers acknowledged that the annual budgeting process was all-consuming; everything else in the organization came to a dead halt during these months as numbers were crunched, objectives set, and budgets prepared.

Another camp argued that the whole organization was built around a production orientation. They reasoned that given the large amount of editorial capability embedded in the organization, BW's whole reason for being was to produce something—anything—and that the sales force would get it sold. This group asked, "If we could produce *product x* really well even if we didn't know whether anyone would buy it, would we produce it?" They suggested that the answer was almost always yes.

A third camp believed that the company was market and customer driven. Their mission statement clearly served the legal market, and all of BW's products were oriented toward helping lawyers understand the substantive and pertinent legal issues of a case.

Finally, a fourth group proposed that BW was a sales- and marketing-driven company. It had the largest direct sales force in the industry and was known for its aggressive yet high-touch sales efforts.

BW management realized that one of the root causes for the company's average performance over the past few years was that all of the arguments were true. BW had "multiple personalities" and never really made choices about or understood its core identity. This lack of clarity resulted in confusion about how to respond to the emergence of new technologies that challenged the organization.

This realization led to BW's developing a clearer identity. Doing so helped the company establish a more coherent internal communications message, make decisions about how to respond to a strong competitor, and prioritize resources across a set of functional demands.

Identity and Change

All b2change organizations need to have identities that focus on the external environment and regard strategic adjustment as "normal." A focus on the external environment is critical to identifying what needs to be changed and how. Establishing what can change and that change is normal is an important part of establishing credibility and realistic employee expectations when change occurs.

Just as some features need to be identified as changeable (for example, needed skills), a b2change organization requires a staunch commitment to some things that will not change. That may sound inconsistent with an approach to management that assumes change is normal, but it isn't. It is a major mistake for an organization to announce change efforts that consistently call for transformational change, radical departures, or fundamental shifts in its strategy.

An organization that boasts of making discontinuous changes in its strategy can create too much uncertainty for organization members and threaten an important source of performance. It is too easy for employees to perceive such announcements as a threat to their future with the company. This problem is a lot like what can happen in psychotherapy. When there is a threat to an individual's basic identity, that individual can become quite anxious as he works to understand who he is, what he believes, and how he will behave.

Understanding its identity allows an organization to anticipate and respond to environmental change in effective ways without being whipsawed by it. When an organization understands its true nature, managers can more easily identify adjustments to strategic intent that organization members will understand and support. For example, an organization that prides itself on legendary customer service is in a good position to identify strategic adjustments that enhance its service and to say no to a strategic adjustment that would cut costs but decrease good service.

When organization members know that announced or intended changes honor the firm's identity, they find it easier to support and commit to new structures and new processes or to building new capabilities. This is particularly true when an organization's identity includes responding to change in the external world. Thus, the best b2change organizations have strong identities that incorporate commitment to both stability and change.

STRATEGIC INTENT

Just as the big rocks create the spaces to be filled up by pebbles, sand, and water, identity provides an important context for strategic intent. Whenever someone asks, "What is the organization's strategy?" they are really asking about intent. That is, how does the organization intend to accomplish its objectives?

The Five Elements of Strategic Intent

Strategic intent is the organization's picture, vision, or bet on how it will develop temporary competitive advantages. It is comprised of the five elements shown in Figure 3.1: the breadth of an organization's activities; the aggressiveness of its operations; the way it orchestrates change; the differentiated features of its products and services; and the logic for making profits.[3] We will discuss breadth, aggressiveness, differentiation, and logic first, and save the important discussion of orchestration for the end.

Breadth. The *breadth* of a company's strategy describes the choices it makes with respect to the range of products or services offered, the different markets served, the different technologies supported, the different segments of the value chain occupied, and so on. The broader the company's strategy, the more complex and diversified it is. GE, for example, has one of the broadest strategies, operating in twenty-three of twenty-six industry categories that are recognized by the U.S. government and supporting technologies ranging from locomotive engines and turbines to light bulbs. WD-40, in contrast, has a very narrow strategic intent that focuses on a particular type of lubricant.

Aggressiveness. A company's *aggressiveness* defines how it develops new products, grows its business, and battles its competitors. It refers to an organization's commitments to courses of action and is reflected in an organization's goals, objectives, and policies. Intel, for example, devotes a very high percentage of its expense budget to the development of new products and to basic research, and Washington Mutual supports its high growth goals through acquisitions. Miller Beer ran aggressive ads during the football season in which referees "penalized" consumers for drinking Bud Lite by embarrassing them and taking the beer away. Budweiser quickly retaliated with ads of its own showing the referees enjoying all the Bud Lite they had stolen.

Differentiation. The *differentiation* elements of a strategy are concerned with the features of a company's product or service and how they match up against competitors' products or services. A product (we'll use the term *product* generically to refer to either products or services) can vary in quality, warranty promises, reliability, or price. GM has a broad strategy because it operates in multiple market segments (Cadillac, Chevrolet, Hummer, Saab, and Saturn, for example), but for each segment, its product has features that distinguish it from other competitors in its class. Differentiation answers the question, "Why would John Q. Public buy a Chevrolet over a Ford or a Chrysler?"

Strategic Logic. Strategic logic refers to the underlying business model used to generate revenue, manage costs, and produce profits. An organization, for example, that chooses an aggressive and broad strategy may be attempting to capture market share and lower unit costs. This volume strategy may seek to establish a low-cost position within the industry and a small margin over many units. Linking the strategic intent to such economic concepts as the experience curve, economies of scale, economies of scope, or global product mandates lends credibility to its specification. Many of the start-up Internet companies in the dot-com period ignored this important principle. They employed an economic logic of "charge people for information they can get for free."

Orchestration. The *orchestration* element is particularly important because it is both an element of strategic intent and a capability. On the one hand, orchestration represents a planning process for how different strategic and organizational initiatives are sequenced. It refers to how changes in breadth, aggressiveness, and differentiation are managed together to bring the organization into proximity with environmental demands over time.

On the other hand, orchestration is a capability in that the organization must effectively coordinate communications, actions, decisions, and events to implement change. A company must also be able to manage and coordinate strategic and organizational changes with technical, customer, market, and a host of other environmental trends that are all changing at different rates and in different ways.

Organizations can change the elements of their strategic intent one at a time, sequentially, or all together. They can alter them quickly or slowly. Microsoft's introduction of the Xbox, the .Net strategy, the tablet PC, Office XP, and Windows XP all happened between June 2000 and November 2002. The decisions to produce these products were made at different times, but each one had to be coordinated with the other and with ongoing, day-to-day operations. Microsoft showed how a variety of decisions can be coordinated when they postponed the next release of Windows to focus on trustworthy computing and other security issues, make an important reorganization, and address customer loyalty.

The orchestration process needs to coordinate changes not only in the elements of strategic intent but also in the processes for designing and creating value. It is no wonder that orchestration is the biggest challenge for most organizations. At best, orchestration is usually conceived of in "cut and paste" terms— "We'll just introduce some new products and run an advertising campaign," as if either of those could happen at any time and in any sequence. At worst, orchestration is an afterthought.

A traditional organization must know how to disrupt the strong inertial forces in it that favor the status quo. Few organizations have a change capability—much less the inclination—to change, and so they fail to invest in orchestration. This is a major mistake. Having the ability to orchestrate strategic intent elements and the capability to manage change is the single most important investment a company can make if it wants to become a b2change organization.

Quality of Strategic Intent

What makes for a good strategic intent? First and foremost, it must identify an environmental path for an organization and an orchestrated sequence of actions, but this is not enough. It has to identify an intent that is robust and that can be implemented.

Robustness and Intent. The primary criterion for a good strategic intent is robustness. A robust intent is one that works well under multiple future scenarios or is flexible in relation to several likely scenarios. Although maintaining flexibility may entail sacrificing some short-term revenue or profit, in most cases the sacrifice will be more than offset by a b2change organization's ability to string together a series of temporary competitive advantages.

With the advent of the Internet, BMG Entertainment faced a variety of alternative scenarios in the recorded music business. Consumers might continue to prefer the experience of shopping for music in a retail environment, might want to be able to mix their own CDs either online or in stores, or might want to download music exclusively from the Internet. It was clear that piracy and intellectual property rights; the power of retailers, artists, and other stakeholders in the industry; and the capabilities of the recording company would all play a role in determining which scenario(s) might emerge as dominant.

BMG's strategy was to be flexible. In addition to forging ahead with an intent that supported the retail channel, the company also started several "low-cost probes" in Web-based businesses, alliances with technology providers, and negotiations with artists. These initiatives adjusted BMG's breadth, aggressiveness, and differentiators to a small extent but kept them connected to the key sources of information that would signal which direction the industry would go.

Identity and Intent. A good strategic intent is consistent with an organization's core identity. A clear example of this is how the Canadian Broadcasting Company (CBC) handled a major change. As a "Crown" corporation, it was largely funded by the government. But as government policies shifted, CBC was encouraged to become more independent. CBC was an icon of the Canadian people, and its identity reflected the country's strong values of diversity and trustworthiness.

CBC's diversity identity made it unthinkable to shift the organization's breadth from the existing four lines of business: French TV, French radio, English TV, and English radio. Minor adjustments were made to aggressiveness by developing new programming tactics and by creating new marketing approaches to generate new forms and higher amounts of revenue. In line with its trustworthiness identity, CBC deepened investments in the differentiators of reliability, stability, and quality. Finally, CBC modified its strategic logic to account for its greater independence from government subsidies. CBC orchestrated these changes thoughtfully and coordinated them with structural changes and initiatives so as to become more of a learning organization. Thus, despite a major shift in the environment, CBC crafted a successful critical configuration by adjusting its strategic intent and honoring its identity.

Capabilities and Intent. The final criterion for a good strategic intent is the extent to which it is supported by the organization's competencies and capabilities. This is a traditional criterion that should not be lost on a b2change firm, but it also goes one step further. In a dynamic view of organizations, capabilities and competencies are not static. They evolve and develop as technology becomes more sophisticated, but more important, they also develop as the organization learns how to use and apply them.

UPS is a good example of how a firm can meet this criterion. As it learned more and more about the relevance of its core competencies and capabilities to the movement of other people's goods, it also learned how these strengths supported a broader strategic intent. As a result, despite an insular and conservative identity, UPS has managed to consistently enter new businesses that involve logistics and delivery.

UPS began in 1907 as a Seattle messenger and package delivery service for department stores. Its next move was to be a competitor of the U.S. Postal Service for the shipment of packages by individuals as well as by retailers. It expanded services to include overnight and international deliveries. As a result of these changes, it became a major competitor of Federal Express. To succeed in this new business, it has had to move from being largely a domestic and ground-based transporter to being a global, air-based operation. Each of these changes was an incremental extension of the basic competencies and capabilities.

To maintain its growth, UPS is in the process of using its logistics competency to enter a new business. It wants to serve as a supply chain expert for corporate America, moving materials from factory to factory, from factory to distribution points, and ultimately from distribution points to retail outlets. It has struck deals with Ford, Jockey International, and Birkenstocks to manage their supply chains in ways that will speed the movement of their materials, lower work-in-process inventory, and reduce transportation costs.

In line with its conservative identity, UPS has grown steadily by understanding and developing its competencies and capabilities and then extending them to new but similar markets and businesses. Despite a variety of environmental and organizational changes, UPS's growth path has been successful because the company's intent was formulated in parallel with its evolving competencies and capabilities.

The Strategizing Process

We began by defining strategy as identity and intent and suggesting that identity was like the big rocks in a jar and intent was like the pebbles, sand, and water. We are now ready to consider how the jar gets filled up—that is, how the strategizing process operates. What distinguishes b2change organizations from traditional ones is their fascination with how the big rocks and the little ones go in. Identity and intent define the content of strategy; strategizing, like other processes in the b2change approach, is agile and flexible—a process designed to change.

Strategizing represents a continuous search for a string of temporary competitive advantages that will drive effectiveness.

It describes how and when to change the pebbles, sand, and water (and sometimes the big rocks). It is important to recognize that there's an irreversible sequence involved. If you fill the jar with water first, you can't add anything else without making a big mess. The same is true with b2change organizations. If the organization doesn't know its identity, there's little sense in making decisions about breadth and differentiators. To do so would increase the probability of formulating a strategic intent that won't be supported by the organization.

The strategizing process is shown in Figure 3.2. We will briefly review the process here, then go into more detail in the sections that follow. Phase 1 is a *strategic review:* a diagnosis of the causes of current performance and an assessment of the strategy's fitness for the future. Phase 2 is *strategic choice:* working with the information generated by the strategic review, the organization decides whether or not a change in strategy is necessary. One possible decision is to affirm the current identity and intent and pursue strategic adjustment. Or the organization might decide to pursue strategic reorientation or even transformation, which leads it to Phase 3, *strategic change.* In this phase, the orchestration process leads as the organization changes its identity, reconfigures its strategic intent, or both.

Phase 1: Strategic Review

Strategizing looks into the future. In Phase 1, the organization examines the credibility of existing alternative scenarios and the likelihood that its current identity and intent will respond to those future demands. Managers and employees need to analyze whether the current strategy will put the organization in close proximity to the most likely future environmental

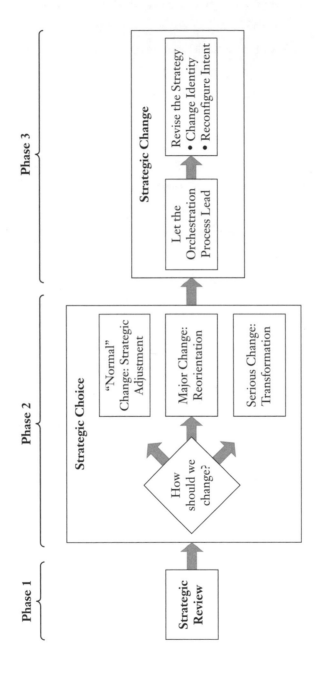

FIGURE 3.2. The Strategizing Process

demands. Looking forward and focusing on the environment are critical. The constellation of breadth, aggressiveness, differentiation, orchestration, and logic needs to respond to future environmental demands—an important condition for creating a virtuous spiral. If the current strategy will not meet the demands of the business environment, then identity or strategic intent (or both) need to change.

There is no rule of thumb about how often strategic reviews should occur. Their frequency should be a function of how quickly the environmental scenarios are changing. The quicker the pace of technological, global, regulatory, and competitor moves, the more frequent the need for strategic reviews.

B2change organizations need to schedule both regular and event-driven strategic reviews. At a minimum, there should be an annual updating of the strategy, even if it is only an affirmation of the existing one. Revisiting it frequently is one way to keep an organization focused on the external environment. A b2change organization should be able to start a strategic review when someone in the organization senses that performance and effectiveness are below expectations, when an unexpected event occurs, or when an assumption changes within the existing set of environmental scenarios that substantively threatens future performance.

Senior managers are often in the best position to initiate a review because they have access to the most information about performance, environmental conditions, technologies, and competitors. But—and this is especially true in a b2change organization—other organization members may also have access to information that could signal the need for a review. For example, a sales representative may learn something about a customer or competitor that warrants a review. Thus, in b2change organizations there needs to be a mechanism—something similar to a "whistleblower" process—that allows employees to signal that a review process should be initiated.

No matter how the strategic review is initiated, broad participation in this early phase of the strategizing process is important. Processes and techniques that involve organization members aid in the diagnosis of the causes of poor performance or the reasons future performance may be at risk. For example, large-group conferences with a variety of stakeholders or "all hands" meetings to discuss current performance, strategic intent, or environmental scenarios can generate valid data; employee and customer surveys help identify areas of concern; and environmental scanning methods, such as technology forecasts, ecosystem mapping, and market analyses, can uncover outdated assumptions.

In general, large gaps between desired and actual performance suggest that some aspect of the strategy is not responding to current environmental demands. In other words, the organization is not proximate with the environmental success path. Review meetings, conversations with key stakeholders, and careful analysis of the existing strategy should determine the problem: the wrong strategic intent or (most seriously) the wrong identity. If the problem is the wrong intent, then intent needs to change. But be warned that adjustments to intent will not lead to immediate performance improvements; these take time.

Small gaps between desired and actual performance are usually indicative of execution problems. There may be little need for a change in strategic intent. Often, small gaps call for an assessment of the creating value or designing processes (or both) and may require only tactical changes. An organization

should be able to determine the source of mediocre performance by assessing its internal operations and looking at its capabilities: Do we have the proper competencies and capabilities?
Are the capabilities adequately supported by the structure, people, rewards, and information systems? This analysis, like all
processes in the b2change approach, should be conducted
through a dynamic lens. Current performance is important, but
it should not distract the organization from planning for the
future.

Phase 2: Strategic Choice

The outputs of the strategic review are the inputs to the strategic choice phase. Here the organization decides whether or not
it needs to alter its identity, the elements of strategic intent, or
both. Depending on the information generated by the review
phase, the firm needs to engage in a conversation that either
confirms the strategic direction of the firm or determines that
the organization needs to reset its identity or intent. As shown
in Figure 3.2, there are three options. If the review process suggests that no major change is necessary, the organization should
pursue *strategic adjustments* to the creating value or designing
processes.

Making strategic adjustments is the status quo condition of
a b2change organization, and something it is designed to handle. These adjustments involve the ongoing implementation
and reimplementation of a particular strategic intent that fits
an affirmed identity. Toyota is a good example of a company
that successfully makes strategic adjustments. It has been building cars, refining its supply chain, and improving quality year
after year for more than two decades. During this time, it has

added new competencies and capabilities, implemented reorganizations, and fine-tuned its reward system. These changes in the creating value and designing processes range from mundane to substantive. They have served to keep Toyota in a leadership position, and highlight the essential point that b2change organizations embrace change as normal.

A strategic review that affirms identity and intent is not a sign that the organization is choosing stability. It affirms the b2change logic that it is the *implementation* of a strategy that changes most often, not the strategy itself. However, if the review suggests that the strategy does need to be revised, then the information from the review is used to determine whether a reorientation or a transformation is necessary.

A *reorientation* reformulates one or more elements of strategic intent within an affirmed identity. A reformulation usually also requires major shifts in the creating value and designing processes. GM's establishment of the Saturn division represented a clear change in breadth, aggressiveness, and differentiation. It required enormous changes in labor relations, reward systems, structure, work design, distributor relations, and other elements of creating value and designing. GM was able to accomplish these changes by starting a new business unit. GM stayed the same, while Saturn implemented the reformulated strategy.

A *transformation* involves changing both identity and intent. From time to time—sometimes by design but more often by accident—organizations shift their identity. This is a rare, important, and risky initiative, even for a b2change organization.

Hewlett-Packard (HP) has found it very difficult to transform itself into a low-cost producer of PCs and consumer electronics. The acquisition of Compaq was resisted mightily by many HP shareholders and devotees of the HP Way. It significantly altered the breadth and aggressiveness of HP's intent, severely challenged what was arguably one of the better orchestration processes among U.S. firms, and probably made the economic logic of the firm too dependent on the Dell-dominated commodity-oriented PC business. The differences in the identities of HP and Compaq were one of the biggest challenges. The merger, by most accounts, was like trying to get gentlemen and cowboys to live in the same house. Despite a well-orchestrated merger integration process, the clash of identities, in combination with the magnitude of the changes in intent, caused many problems.

Phase 3: Strategic Change

The third phase in the strategizing process is analogous to filling the jar back up by revising the organization's strategy—both its identity and intent in the case of a transformation or only its strategic intent in the case of a reorientation. As was true of the review phase, the number and type of employees that should be involved in revising the strategy and just how active they are depends on the size of the organization, the expected scope of change, and the likely targets of change. A transformational change is likely to require broad participation and deep levels of involvement. In contrast, a small reorientation that changes only aggressiveness, for example, might limit involvement to the sales and marketing departments.

As a general rule, more involvement is better, and particularly in b2change organizations. The more employee input an organization gets to the strategy formulation process, the more likely employees are to understand and accept the new strategy and find it useful as a guide to their behavior.

Orchestration Leads the Change. The characteristics of the change phase depend on the type of shift anticipated, with one exception: all strategic change efforts should be initiated by the orchestration process. For a given strategic intent to be effective, managers and employees in a b2change organization must share and support it.

When a company determines that a transformation or reorientation is necessary, the single most important thing for organization members to know is that the strategy is going to change. This resetting of the identity or intent must be initiated by the orchestration process—its first order of business is to alert the rest of the organization of the shift about to take place. The orchestration process is charged with communicating to the organization that it is going to "change the way it is changing." Because the earlier review process was conducted with broad participation—in fact, there may have been multiple review processes—there should already be a good understanding among the members of the organization of why a change in strategy is necessary. The orchestration process spreads this understanding deeply into the organization and begins to involve people in the specification of the new strategic identity or intent.

Communication is one of the banes of organizational life. Very few, if any, organizations do enough of it, at least in the eyes of their members. Recent research on social change suggests a view of communication that complements our b2change approach.[4] It provides guidance about how to ensure that the organization is alerted to the impending change in identity or intent. It argues that changes in strategy are facilitated when organizations take advantage of their *connectors, mavens,* and *salespeople.*

Connectors are individuals who occupy central positions in the social network. When a connector knows that a change in intent is being formulated, everyone inside and outside an organization will know it too.

A b2change organization should also leverage its strategy mavens. Strategy mavens have extensive knowledge about strategy in general and the likely changes in intent or identity. Mavens are willing to tell anyone who is interested everything they know about a subject. The key to the maven's role is trust. People who speak to mavens must know that they are getting unbiased information—that there is no "hidden agenda," just good data.

Finally, the organization needs to take advantage of its salespeople—that is, the individuals in the firm who are able to influence others to contribute to or buy in to the new strategy. They usually can be found anywhere in an organization.

Connectors, mavens, and salespeople exist in all organizations—there is no need to worry about creating them. The difference in a b2change organization is that the company makes a point of using these resources to communicate change. These individuals need to be involved in the review process so that they are informed about the change.

In addition to keeping open these channels of communication, the orchestration process needs to ensure that the message about change is "sticky" and relevant. To capture people's attention, the message must be memorable. B2change organizations need to leverage the expertise in their marketing and communications departments to create sticky, relevant, meaningful messages.

The source of meaning is that the organization will be changing its strategy and that people will need to behave differently. Members of a b2change organization are sensitive to information about strategy because it is central to their day-to-day activities. When the right people communicate an important message, organization members can hear it and adapt quickly. As we will discuss later, this is why leadership is a team sport and b2change organizations need a "surplus" of leaders.

Reorientation Needs to be Planned. When an organization engages in a reorientation, it redefines one or more of the elements of strategic intent: breadth, aggressiveness, differentiation, logic, and orchestration. A relatively small change, such as a modification in a warranty (a differentiator), has few, if any, implications for the competencies and capabilities an organization needs. But changing multiple strategic intent elements is much more complex and often requires change in the organization's design and capabilities. The criteria described earlier of a good strategic intent apply here. Does the new intent position the organization well for a variety of different scenarios? Does it complement the organization's identity? Are the organization's current competencies and capabilities up to the task of implementing the intent? Can needed new competencies and capabilities be developed?

There is a right sequence for making strategic intent decisions. The first element to specify is strategic logic. The question should be: Do the changes in the environment require a shift in the way the organization drives revenues, controls costs, or produces a profit? If a change is required, this element should receive early attention in the reconfiguration process;

the other elements of the intent are then prescribed and aligned accordingly.

Xerox's early economic logic—a clever plain-paper copy machine rental contract paired with patent protections that created large financial barriers to entry—helped commercialize the company's copying technology quickly. But as new business venture proposals for personal computers and software emerged from Xerox's PARC research facility, this same logic was an inappropriate model for evaluating if and how to invest. What was patentable and what could be rented proved poor templates for evaluation. By failing to understand the appropriate models for these new businesses, Xerox lost out on important new opportunities, including the mouse and other computer technologies.

Once the organization determines its logic, it should then describe its breadth, aggressiveness, and differentiators. Once Jack Welch established the logic of being number one or number two in every business, GE had important decisions to make about what units to keep and divest (breadth), how to defend current positions or invest to achieve the desired position (aggressiveness), and what it would take to build that kind of market share (differentiators).

Finally, the orchestration process needs to coordinate the design and implementation of the changes and see that they become manifest in the competencies, capabilities, and design of the organization. When and how these changes are implemented requires carefully orchestrated timing. When should the firm lead change in the industry, and when should it move with change in the industry?

Offensive reorientations can create havoc for competitors and set the rules of the game. This is an important function of crafting and implementing strategic intent—it can set the organization (and sometimes the industry) on a new path.

Merck's acquisition of Medco radically shifted other pharmaceutical companies' perceptions of the industry. It suggested that a new value chain was emerging and pushed in the industry into a short-term consolidation. Similarly, Apple's introduction of the iPod and of iTunes.com shifted the definition of hardware and software companies.

Sometimes a strong follower position is best. A b2change organization must be ready both to lead and to adjust.

In the case of substantial adjustments, the key orchestration issues involve coordinating and sequencing the changes in the intention elements and addressing the implications for competencies and capabilities. For example, TWA, prior to its acquisition by American Airlines, announced changes in the differentiators of improved service and more leg room on its domestic flights but did not alter its competencies and capabilities to support the changes. The result was a failure to change and ultimately a failed airline. When there is little or no coordination between strategic intent and the creating value process, customer satisfaction and corporate value can fall quickly.

The orchestration process must address the speed of the change process and the amount of effort needed to make it happen. The quality of execution should be determined by assessing the size and expected duration of the environmental opportunity. For small to moderate-size opportunities of short duration, speed is more important than quality. In most cases, though, an 80 percent execution is probably more than enough. In the pursuit of a string of short-term advantages, b2change organizations need to avoid exhorting members toward perfection, excellence, and other sensationalist metaphors. These labels ignore or mask the realities of implementation (which are that no one can do it perfectly), often do not align with the organization's identity, and create cynicism.

Transformation Is Risky. As we've discussed, a strategic transformation that changes identity is needed when the strategic review shows that the organization's identity is not viable. Typically in these cases, the review has identified an environmental shift or organizational event of such magnitude and importance that the very core of the organization is viewed as obsolete. For example, imagine being Stasi, the East German secret police after the fall of the Berlin Wall. The emergence of a unified Germany clearly challenged Stasi's legitimacy. The whole organization needed rethinking. Similarly, Prime Minister Margaret Thatcher's decision to end subsidies to the coal-mining firms in Britain required all the firms to rethink their identities, including whether they should remain in the business. In the United States, how about being AT&T when the telecommunications industry was deregulated?

Successful change of a firm's identity is a rare event, but it does occur. More often than not, it coincides with dramatic shifts in technology, a fundamental change in the environment, or a merger or acquisition. These "inflection points" in an industry's or organization's life cycle can be obvious or subtle: environmental scanning, scenario planning, and due diligence processes can provide important information about when transformational change will be needed.

In a classic case of identity change, the March of Dimes organization, which had been dedicated to the eradication of polio, lost its reason for being when a cure for the disease was found. In response, the organization successfully repurposed itself to address a mission of preventing birth defects and infant mortality.

The issues involved in thinking through a new identity and strategy are so complex and difficult that it is a good choice only when no other options exist. As we've discussed, identities are deeply rooted in the basic assumptions of an organization and are very difficult to change. The one thing that increases confidence in any decision to shift identity is an intimate knowledge of the existing one. There is simply no substitute for knowing the organization's culture and character.

The story of American Healthways (AMHC) is a good example of how to intentionally clarify and leverage identity for transformational change. Founded in 1981 to own and manage hospitals, AMHC had transformed itself by 2004 into a proactive health support provider.

The health care market is a rapidly changing, complex, and cost-conscious industry. Health care reforms and reimbursement changes in the 1980s pushed more and more services into outpatient clinics. As an operator of hospitals, AMHC noted this change and decided to look for a better business.

In 1984, AMHC launched the Diabetes Treatment Centers of America, outpatient clinics within hospitals, which became centers of excellence in the treatment of this disease. In 1993, AMHC repackaged the clinic's services into the Diabetes Healthways plan and sold it directly to health insurance companies as a proactive product. Rather than waiting for patients to schedule treatments, appointments, and other types of care, the organization proactively contacts patients to remind them about treatment options and coach them in treating diabetes. This marked the beginning of AMHC's shift from hospital operator to proactive provider of health support.

AMHC introduced additional proactive products in 1998 and 1999. Just six years after their introduction, the proactive disease management programs outside of hospitals earned higher revenues than the hospital-based programs. By 2003, AMHC was ranked fifth in *Fortune*'s list of America's fastest-growing companies and second of one hundred companies in total return on investment. In addition, in 2003 and 2004, it was ranked number one on *Fortune Small Business* magazine's list of fastest-growing publicly traded small businesses.

From our perspective, what is more interesting than AMHC's financial success is the way it achieved that success and the role that identity played in the change. The projected growth for the proactive business clearly pointed to the need for a new organization design. The existing structure and systems simply would not support the future organization.

As part of an organization redesign effort, AMHC realized that its strategic intent was not clear enough to guide organization design. For example, the proactive disease management strategy by itself could not answer questions about how to drive the account management function; whether a network, front-back, or process-based organization structure would serve it better; or whether to outsource the IT function. A cross-functional task force, charged with specifying the new organization design and its structure, ended up focusing on AMHC's strategic intent and eventually the very identity of the firm.

The identity conversation included debates about the core values and assumptions driving the organization's growth, discussions of important biases and tendencies in decision making, and reflections on the organization's strengths and weaknesses. After a number of formal and informal conversations with a broad range of stakeholders, the task force produced the necessary epiphany and consensus that AMHC was truly a market-driven company.

The task force realized that being market driven was the only way the company could be successful in the proactive business area. Moreover, it realized that even before the proactive disease management strategy was formulated, the old "hospital" strategy was effective because it too was market driven. With this new information in hand, it became much easier to make important organization design trade-offs and strategic choices about how best to implement the new strategic intent. The IT outsourcing decision, for example, became a nonissue. If the organization was market driven, it had to possess the ability to adapt its proprietary software applications; outsourcing IT was out of the question.

Conclusion

Strategic adjustments and reorientations are the *point forte* of the b2change approach. B2change organizations develop and resource strategic changes with appropriate urgency and expectations. Their identity, strategy, competencies and capabilities, and organization design all support the mind-set and reality that change is a normal and routine process.

B2change organizations have many important strategic features that distinguish them from traditional firms. They

- Are concerned about the future and use environmental scenarios as important inputs to any discussion of strategy.
- Comprehend the power of a well-understood identity and take the time to be clear about what their identity is, where it comes from, and how it contributes to success.

- Have an identity that focuses on the environment and supports change.

- Have a robust strategic intent that is likely to bring the organization into proximity with a variety of future environmental demands.

- Make changes in their strategic intent in anticipation of shifts in the environment. Intent is not changed randomly or frequently but is informed by analyses of what the future is likely to hold.

- Ensure widespread participation and involvement in the review of strategy, the communication of changes in strategy, and the reconfiguration of strategy.

- Rely on a vibrant orchestration capability not only to manage strategic adjustments but to initiate changes in intent.

- Find the positive aspects of their current identity and leverage them when change is needed.

The next seven chapters describe the designing process. Together, these seven chapters are aimed at creating a dynamic alignment that supports the intent and identity of a b2change organization.

Chapter 4

Structuring for Effectiveness and Change

Built-to-Change Strategy:
Create Jobless Structures

The structure of an organization is a visible and important determinant of performance. It is often the first issue that comes up when managers think about change. Indeed, structure is often the *only* issue that comes up when change and organization design are considered. Executives assume that if boxes are moved around or reshaped and resized, successful organizational change will occur. Obviously this is an incorrect assumption, but it is nevertheless true that an organization's structure is a critical determinant of organizational effectiveness and in most cases needs to be altered when an organization's strategic intent changes. It therefore needs to be designed not just to meet current needs but to change.

Often we think of organization structure primarily as a way to distribute the work (you folks do shipping; you over there get some sales) and to distribute authority (OK, everyone, Maria runs marketing). A better way to think about it is that an organization needs a structuring process that enables it to develop the competencies and capabilities it needs to execute its strategic intent. Thus the major consideration in designing and structuring is finding the best approach to creating value.

For example, most prescription pharmaceutical firms have a strategy that calls for an organization that is highly focused on one sales channel, doctors. So we should see—and do see—a structure that is focused on that channel. If the strategy calls for low costs, which is Wal-Mart's strategy, the structure needs to focus on reducing costs in everything the organization does. In the case of Wal-Mart, this means a structure that, among other things, focuses on key suppliers and the management of inventory.

Given that the structure of an organization needs to be strongly determined by identity and strategic intent, what about structuring an organization for change? If there is reason to believe that some element of intent will change, as there almost always is, it is important to create a structure that is flexible enough to allow for strategy-driven changes. A number of structural features make strategy-driven change easier. All of them reduce the all-too-common resistance to change that is generated by most organization designs.

External Focus

The many possible approaches to structuring organizations differ significantly in the degree to which they focus on the external environment. In particular, they differ in the degree to which the focus is on customers and in how effectively different parts of the organization satisfy customer demands. We are being overly kind when we say existing approaches "differ in degree," because books on organization structure often do not consider customers at all. Pick up a text on organization design and look for the word *customer* in the index. In most cases, customers just don't enter into the thinking. Our colleague, Jay Galbraith, has done an excellent job of describing in his recent book the importance of the customer dimension in organization design.[1]

For a variety of reasons, structures that focus on customers are much easier to change than those that are focused internally. This holds true even if the organization is designed around the idea of some departments' satisfying internal customers. Having to satisfy internal customers is superior to being held accountable only for internal standards and budget performance, but it is not the same as having external customers.

The best design puts as many employees as possible in direct contact with the external environment. In other words, employees should have few, if any, degrees of separation from external customers. A good rule of thumb is that no employee should have more than two degrees of separation from a customer. The reason for this is straightforward. Direct exposure to how well the organization is satisfying its customers gives employees credible and powerful feedback about how well the organization is performing.

The wisdom of this idea may seem self-evident, but it is a radical one. How many organizations have systems that put HR, research and development, production, accounting, audit, or procurement in touch with customers, or even with someone who deals with customers? How many organizations have automated telephone answering systems that are designed to ensure that contact with customers is kept to an absolute minimum?

Feedback from the external environment is particularly important for employee motivation. Hundreds of studies on work design have shown that work can be highly motivating when individuals are doing tasks that challenge them and provide feedback about how well they are performing.[2] Who provides the most credible feedback? Customers. We saw an interesting example of how to open up feedback channels when we studied an electronics firm. To give the production teams customer contact, the company had them visit their customers to see how their product was being used. They also gave the customers an 800 number that put them in contact with the manufacturing team that built the product.

Feedback can also be a source of motivation for change. When customers tell employees that the organization is not performing well, employees are far more likely to be motivated to change than if they hear it from executives. Employees don't enjoy dealing with unhappy customers or delivering poor service. This is true whether the employee is a computer programmer or a sales clerk. Customers also often provide information about *how* the organization needs to change in order to be successful. Thus the more feedback employees get from customers, the more the organization will know what to change and will be motivated to change it.

STRUCTURING FOR CHANGE

What does a dynamically structured organization that is focused on the external environment look like? There is not a single answer to this question, but it is possible to identify a number of structural features characteristic of organizations that are designed to change.

Structures Without Jobs

The fundamental building block of most organizations is the job. Traditional job descriptions are long, elaborate, detailed, and often badly out-of-date. They cover what the job holder is supposed to do, the kind of skills needed, and, in some cases, how performance can be measured. Changing a job description usually requires a major effort. A new job description needs to be written, reviewed for accuracy, and ultimately processed in terms of its implications for hiring, pay levels, and reporting relationships. Once a new description is approved, individuals are expected to do what it says, nothing more and nothing less. To be sure that employees are following their job descriptions, "auditors" are sent to check on what they do.

When an organizational restructuring occurs and employees have to do different kinds of work, report to different supervisors, and perform new procedures, it is definitely not business as usual. It is a major event, not an ongoing, continuous reality. It also often is resisted by employees, because of the loss of certainty and clarity and the "extra" work involved in implementing the change. One result of restructuring often is a costly dip in an organization's performance.

When we teach executives about organization design, one of our favorite questions is whether their organizations have job descriptions; virtually all of them raise their hands. But when we ask how many of them have job descriptions that are up-to-date, only a few hands go up. This is neither surprising nor necessarily a problem; in fact, in some respects it may be positive, because it means the company is changing.

Increasingly, organizations are recognizing that job descriptions are not only costly to maintain but also obstacles to change. They become hard-wired in an organization and calcified, rendering change difficult. That said, change still occurs, because people often do what they have to do in order to get things done, so job descriptions become badly out-of-date and irrelevant. Instead of worrying about this, b2change organizations simply abandon the fiction that fixed jobs and job descriptions are a good thing. Capital One did this by stating "that every job has an expiration date."

The best alternative to having fixed jobs and well-developed job descriptions is a structure that is characterized by dynamic work assignments and relationships. With this type of structure, individuals are assigned responsibility, on a temporary basis, for performing groups of tasks. As people's skills change and the needs of the organization change, the task mix that individuals are responsible for is adjusted. The kind of projects individuals work on and the kind of tasks they perform change depending on what is happening with a particular customer or a particular product.

As a result of being in an environment of continuous change, individuals are experienced in the art of organization change. They are not led to expect, nor do they experience, structural change as a disruption of their lives. Instead, it is a matter-of-fact part of the way the organization does business.

We often see this kind of structure in consulting firms and in other professional service organizations where individuals are continually moved from project to project with a different project lead for each assignment. Instead of reporting to a single manager of marketing, production, or other function, individuals report to multiple managers—for example, one who represents a function and another who is managing a customer relationship or a product development process.

Clearly this approach to organizing puts a heavy demand on individuals and their supervisors to continually redesign their work. It is, however, far better than the alternative of having job descriptions that are limiting, difficult to change, and out of date. It also changes an important aspect of how individuals define themselves: instead of being known primarily by their job, they are viewed in terms of what they *can* do as well as what they *are* doing.

Teams

The use of teams has a number of advantages that b2change organizations can leverage. Working in a team helps individuals develop skills they will need when the organization changes. In particular, the ability to establish relationships, to manage interactions with different parts of the organization, and to adjust to changes in the business situation can all be developed in a team-based organization.

Teams that are multidisciplinary and focused on the external environment are particularly likely to help individuals understand the organization's strategy and business model. These teams also provide people with feedback about how well their part of the organization is performing.

Temporary teams can greatly enhance the agility of an organization. They can allow an organization to focus quickly on new products, customers, capabilities, and competencies.

The key is to charter teams as temporary structures that have deliverables and limited life expectancies.

Project teams and temporary problem-solving teams can be very powerful aids in developing the kind of skills that are needed to implement organizational change. In essence, individuals learn about building new working relationships and performing new tasks every time they are on a new project team.

To be effective, project teams need to have clear accountability and produce results that are visibly tied to customer satisfaction and business performance. For example, creating a team to launch a new product is a powerful way to motivate individuals, encourage them to learn new skills, help them to understand the business, and ultimately help them be more accepting of change.

Permanent teams can facilitate tactical change, although they probably aren't as useful as temporary teams in supporting strategic change. There is quite a bit of research suggesting that self-managing teams in which individuals can perform multiple tasks are particularly good at tactical change.[3] For example, they respond well to unusual customer requests, equipment breakdowns, new processes, and service failures. The major reasons for this are that they have regular customer contact and are trained to understand the work flow.

Virtual Work Relationships

A third important structural element that b2change firms use is virtual work relationships. With the capability of connecting employees through electronic means growing all the time, organizations are increasingly using teams whose members are scattered across different locations.[4] For example, Sauer-Danfoss, which designs and manufacturers engineered hydraulic and electronic systems for mobile equipment, regularly uses virtual teams that are spread across the globe so that projects are driven forward twenty-four hours a day. P&G uses global virtual teams to speed the development of new products. Virtual work relationships do have an important downside. Individuals can feel disconnected and may not be well integrated into the organization.

When it comes to organizational change, virtual working relationships have a number of advantages. With virtual structures, reporting relationships and team formations can be changed without many of the usual problems. Individuals do not have to change their offices, nor do they have to disrupt their personal lives by moving to a new location. One result is that they are less resistant to change.

Innovative companies like Sun Microsystems and SEI Investments don't want employees to think in terms of having a permanent physical location. Sun Microsystems expects most of its employees to work from multiple locations and to communicate with coworkers electronically. SEI Investments has designed a workplace without walls or even partitions—everything is on wheels. Employees reconfigure the office any time there is a need. The whole point is to make change an easy, everyday activity, not a disruptive event.

Business Units

There are a number of advantages to designing an organization with multiple business units. Business units create more "surface area" between the company and the environment. Employees are closer to the customer, which, as we have discussed, can be highly motivating. Particularly when business units have considerable autonomy, employees take ownership for results and willingly adapt to change. In essence, business units are a way to get the parts of a large organization focused on the external environment and tied into performance results that they can control.

Contrast a constellation of business units with a large functionally structured organization. In a functional structure, most employees do not have a clear line of sight to the business results, nor do they get feedback from customers. Instead of creating a product or service for a customer, they perform functions for other parts of the organization. Thus, if they have a customer at all, it is an internal one.

Multiple customer-facing business units have one more advantage that is rarely recognized. They create a much larger number of employees who understand "their business." These people understand their business because they have control over a total business experience. All too often, business understanding is missing in large organizations, even among experienced managers. Managers tend to focus on understanding the function in which they are embedded, not the total business equation. They are thus poorly positioned to understand when and why change is necessary; they also lack the skills to execute a major change effort.

The business unit model has one final advantage for a b2change organization. In order to implement strategic reorientations or transformations, individual units can be subtracted or added to the organization's portfolio of activities with minimal disruption to the rest of the organization. In essence, if a particular market is growing or disappearing, the organization can adjust to it simply by changing one of its business units.

The rest of the organization can continue to do business as usual.

The extreme version of an independent business unit model is the well-known Berkshire Hathaway corporation, which has totally independent business units. Its corporate center is so small that it doesn't have to alter itself at all when it buys or sells a business, and the business units are so independent that they are not affected by the addition and subtraction of other business units.

A less extreme version is Johnson & Johnson (J&J). It has multiple independent business units, each of which has its own board of directors that is staffed by executives from other J&J businesses. Unlike Berkshire Hathaway, J&J has a significant corporate staff that provides services and supports synergies among the units.

L-3 Communications is an example of an organization able to acquire a new business every month because it lets each new division run fairly autonomously—it couldn't possibly manage that kind of growth if it had a functional structure.

GE is another example of an organization that is comfortable adding and eliminating business units. A look at the company's history shows that it has done so many times every year for decades. For example, it has eliminated a computer business, a uranium business, and a household appliance unit that was one of its original businesses. The organization has entered numerous financial service businesses and the entertainment business.

Like J&J's, GE's units are not as autonomous as those of Berkshire Hathaway, and as a result there are some repercussions throughout the rest of the organization when units are added or subtracted. The corporate staff needs to change according to what happens in the business units, and often the human capital management plan needs to change. In the GE model, the top managers from each of the business units are considered to be corporate property, so their careers are managed centrally. Thus a change in the business mix may change who is developed and how he or she is developed. Overall, however, these adjustments are not a serious obstacle to change.

Perhaps the major disadvantage of the multibusiness model is investor skepticism. Because of the management problems that some megaconglomerates experienced in the 1980s, investors are understandably suspicious of them (remember ITT and Westinghouse). It is important, however, not to overlook the success stories or the issue of relatedness among the business units. GE is well known, but how about United Technologies Corporation? It is a $37 billion multibusiness company that since 1984 has generated greater returns to its shareholders than GE.

Managing a multibusiness corporation is a capability that has to be developed. If a company does develop such a capability, it can produce a significant competitive advantage, not the least of which is the ability to change.

Matrix Structures

Simplicity is desirable in an organization's structure, but it is not the be-all and end-all. Functional structures are simple. Business unit organizations are simple. Matrix organizations are clearly more complicated to design and operate. Nevertheless b2change organizations often choose a matrix structure over the others. The reason is that when a matrix structure is performing correctly, it can implement strategy and change in ways that the others cannot.[5] Why? Because matrix organizations can develop competencies and capabilities that more traditional structures simply cannot.

When a matrix structure works well, it gives the organization both a focus on current performance and the ability to change—the yin and yang of a b2change organization. Change is built in because individuals are responsible for projects and business areas that are constantly changing in response to the environment. A matrix structure supports changing both the knowledge base of the organization and its operations. Thus it can be a structure that supports tactical as well as major strategic change. And although a dual reporting relationship is complicated, it creates a business environment that challenges employees and provides them with feedback. Employees have a sense of stability because they have a career home and someone who is worried about their development.

The complexity of matrix structures often generates criticism, but they have been working for over thirty years in such organizations as Boeing and Northrop Grumman. This longevity proves that matrix structures can provide a competitive advantage. The combination of many close-to-the-customer business units and a matrix structure is often the best way to design a large b2change organization.

Front-Back Structures

The front-back structure is not well known, but it can be the right approach for a b2change organization. As the name suggests, the organization has a "front": a customer-facing piece that deals with all customer-related activities, including sales, most of marketing, and the delivery of products and services. The rest of the organization, the "back," produces the products and services that the front sells and delivers to the customer. In essence, the front of the organization becomes a customer to the back. In some respects, the front is not the best customer for the back, because as we noted earlier, no internal customer is, but it can be a reasonable proxy for an external customer. When the front is properly designed, it can reflect the needs and desires of the ultimate end user of the organization's products and services.

B2change organizations often choose front-back structures because customers want to deal with only one representative even when the company sells a complex array of products and services. Information technology firms (for example, IBM, HP) and financial services institutions (for example, Merrill Lynch, Citibank) sell a wide variety of products and services. Many of their best customers, large companies, want to deal with a single representative who manages the overall interface between the two organizations.

The same situation exists with many individual customers; they want a single person when interfacing with large financial service organizations and other complex service delivery organizations. They don't want to have to work their way through the various product offerings and the individuals representing the products to buy a mix of services and products.

For many types of tactical change, such as eliminating selling to particular segments of the market or discontinuing products, the front-back organization is relatively easy to change, because it has a kind of modular structure. This is particularly true when change affects the customer-facing part of the organization, which has a good sense of how the market is changing and therefore is motivated to adapt. For example, if the organization no longer wants to sell to a particular kind of consumer or to a particular geographical area, it can eliminate or reassign those employees who are the "front" for that particular type of customer.

A similar situation exists with respect to the back of the organization. If the organization wants to reduce its services and products, "all" it has to do is eliminate the particular piece or pieces of the back that produces them. The rest of the organization doesn't need to change. If the organization wants to add a new product and enter a new market, it can simply add a production module or a sales unit.

Sometimes the front-back structure is easier to change than to operate. Those organizations that have tried this model find managing the interface between the front and the back to be a major challenge. All too often, the back does not want to listen to the front, and the front is frustrated by its relationship with the back. The front may even end up demanding to go to other suppliers to satisfy the customers' needs. Some of this tension is clearly healthy—it calls for improved performance, and the front is behaving exactly as external customers would—but not all of it is.

When all is said and done, the strengths of the front-back organization usually do outweigh its complexity and the disadvantages that stem from it. In many respects it is not surprising that organizations using this structure are in complex businesses, with customers who buy multiple, often complex products and services.

Organizations in complex businesses face an interesting choice: they can either pass complexity on to their customers and ask the customers to sort it out, or reduce the complexity their customers experience by managing it themselves. Managing complexity is a capability that can produce significant dividends. Customers usually prefer to have a supplier manage complexity and will pay accordingly. Because the front-back organization has an advantage with respect to change management, it can keep ahead of its customers' abilities to self-manage the complexities of their products and services. This can allow front-back organizations to enjoy high revenue and healthy profit margins on a sustainable virtuous spiral basis.

Business Process Outsourcing

The structural elements we have looked at so far involve only one party: the b2change organization itself. However, one of the fastest-growing industries in the United States is business process outsourcing (BPO). It is particularly popular in finance, accounting, HR management, and information systems management.

The BPO model is a simple one. An outsourcing firm agrees to take over one or more entire functional areas for a company. The outsourcing firm creates and runs the systems that provide information services, HR, or whatever traditional internal staff services the organization decides can be done better by an outsourcer. Recently, P&G, IBM, Bank of America, International Paper, PepsiCo, and BP have all outsourced HR administration, despite the fact that each of them has been acknowledged as having "best practice" HR functions.[6]

BPO arrangements can produce real cost savings because of the economies of scale an outsourcing firm can achieve. There is also a core competency advantage which argues that an outsourcing firm, because of its scale and focus, will always have more of a core competency in an area like HR management than any single company is likely to have.

Finally, and most relevant to a b2change organization, another potential advantage has to do with managing change. Some outsourcing firms not only have expertise in managing change but are in a position to make change less painful for their customers. If the customer wants to grow or contract quickly, it simply goes to its outsourcer and says that it would like to change the level of service. The outsourcer is then responsible for handling the change. By shifting responsibility from an internal staff group to an outsourcer, the firm makes its own change effort less complicated and avoids the political pressure that in-house units would exert against change.

There is another reason why both tactical and strategic change can be more effective when a process is outsourced. The firm that is either upsizing or downsizing doesn't have to worry about whether its systems need to be revised or whether new knowledge and skills are required to operate them with its new business model. It relies on its outsourcing firm to provide this kind of expertise and indeed to revise processes so that they fit the new business model.

For example, if an organization shifts from a functional structure to a matrix structure, it will need to change its performance management system. If the company outsources its performance management design and operation, then the outsourcer will be expected to have the knowledge and systems to handle this new structure.

BPO fits very well with the front-back approach. The customer-facing part of the organization stays intact while parts of the back and the corporate staff are gotten rid of altogether through outsourcing. The relationship between the front part of the organization and the BPO provider is a true customer-client relationship, not the weaker internal customer relationship. Thus b2change organizations may move toward using BPO not just for cost savings but because it enables them to make change an ongoing activity.

B2Change Structure

At this point we can begin to envision the shape of the b2change organization. It will have internal elements that facilitate change when it is needed: teams, virtual working relationships, and a jobless structure. It will stay close to the customer with either small business units, front-back structures, or possibly, a combination of these. It may have matrix structures and BPO providers that create integration and competency excellence. All of these will be explicitly seen as tools for day-to-day success but also as essential ingredients for creating a b2change organization.

CREATING NEW BUSINESSES

Perhaps the most difficult challenge for any organization is orchestrating the development of new businesses that require new competencies and capabilities. As was mentioned earlier, traditional organizations often have trouble capitalizing on new technologies, such as silicon chips, search engines, fuel cells, digital imaging, and computers, that create whole new businesses. They seem to have the problem even if they develop the technology themselves and have a head start over new businesses.

B2change organizations must constantly attend to the processes of the day while also developing scenarios based on the innovations that will define their future. This is a difficult balance to get right. Giving the right amount of attention to these two agendas seems to require a mental and operational agility that most organizations don't have. Sony, for example, traditionally exceled at innovation, but missed the boat on MP3 players because their policies for protecting their music division got in the way of the new products.

Business writers have coined the term *ambidextrous organization* to describe firms that operate effectively both in slowly changing traditional businesses and in businesses that require major strategic change. But as is true of people, few organizations are ambidextrous.

Most organizations are much better at exploiting their existing capabilities than at looking forward and determining which new capabilities to develop. They thus often falter in developing and marketing new products and services. They particularly stumble in implementing transformational change that requires a new identity; one result is that start-up organizations often win out. The reason for this is simple to identify, but hard to overcome. Existing businesses often have practices and policies that are built to serve an existing set of environmental demands and are designed for stability, whereas start-ups don't have a burdensome legacy of practices and policies.

New businesses in old organizations are often weighed down by expenses and controls imposed by the existing corporate structure. It's almost a cliché that successful start-ups are launched in the zero-overhead environment of an entrepreneur's garage, free from the burdensome costs of existing firms. Everyone knows the stories of HP and Microsoft.

Further, when start-ups are a part of a large existing firm they often lack the decision-making authority for the quick "make or break" decisions that are characteristic of new businesses. The Honeywell case, which was discussed in Chapter One, is an example of this; its computer business did not have the authority to move as fast as that volatile industry demanded.

New Business Units

Often the only viable approach to starting new businesses within an existing organization is to create a special business unit that is "independent" of the existing corporation, much like the businesses in Berkshire Hathaway. The degree of independence can vary, but clearly it needs to be high. This may mean that, for example, only the CEO of the new business venture reports to the CEO of the existing company. The rest of the new venture has no reporting relationship to the old organization, so that it is protected against "infection" from parts of the old.

Even though the use of new venture business units sounds like a good approach for a b2change organization, it may not be. It has been used by a number of companies, including Intel, Mead Paper, and P&G, but it is not clear that it has been highly successful. We know of no good research data that has addressed the question of whether new venture units are more likely to be successful than new firms that are founded to enter the same business area. Our guess is that they are not and that in fact they may even be less successful.

In a new venture that we worked with, the people in the new business were transferred from the existing business and still saw themselves as working for that company. Thus, unlike people in a truly entrepreneurial venture, they didn't see the failure of the business as a big threat, because they could always go back to the existing organization. In addition, their compensation followed the practices of the existing organization rather than being like that of the typical start-up venture in which individuals could lose everything or become very wealthy. But perhaps the biggest limitation of the venture was that most individuals came to it laden with a "big corporation" mind-set. When it comes to expenses and speed, what works in a big company can be fatal for a start-up.

The risk associated with creating new business units can be reduced to some extent by building good links between the new organization and the existing organization. A successful example of using the independent unit model to spur growth is Ciba Vision, a business unit of the Swiss pharmaceutical company Novartis. Ciba Vision sells contact lenses and eye care products. Searching for innovative breakthroughs in the markets where it was not performing well, Ciba Vision launched six new venture units, each focused on new product areas. These autonomous units each had their own R&D, finance, and marketing; in short, they were full, functional organizations.

Ciba Vision staffed them with leaders who were willing to challenge the status quo and operate independently. Each of the units had their own uniquely structured processes and organization designs. To ensure that the knowledge generated in the new ventures would be shared and integrated, a single executive was put in charge of all the new units. This approach has paid off for Ciba Vision. The company launched a number of new products and even overtook J&J, the market leader, in some market segments. Its ability to operate in an ambidextrous way also allowed it to maintain its conventional business.

Overall, new business units are a way to produce major change in a b2change organization. They are particularly appropriate when the future scenarios and strategic intent favor getting into a new business area and the organization realizes that its existing business units do not possess the appropriate competencies and capabilities. It is probably the best approach for existing organizations to use when they want to make a major entry into a new business area, but there is no guarantee of success—quite the opposite, in fact: it is a risky strategy. Because it is risky, an organization would do well to consider the options, described in the next sections.

Joint Ventures

Joint ventures are an approach to creating new businesses that is often favored by b2change organizations. Corning, for example, has successfully used them as a way to bring technical innovations to market. Joint ventures typically benefit from having relatively high levels of autonomy, and when this is combined with the right transfer of competencies and capabilities, they can be very successful.

B2change organizations need to see the creation of joint ventures as an important capability. In the future we expect to see more CEOs drive joint-venture capabilities through their organizations just as Larry Bossidy and Ram Charan argue that organizations should drive execution capabilities through organizations today.[7] It's all a question of mind-set. Is change an occasional event—in which case we don't need strong joint-venture capabilities—or is it an ongoing part of an organization's life?

Acquisitions and Mergers

Acquisitions and mergers are two of the most obvious and frequently used ways to produce major strategic change in a corporation. They have a number of obvious and very attractive advantages. They can, for example, provide an entrée into a new market, allow an organization to increase its scale, and provide new core competencies. B2change organizations are cautious about acquisitions and mergers because they have a certain "fatal" attraction. They seem to offer quick and easy reorientation and in some cases transformational change. They can indeed change the very identity of a firm, but, more often than not, they fail. Depending on the scoring system used to measure the success of acquisitions and mergers, the failure rate varies between 60 and 80 percent.

As a general rule, mergers, as contrasted with acquisitions, are particularly difficult to manage. In fact, many have argued that there are no such things as mergers, there are only acquisitions that are mislabeled. All too often, mergers are accompanied by statements that they are "a merger of equals" and that the best people and practices from each organization will be continued in the new merged company. In reality, there is often extreme competition for jobs between the members of the two merged organizations. People often have a strong attachment to the way their organization was run, and they fight to have that way adopted. The result is often conflict and the adoption of a set of practices and policies that really don't fit together to form a coherent whole.

Acquisitions, particularly those in which one organization is significantly larger than the other, present a different set of issues than mergers. They represent a better way for b2change organizations to grow and develop. B2change organizations typically employ one of two acquisition strategies. The first is a hands-off, "We won't touch it; it will operate as an autonomous business unit" approach. This has worked well for Berkshire Hathaway and other true holding companies that buy good businesses and run them independently. The major problem with the hands-off approach is that it really is roughly the equivalent of buying stock in a company or managing an investment fund. It only rarely creates synergies that enhance the value of the acquiring organization.

The second approach is to look for the synergies that can occur when a b2change organization buys a smaller business to bring in a key skill, group of customers, or perhaps technology. When this type of acquisition is handled correctly, it can indeed create a new core competency or at least supplement the core competency of the existing b2change organization. It also can create new customers.

Limited Brands (The Limited) is an organization that has successfully used a mixture of acquisitions and internal development to enter new businesses. Most of its sales came from apparel in the 1990s. Today, as a result of its acquisitions of Victoria's Secret and Bath & Bodyworks, 70 percent or more of its sales come from skin care products, cosmetics, and lingerie. In many respects, these are better businesses than apparel, which suffers from strong competition, relatively low margins, and hard-to-predict fashion trends.

A number of The Limited's existing capabilities, such as store management and location, were directly applicable to the new businesses. But to get a head start with recognizable brands and product expertise, the company felt acquisitions were necessary. The approach has been successful in developing new businesses while allowing The Limited to stay true to its existing identity.

As a rule of thumb, b2change organizations make clear to everyone that an acquired company is going to become part of the acquiring company and is going to operate like the acquiring company. In this type of acquisition, integration can be quick, thorough, and strategic. It rarely changes the operating procedures of the acquiring company, but it may change elements of its business model.

One company that has done an excellent job with acquisitions is Cisco. It has acquired numerous companies, thus building its business, increasing its customer base, and adding important new technologies. In each of its acquisitions, Cisco has been clear that its systems and practices are going to dominate. What Cisco is buying, in essence, is the intellectual capital, human capital, and customers of an existing organization. As the CEO of Cisco explains it, buying an existing group with existing relationships and existing capabilities is cheaper and in many ways easier than building new groups and capabilities.

Sysco, the food-service firm, is another company that has done an excellent job with acquisitions. It has used them primarily to enter into new geographical areas. They have found that buying an existing food-service operation and integrating it into the Sysco network is much quicker than coming into a new territory and starting from scratch.

Sysco has expanded nationally by systematically acquiring companies in key markets. In all of its acquisitions, Sysco has made it clear that the acquired company is expected to adopt most of Sysco's practices. Because the core competency of Sysco is its ability to handle the logistics of wholesale food sales and distribution, it makes good business sense for the acquired companies to adopt Sysco's practices. Occasionally the company picks up a great idea from one of its acquisitions, but given its years of experience and many acquisitions, Sysco simply has more knowledge about wholesale food distribution than the companies it has acquired.

Cisco and Sysco show that acquisitions can be a powerful technique for a b2change organization. However, the very high failure rate of acquisitions warns that for most companies they are unlikely to be successful. Thus, unless an organization has developed the capability of managing the transition from two organizations to one, new business development and strategic change should come from other approaches.

Alliances

One final approach to creating new businesses is to use alliances. Alliances, like acquisitions, can be a quick and effective way for a b2change organization to add to its capabilities and competencies. One recent study found that U.S. companies announced 74,000 acquisitions and 57,000 alliances from 1996 to 2001. Clearly these two structural options are on the agenda of most organizations. The pace has slowed some since 2001. In 2002, for example, U.S. firms announced "only" 7,795 acquisitions and 5,048 alliances. But that was a period when the economy was weak, and in 2004 and 2005, activity picked up.

There are many different kinds of alliances, but most of them have in common an agreement between two or more organizations that, at least at the beginning, is seen as mutually beneficial. Organizations may, for example, market each other's products or share technologies and core competencies, potentially gaining such advantages as market share and visibility.

The Star alliance of major air carriers is one of the most highly visible alliances. The members (United, Lufthansa, and others) share a great deal of information, conduct joint marketing, and coordinate operations. The alliance has allowed members to offer customers a global capability, giving them an advantage over airlines that serve only regional markets. They can offer connections and access to flights and flight information around the world. Given the difficulties of expanding airlines to new countries, the Star alliance has allowed its members to become global players much more quickly than they could have otherwise. Had they tried to do it through acquisitions or internal growth, they would still be decades away (perhaps an eternity away) from achieving this objective.

Alliances are often difficult to create and are certainly not an automatic success. Before b2change organizations enter into alliances, they need to conduct a great deal of due diligence on their prospective partners and protect themselves against their alliance partner eventually becoming a competitor as a result of what it learns from the alliance. This happened in the Fuji/ Xerox case, in which Xerox's core competencies and intellectual property were shared and Fuji desired to expand into manufacturing products similar to the ones it was getting from its partner.

Like implementing acquisitions and mergers, the ability to form effective alliances may best be thought of as a capability that an organization needs to develop. Forming alliances is not something organizations naturally do well, but having the ability to do it can enhance both current organizational performance and the ability to change. For example, it is much easier to exit a market if it means severing an alliance than if it means closing down your own operations in that market. It is also easier to grow into a new market by forming an alliance than it is by following a build-from-nothing strategy. This is particularly true if entering that market requires developing a new core competency or organizational capability.

Acquisition or Alliance

B2change organizations view alliances and acquisitions as alternative ways to accomplish the objective of quickly changing their performance and capabilities. The change can be minor or transformational. Ideally, b2change organizations should be capable of structuring and operating both acquisitions and alliances, enabling them to choose the one that best fits what they need to accomplish.

As was mentioned earlier, Cisco has for years followed an acquisitions-based growth strategy. It also has entered into a large number of alliances. The company has a director of corporate development who is responsible for both acquisitions and strategic alliances. This puts the decision about whether to pursue an acquisition or alliance in the hands of a single, knowledgeable individual. When the decision options include the possibility of developing a particular technology or capability internally, this structure makes a great deal of sense and increases the likelihood of a good decision.

Cisco is particularly likely to use alliances where the competency or capability it needs is not central to the organization's future. The rationale here is rather obvious: the company doesn't want to trust critical core competencies and organizational capabilities to an organization that it doesn't completely control. If it is acquiring a support technology or something that isn't critical to the business, then an alliance may make a great deal of sense, as an alliance can often be activated and terminated with less cost.

Interestingly enough, alliances may be particularly effective when "soft" or human resources are a critical part of the the desired competence. Even a company that is very skilled in integrating soft resources, such as human talent, can very easily lose those resources as a result of an acquisition. This is much less likely to happen with alliances, because they are less disruptive and require less change on the part of the partners. There is rarely a reason, for example, to significantly change reward systems or career tracks as a result of an alliance. Ultimately an organization's choice between an alliance and an acquisition may best rest on the degree of uncertainty the company faces. The greater the uncertainty, the more that alliances make sense.

Conclusion

We began this chapter by stressing the importance of organizations having an external focus and structuring for change. It is clear that there are multiple structural approaches to organizing. Each structural option that we discussed (for example, customer-focused, alliances, and acquisitions) requires an organization to have an orchestration capability to successfully execute it. One clear implication for a b2change organization is that unless it is sure of its long-term structure, it may want to develop the capability to operate several different structures so that it can change its structure when necessary.

The structural approach that a b2change organization takes must reflect its current and future environments, identity, strategic intent, approach to creating value, and expectations about the kinds of changes it needs to make. As we will see in the chapters that follow, the structural choices an organization makes have important implications for the processes, people, and reward system it needs.

Chapter 5

Developing the Right Information, Measurement, and Decision-Making Processes

Built-to-Change Strategy:
Move Business Decision Making Down the Organization

T he designing process in the B2Change Model must address three important questions that form the basis of an effective dynamic alignment:

1. What kind of information do you collect, and how do you communicate it?

2. How do you measure individuals, units, and the organization as whole?

3. Who should be involved in making decisions?

Each of these processes needs to be actively coordinated with the organization's structure and with each other. Like every other feature of a b2change organization, they need to support both organizational effectiveness and change.

INFORMATION

The information processes of an organization are roughly equivalent to the nervous system of a human being. They permeate every part of the organization as well as sense key areas of the environment. The better the information an organization gathers about its performance, its capabilities, and its environment, the better the organization will perform and the more effectively it will be able to change. What information should b2change organizations collect?

- Performance: How are we doing?
- Capabilities and competencies: How strong are we?
- Environment: What's going on and what does it mean?

Information systems need to monitor company operating performance and the strength of its competencies and capabilities. For example, a company that has quality as a capability needs to gather ongoing data showing how the quality of its products compares with that of competitors. It also needs measures of how well its quality processes are operating.

The best information systems produce metrics that can be used for goal setting and, as we will discuss in later chapters, for reward allocation. They also provide an organization with feedback about how it can improve its performance and manage change. Having an information system that calibrates costs and performance for major competencies and capabilities is an ambitious goal, but one b2change organizations strive to achieve.

In addition to information about how the organization is operating, data need to be gathered on what is happening in the business environment. The nature of the data needs to be specific to each organization, but two points are clear. First, b2change organizations gather data on how their competitors are performing. Benchmarking an organization's performance against the performance of its competitors can be a powerful source of motivation to perform better as well as an indicator of the need to change. Second, b2change organizations gather data about how the environment is changing (and is likely to change) and reflect on the change implications of the data, so that they can respond with changes of their own.

One weakness of many organizations' information systems is that they operate in silos. Comprehensive data gathering needs to cut across an organization and look at multiple activities.

A simple example of the silo problem is the staffing function's perennial challenge in determining which hiring methods are best—for example, does it make sense to hire from prestigious universities, or are local colleges just as good? In many organizations, recruiters have a hard time making an assessment because they don't have employee performance data. However, the department next door, the one that runs the performance management system, does have data on how hires have performed. The solution is simple but hard to execute for organizations that are designed for stability: the two departments need to work together to determine the success rate of hires from different colleges.

One company we worked with did just such an analysis of their hires, and to their surprise the most successful hires came from one of the less prestigious schools. Graduates from this school cost less, stayed longer, and performed as well as those from more highly regarded schools. This is a simple but poignant example of how information gathering that cuts across silos is essential for understanding performance.

Information Transparency

Transparency is key to the effectiveness of a b2change organization's information processes. (This is also true in decision making, which we will consider later in this chapter.) Metrics need to be visible to those who influence them, who are affected by them, and whose performance can be improved by knowing them. Keeping measures secret not only makes it difficult for individuals to correct their behavior but also takes away a potential motivator of change.

In traditional organizations, information about competitors and the business environment goes to senior management, who ponder it and, if it is disturbing enough, launch a change initiative. In a b2change organization, this information goes to all employees in order to create a culture and a structure where organization members are connected to the environment.

Employees need to be encouraged to ask, "What are we going to do about these new technologies? How can we reduce our costs? How can we respond to the rise of competitors overseas? What capabilities do we need to counter a competitor's new products?" Well-informed employees will push for constant change; they will not sit in a cocoon of ignorance that is only irregularly punctured by management's change programs.

Of course, there are limits to how public business information can be, but as a general rule, the more public the results are, the more effectively they can be used to improve current performance and the more they can be a motivator of change. This is, of course, particularly true with respect to information that compares an organization's performance with competitors' performance. There is nothing like competition when it comes to motivating an organization to perform better.

Communicating Information to Employees

Encouragingly, there is evidence that organizations are providing more performance information to their members than in the past.[1] Table 5.1 presents data on this point. From 1987 to 2005, there is a significant increase in the information that Fortune 1000 firms provide to their employees, particularly with respect to data about business unit results and business plans and goals. According to these data, most (but not all) employees now get information about corporate performance, business unit performance, and business plans. They are much less likely to get information about new technologies and competitors' performance. The failure to share data about the performance of competitors is a serious omission, given the role it can play in motivating performance and change.

Often it is difficult for individuals to understand how they can influence the results of a large organization; thus giving them information about the performance of their own business unit is critically important. Doing so allows managers to establish meaningful goals for individuals—goals that individuals can understand and influence. It also allows all members of an

TABLE 5.1. Information Sharing

	1987	1990	1993	1996	1999	2002	2005
Corporate operating results	4.3	4.1	4.4	4.5	4.2	4.3	4.4
Unit operating results	3.6	3.5	3.8	4.0	4.1	4.3	4.2
New technologies	2.7	2.4	2.8	2.8	2.7	3.0	3.4
Business plans and goals	3.3	3.2	3.5	3.7	3.9	4.2	4.1
Competitors' performance	2.2	2.3	2.5	2.6	2.7	2.8	2.9

Percentage of employees getting information: 1 = 0–20 percent to 5 = 81–100 percent

organization to talk about the business and the business strategy in a meaningful way. Everyone is encouraged to understand how their particular unit is operating and to make needed improvements.

There are numerous ways to communicate with employees. B2change organizations leverage one of the most underutilized forms: face-to-face communication. This is particularly the case when the subject of the communication is organization strategy, business results, and improvement opportunities. Too many traditional firms have become lazy, communicating only through email or press releases. These methods are cheap, but they are inadequate for a b2change organization.

For there to be meaningful employee involvement and understanding, managers need to talk about business data face-to-face, stress what is most relevant, and answer questions. There is no doubt that this costs money and takes time, but managers in a b2change organization know it is precisely the kind of investment that needs to be made. Communicating is a necessary process for creating a change capability, and senior management must assume the responsibility for it. The top management team at Deploy Solutions, for example, recognizes this. They spend one to two hours *every week* discussing what information will be useful to the employees and how to present it effectively. This is a big investment in education and motivation, an investment that helps create a capability for ongoing change.

Where it is possible to get employees together for town hall meetings, it is well worth doing. Wal-Mart, for one, has used Saturday business reviews as a key technique for driving its business. At a smaller company, Planar Systems, the CEO routinely asks questions and debates strategy in town hall meetings. In addition to these meetings, he holds a monthly meeting with fifty to sixty managers in a room where everyone can see each other and where they constructively discuss operations and strategy. Because it is a technology company, Planar also uses email and encourages employees to "ask the expert" about the business. Face-to-face meetings and town hall sessions are not practical in all organizations because of geographical dispersion. Possible substitutes include video, voice mail, and email.

Samuel J. Palmisano, CEO of IBM, has run what IBM calls "jam sessions." They focus on IBM's values and other issues. IBM, like many companies, faces the challenge of maintaining their strong identity while adapting to a changing business environment. It runs jam sessions to sense which of its traditional values and practices need to be updated. These are not just one-way communication sessions—they are also an information-gathering activity.

One of IBM's major jam sessions was a three-day live intranet debate. At the heart of the session was the question, "What should IBM preserve from the old IBM culture, and what do we need to change?" It had broad participation—over fifty thousand employees logged in and posted ten thousand comments. The session was only one step in a transformational change, but a positive one, and it helped IBM reinvent itself as part of its transition from a hardware to a service company (over 60 percent of its revenue now comes from services).

. . .

Here is a list of the seven most important characteristics of a good information system. Compare them to what your organization does, to determine how close you are to having a b2change information system. Good information systems:

1. Provide comprehensive data on key processes
2. Integrate data across departmental boundaries
3. Monitor capabilities as well as performance
4. Are linked to goal setting and rewards
5. Include information on competitors
6. Provide trend data on the business environment
7. Make measurements visible throughout the organization

MEASUREMENT

A b2change organization addresses two issues in the development of its performance measurement system. The first concerns what *units* to measure. The potential variation here is enormous—measures can and, in most cases, need to focus on what individuals do, what teams do, what departments do—all the way up to how the organization as a total entity performs.

The second issue concerns *what* to measure. As discussed above, every organization needs to focus on measures of current performance, but what distinguishes the b2change organization from others is its emphasis on measuring *predictors of future performance*. Most companies are comfortable if measures show they are doing well now. In the b2change organization, which has truly internalized the notion of continual change, comfort comes only when measures show that the company is on track to do well in the future.

In the sections that follow, we will build on our prior discussion of information systems that addressed "what to measure." We will look extensively at how b2change organizations measure individuals, followed by a look at how they measure teams, business units, the total organization, and key processes.

Measuring Individuals

Virtually every organization has a performance management system that, among other things, is intended to provide data about how well individual employees are performing.[2] The systems that are actually in place in organizations vary enormously in what they are supposed to accomplish, what measures they use, what is communicated about the results of the appraisal, and what is actually measured. Measurement of individual performance is an area where organizations seem to be constantly changing their practices, usually in response to dissatisfaction with their existing system. Organizations always seem to hope that the next system they develop will be the answer.

There are three major reasons organizations have so much trouble with the measurement of individual performance. First, there are many design options, so there are many opportunities to make design mistakes. Choosing the right tool is only one of many design decisions that need to be made. Second, in most circumstances both the evaluator and evaluated are uncomfortable with the process and have not received any training in how to do it. Third, in many situations the measurement of performance is a difficult task that requires complex judgments.

One option that b2change organizations should consider, given the difficulty of measuring individual performance, is simply not to use measures and information processes that focus on individual performance—in other words, to not do it. In most U.S. and European organizations this is not a realistic option. Legal requirements and cultural beliefs support the notion that individual performance should be measured and should have an impact on compensation and promotion.

Despite these constraints, b2change organizations have options that most other organizations do not.

As you'll recall, two of the structural elements of the b2change organization are teams and small, close-to-the-customer units. These elements, when combined with the elimination of individual job descriptions, shift the performance focus away from hard-to-execute individual measures toward group measures. Thus b2change organizations can consider the possibility of not measuring individual performance in situations where the way work is designed renders it difficult or impossible to develop adequate metrics of individual behavior. This is likely to be true, for example, in a highly interdependent work arrangement such as a software design team or a process production team that is operating a chemical plant or a paper machine. In these cases it is difficult and dysfunctional to separate the performance of individuals from the performance of the total team. If you are a sports fan, think football, doubles tennis, soccer, or basketball—not track and field or golf.

We will look at measuring team performance later in this chapter, but what about organization designs where individual performance *can* be managed? In these situations, we believe it is very important to measure individual performance, but clearly it's better not to do it at all than it is to do it poorly. With this point in mind, here are a set of practices that b2change organizations can use to make the individual measurement process run smoothly and produce good data.

Conduct Top-to-Bottom Appraisals. B2change organizations not only conduct performance appraisals well, they start at the top of the organization. All too often the senior executives in an organization are not appraised and do not appraise their subordinates. The result is that performance appraisals become something senior executives tell middle management to do to lower-level employees. Needless to say, this sets up a negative dynamic in the way people think about and conduct appraisals. Among other negatives, employees see no senior management role modeling, and senior managers are not held accountable for their performance. For these reasons, the performance appraisal process needs to start with the board of directors doing a thorough and rigorous appraisal of the CEO and to cascade down from there.

CEO Michael Dell provides a good example of taking assessment at the top seriously. His appraisal includes a survey that collects data from a broad range of employees. Recent results showed that a large number of employees felt Dell was impersonal and was emotionally detached from the workforce. What happened next says a great deal about Dell's efforts to continuously improve his performance and that of the organization.

Dell immediately faced his top management team and offered a frank self-critique, acknowledging that he is very shy and that this can make him appear aloof and unapproachable. He vowed to change and followed up by showing a videotape of that talk to every manager in the company. Further, he put some desktop props in place to help remind him and others of the change he was committed to. For example, he put a bulldozer on his desk to remind him not ram ideas through before testing them with others.

In addition to the behavior changes that may result from Dell's efforts, the symbolism of his being appraised is very important. It sends a message to the entire organization that improvement is expected and is standard operating procedure for everyone in the organization, not just the lower-level employees.

Measure Appraisal Effectiveness. B2change organizations evaluate how well appraisals are done by managers. This makes a significant statement about their importance to the organization, gives managers feedback about how well they conduct the appraisals, and motivates them to do a good job. Systematic measurement of appraisals should include three elements: an audit of the quality of the written documents produced in the process, a gathering of survey data on how the individuals who are appraised feel about the appraisal event, and measures of the timeliness of the appraisal meetings and reports.

Set Goals in Advance and Keep Them Current. B2change organizations establish specific and quantifiable goals for acceptable levels of performance. Managers and their subordinates sit down before the performance period begins and establish what measures will be used in the evaluation and what levels of performance are challenging but achievable. Research suggests that the more interactive the goal-setting activity is, the more likely people are to accept the goals, be motivated by them, and see performance appraisal as a fair and reasonable process.[3]

When managers set goals, they need to keep in mind that the difficulty of the goal is a key determinant of performance. Easy-to-achieve goals tend to lead to poor performance, but so do goals that are too difficult. When goals are set low, individuals settle for low levels of performance. When goals are set too high, people give up because they do not believe they can achieve them, or they cheat in order to give the impression of achieving them. Goals that are perceived to be achievable but challenging should be the objective because they are the most motivating and produce the highest levels of performance.

You may have thought of a potential problem that goal setting creates for b2change organizations. Most organizations set annual goals. Annual goals presume a reasonable stability for the next twelve months. That stability may occur, but b2change organizations never work on the assumption of stability. They engage in frequent reviews of goals.

The Orvis Company reviews each individual's key performance measures *every month*. It is a big investment, but a necessary one. It's not that common that goals need to be changed, but Orvis is always monitoring the environment, and the reviews ensure that the company does change goals when the environment demands it.

Listen to the Individuals Being Appraised. B2change organizations allow the people who are being appraised to respond and provide input at the end of the performance appraisal period. They can present their version of how well they have performed their work assignments against preset goals. Our research supports the value of giving people this opportunity *before* their appraiser reaches a performance judgment.[4] It leads to more accurate appraisals and to individuals believing they have been fairly appraised.

Use Objective Performance Measures. Many appraisals fail because the performance measures consist of vague ratings with such terms as "excellent," or poorly defined general traits or personality dimensions such as "reliable," "communication skills," "customer focus," and "leadership." These traits are difficult to judge and almost always lead to communication breakdowns and misunderstandings between appraisers and individuals who are being appraised. B2change organizations adopt a balanced scorecard of behavior- and outcome-based measures that quantify, or at least clearly identify, what performance and behavior are being judged. For example, rather than assessing the general dimension of reliability, the appraisal should focus on whether critical work has been completed on time and whether preset goals were met.

Here is a simple example of how agreement between rater and ratee can be increased when the appraisal focuses on observable behaviors and the business outcomes they produce. Assume that growth is an important business objective for a company; given this, the behaviors that lead to growth need to be identified and each person assessed against those behaviors. For instance, a saleswoman in the company might be appraised on such behaviors as the proportion of her sales that come from new products, the number of suggestions she made for product innovation, or her opening of new sales territories and customer accounts. These types of specific measures establish the strongest link between the organization's business strategy and the appraisal process. They also provide objective data on which to base an appraisal.

Employ Meaningful Ratings. B2change organizations reject the notion of ranking subordinates and using rating scales that require the rater to place a fixed percent in each category. Traditional organizations, in keeping with their stability-oriented and bureaucratic assumptions have come up with a variety of measurement schemes that go way beyond the precision that is necessary or justified by the process. For example, they rank order hundreds or thousands of people from 1 to whatever the total number of individuals is. It is like trying to measure the length of an object to the closest thousandth of an inch using an ordinary straight ruler; the data needed to compare people so precisely just isn't available.

B2change organizations do need to rigorously assess the performance of their members and ask whether they are better off retaining the individuals or replacing them with somebody from the outside. In most situations, a three-tier rating system (some version of, "walks on water," "swims," "drowns") typically provides all the information needed to handle pay increases and to identify candidates for promotion and dismissal. In certain instances, a fourth category ("too new to judge") is needed for employees who are new to the job and just learning how to perform it.

PECO Energy Corporation is one company that uses only three categories: "great," "OK," and "needs improvement." This simple system provides all the information the company feels it needs to manage its employees. It replaced a five-point scale that had produced ratings that were more complicated but not more useful.

One rating practice that b2change organizations should never use is forced distributions. Many organizations (for example, GE, EDS, and Accenture) require their managers to identify a certain percentage of employees who are failing, often 5 to 10 percent, and a certain percentage who are doing particularly well, often 15 to 20 percent. Jack Welch used this practice at GE, and he has argued that others should use it as well.[5] He also goes on to say that in his view, organizations should fire the employees who fall in the bottom category.

The forced distribution approach ignores the reality that in some work groups there are no poor performers and in others there are no good performers. It causes managers to disown the appraisal event and essentially to say, "I was just following the rules" when they deal with a "poorly" performing employee. Further, it moves the organization significantly away from a virtuous spiral environment. Instead of employees asking how they can improve it, the method fosters competition and survival of the luckiest or most political.

Given these problems, why do companies use the forced distribution approach? The answer is simple but not particularly flattering to many managers. It represents an easy answer to solving a classic problem: rating inflation. Just as in universities where professors tend to give high grades to everyone, many managers find it easier to be generous with high ratings, and, as a result, many organizations suffer from top-heavy performance appraisal scores. Instead of dealing with the problem as a failure of leadership, some companies adopt a dysfunctional bureaucratic solution, mandating a result. Because it is a leadership problem, the best solution rests in creating effective leadership rather than in the top-down bureaucratic mandate of a forced distribution system.

Managers need to be held accountable for the ratings that they produce. It has to be clear that ratings must be justified by operating results that are correspondingly high. It often helps to set up cross-organizational meetings in which managers have to justify their ratings to their peers and top executives. Capital One and Intel call these "cross-calibration" meetings. Both companies have effectively used them to control rating inflation and to develop consistency in how managers use the rating scale.

Overall, the best solution to rating inflation is not a bureaucratic rule; it is a set of behaviors and processes that are put in place and modeled by the leadership of the organization. In other words, senior executives need to be leaders, not bureaucrats.

Assess Skills and Competencies. From a change perspective, it is particularly important for an organization to develop good measures of an individual's skills, knowledge, and competencies. Without these indicators it is difficult to know what the human capital resources of an organization are and, therefore, what type of changes and performance an organization is capable of. Knowing the characteristics of the human capital that can be deployed is vital in developing and implementing new strategies. At the very least, such knowledge can help a company decide how many existing employees can contribute to a new strategy, how much training needs to be done, and what kind of hiring is necessary to yield the skill mix the organization needs to move forward.

Information about skills and competencies also is critical in diagnosing what the problem is when strategies run into difficulty. As we discussed in Chapter Three, it may well be that the strategy is not flawed but that the organization simply doesn't have the capability to execute it. The skills of the individuals who are charged with executing the strategy may be at the core of an organization's performance problem.

Change, even minor change, almost always requires individuals to learn new skills. This requires a performance appraisal system that helps individuals understand what skills they need, provides them with a development plan that allows them to acquire those skills, and, of course, sets the stage for their being rewarded when they develop the new needed skills. Thus a performance management system that evaluates the skills of individuals and gives them advice on their development is a critical support process when virtually any type of change is called for.

Discuss Development and Rewards Separately. B2change organizations separate the discussion of pay for performance from the discussion of development needs and activities. This means that the appraiser and the person being appraised should hold two separate discussions—one that covers past performance and the resulting pay increase or bonus, and a second, separated by at least a week, that reviews the future development and career situation of the individual.

Use the Web. Information about the assessment of individuals needs to become a matter of record in the organization. The best way to do this is an intranet-based system that profiles each individual in the organization, including his or her task assignments, performance goals, and recent results. It also needs to include information about skills, competencies, and plans to develop new skills.

Intranet systems can also facilitate an efficient internal labor market—something that is more important to b2change firms than to traditional firms, as b2change firms expect ongoing redeployment of talent. When employees can access information about the skills needed for various kinds of work—and the programs available to teach those skills—they can take the initiative in their development.

When managers can access information about the skills of employees, they can seek out the talent they need. Having a searchable database of skills is much more efficient than the traditional word-of-mouth, hit-or-miss approach that is used by most organizations to fill new openings.

Some of the major professional service firms (for example, PricewaterhouseCoopers, McKinsey) do a good job of using information systems that profile the skills of individuals. They have online profiles of all their professional staff. These profiles can be accessed by managers looking for individual skills that fit a project team or a job opening. For example, if somebody needs an accountant who speaks Russian and understands international accounting practices, he or she can go to a database and see if any employees have this particular skill set.

SAS, the very successful software company, has an extensive skills database that helps managers analyze the fit between the skills the organization has and the skills it will need in the future. This helps them manage change as well as assess how likely it is that SAS can make specific changes.

Measuring Teams

As we indicated earlier in this chapter, b2change organizations tend to prefer processes for measuring teams. Some of the most important, and most complicated, performance measurement systems are those that focus on groups of individuals who have responsibility for a particular business process, customer, or geographical area.

In many respects, the same principles that apply to measuring individual performance are appropriate for team performance. Measuring team performance is particularly important when a team has a high level of interdependence, such that individuals on the team need to work together closely to produce a product or a service. In these cases, it is critical that the team as a whole be assessed and that the process focus on both its performance level and its capability level. It is also important that the results of any assessment be given to the team so that it has the chance to improve its performance.

Assessing the performance of the members of a team may or may not be desirable, depending on the situation. Doing so can take attention away from the performance of the team as a whole. B2change organizations often have the team members assess each other. This can be quite powerful both as a team-building activity and as a motivator of performance improvement by individuals. But—and this is an important but—peer assessment requires the right measures and methods. It is not something that should be "just done."

In most cases, it is not possible to generate a profit-and-loss statement for a team. Instead of being responsible for a whole business, a team is usually responsible for part of a business or a particular customer segment. Nevertheless, it may be possible to get at least some financial numbers as well as production numbers for a team. Obviously these are desirable, as they help team members see the team's impact on the performance of the organization. Financial data also make it easier to set performance goals for the team and to reward the team based on its contribution to the overall performance of the organization.

Measuring Business Units

One of the advantages of having business units in organizations involves measurement. It is often possible to generate a profit-and-loss measure for business units. This is an obvious advantage from both a current operating perspective and a change perspective. It allows an organization to get good feedback about how each of its parts is operating and can provide a powerful incentive to improve performance and to change. As we will discuss in later chapters, this is particularly true when rewards are tied to business unit performance.

When measuring business units (or organizations for that matter), it is important that performance be measured not only in terms of financial performance but also in terms of capabilities and competencies. In the B2Change Model, competencies and capabilities are a firm's means of creating value. Measuring them is as important as counting inventory. To do an adequate job of measuring competencies and capabilities, each business unit needs to identify what its most important competencies and capabilities are and how they can be measured. Again, in the B2Change Model, such measurement is expected; it's tied into the ongoing strategizing process and isn't some optional or an off-to-the-side activity.

It's a good idea to be explicit in identifying the link between individual skills, business unit competencies and capabilities, and financial performance. One of the advantages of having business units is that these links are more obvious and hence easier for employees to act on than are corporate level links.

At the risk of being tedious, we must make one more point: as we noted earlier, it is critical that the results of business unit assessments be shared with employees. The sharing process is central to creating motivation to perform well and to change when performance falters. Poor performance rarely leads to any motivation to change if employees don't understand what performance is needed or have information about results. Indeed, often individuals' resistance to change in traditional firms is a direct result of their not understanding why change is necessary and how their behavior can affect performance.

Measuring Organizational Performance

Public companies spend a great deal of money and time preparing financial statements that they issue to their shareholders. B2change organizations do more; they make an active effort to share these results with all of their employees. Sharing performance results with all employees has a number of advantages, most notably that employees understand the business better and as a result understand when and how they need to change.

The major issues surrounding the reporting of organizational performance go beyond whether organizations share financial results with their employees. One set of issues, which was addressed by the Sarbanes-Oxley Act, involves the accuracy of the financial reports that are issued. Clearly, transparency and better audit controls are needed, but from the point of view of organization change, the most important issue concerns something that is not reported to investors: intangibles.

Measuring and Reporting Intangibles. What is not reported to the public are metrics that reflect on the intangibles that influence organizational performance and the value of a company. Organizations are not required to report on intangibles, and most do not report either internally or externally on metrics other than accounting metrics. In many cases, this is because they simply don't have the measures; in other cases, it is because they have chosen not to. Yet measures of intangibles are often precisely the kind of leading indicators that a b2change organization needs.

B2change organizations crave data on employee motivation, satisfaction, and involvement, but reject the traditional survey approach because it can be too slow and infrequent. Rather, they utilize the intranet to obtain regular (weekly or monthly) online pulse surveys that measure reactions to change as well as motivation, understanding of the business strategy, and involvement. The results are instantly available and used by organization members to implement change.

The balanced scorecard approach to measuring and reporting organization performance has had a positive impact on internal and external reporting. Although the implementation of this approach varies enormously from company to company, it always includes nonfinancial metrics: customers' perspectives, internal processes in the organization, and the learning and growth activities of the organization. The details of what is measured under these three nonfinancial areas vary significantly from organization to organization, as they need to reflect a company's particular identity and strategic intent.

It is beyond the scope of this discussion to go into detail about the types of measures and measurement areas that are appropriate for different types of organizations. It is appropriate, however, to note that b2change organizations develop and utilize lead indicators that focus on their organizational capabilities and core competencies.

Measuring Capabilities and Competencies. An example of how an organization can use metrics of organizational capabilities is described by Dave Ulrich and Norm Smallwood in a 2004 *Harvard Business Review* article.[6] They asked the

InterContinental Hotels' executives to assess their company on both the actual state and the desired state of their capabilities. The results showed that for the firm to execute its current strategy there needed to be a great improvement in collaboration and speed. In the areas of shared mind-set and accountability, however, the company was already at a satisfactory level. This analysis provided momentum toward change, particularly when the results were broadly shared within the organization. Unlike financial analysis, which often shows only that "you need to change," analysis of capabilities shows *what* you need to change and can be an indicator of performance long before the financial numbers show what is happening.

B2change organizations need to think hard about which competencies and capabilities are important enough to warrant measurement at the business unit or organization level. The organization's strategic intent should drive this decision. Kaplan and Norton's *Strategy Maps* provides a disciplined way to decide which capabilities to measure.[7] A completed "strategy map" shows how key competencies and capabilities lead to the implementation of strategy.

The important point is that a b2change organization must measure and constantly monitor its make-or-break competencies and capabilities. Measurement is necessary from the point of view not only of strategy development but of process improvement. As work on quality has shown, it is very difficult to improve a process without good metrics on how the process is operating and how it performs. Providing the results of metrics to individuals who are responsible for the key capabilities in an organization can be a powerful source of motivation to improve those capabilities, particularly when the metrics are used for goal setting and are tied to rewards.

Only if capabilities are measured and their outcomes known is it possible to increase their effectiveness. In addition it is difficult to alter them when an important change in the environment calls for improved levels of performance. Good measurement of capabilities is important both from an operating performance perspective and from a change management perspective.

Using Budgets as Performance Measures

We have reserved a discussion of budgets as part of organization performance measurement until now because they don't fit in a b2change organization. Most traditional organizations use budgets to measure organizational performance as well as individual group and unit performance. But more often, budgets are used to exercise control and become a force against change for several reasons.

First, they are set once a year and difficult to change after they have been set. This is particularly true when they are very detailed and specify all possible expenses. In the past, annual recalibration of spending levels may have made sense because it matched the pace of change, but today it doesn't. Change in the business environment doesn't wait for the earth to make a complete revolution around the sun.

Second, when managers are held accountable for the results of their budget, they are hesitant about over- or underspending them. Two all-too-common results are that badly needed changes don't get funded and individuals spend money in categories that don't warrant it simply because if they don't spend it, it will be lost when the year ends. Because of the rigidity it produces, the traditional budget process has no place in a b2change organization.

Of course, budgets don't have to be rigid and unchangeable during the year. B2change firms have two options with respect to budgets: alter the budget process so that it is more change friendly or eliminate it altogether.

One way to make budgets more change friendly is simply to put some slack in the budget and to avoid detailed budget categories and numbers. Another approach is to give individuals a budget for innovation and new initiatives that they can use or not use during the year depending on what kind of changes come along. Among the best practitioners of this method are 3M, Intel, and other technology firms, which have budgets for local innovations in particular work groups and work areas. They also have money budgeted that can be applied for by individuals or groups of employees anywhere in the corporation if the money in the particular area is not sufficient to support their change or if they are denied it but believe strongly in their innovation.

3M is a company that has received a considerable amount of publicity because it gives individuals 15 percent of their time to pursue changes that they think are appropriate. This is not a "cool idea" 3M recently implemented; it is an entrenched method 3M has used for many years. This approach has helped it continue to be a leader in new product development and innovation.

The adoption of activity-based costing methods is another good alternative. Many traditional budgets are built around categories of spending, such as salaries, supplies, and travel, rather than on a business process. There are a number of problems with this approach. All too often it means that an organization gains no understanding of the relationship between money spent and the outcomes produced. With activity-based costing, expenses reflect processes, such as hiring new employees, developing new products, and delivering customer service.

Activity-based costing complements nicely the focus on measuring competencies and capabilities described earlier. By developing activity-based costing, organizations position themselves to make good decisions about whether costs are reasonable and whether to change or alter the process. In some cases, they can benchmark the costs against the costs incurred by other organizations for similar processes.

Today a number of companies measure the cost of HR administration, as well as other administrative services, and share benchmark data. Doing so helps them evaluate their spending and performance in such areas as salary administration and training. In the case of Prudential and International Paper, activity-based costing played an important role in their decision to outsource HR administration.[8]

The second option for b2change firms is to eliminate budgets entirely. There is a group of companies in Europe that has gotten together to explore and experiment with the creation of budgetless organizations. This is not to say they eliminate measurement; but they do eliminate the detailed budgeting process that occupies so much time at certain points of the year, produces organizational rigidity and, often, generates mountains of reports that people rarely look at.

The budgetless approach is described in the book *Beyond Budgeting*, by Jeremy Hope and Robin Fraser.[9] At the heart of the beyond-budgeting movement is the insight that when an organization uses a budget as a rigid control mechanism, the result is all kinds of counterproductive game playing and, what is most salient from our point of view, stifled change. A budget is in practice a fixed performance contract between one level of an organization and another. The operative word is "fixed," which is why it is very hard to create a b2change organization without adopting some of the beyond-budgeting philosophy.

A leader in the beyond-budgeting movement is the Swedish bank Svenska Handelsbanken. The bank trusts that managers will work to optimize profit—and hence do not need a fixed contract under which they promise certain results in what we all know is an uncertain future. Managers still set cost and revenue targets—and these are very much stretch targets—but they are not judged against what they guessed they could do. Rather they are judged against the performance of a peer group within the firm, an external benchmark, or what the market has done in its sector. Hope and Fraser point out that although finding the right comparator is always an issue, you can often find comparators within the firm if you look.

Instead of engaging in an annual planning process, beyond-budgeting firms continually go through four steps:

1. Check: How are we doing?
2. Aim: Should we reset our goals?
3. Plan: How will we achieve our goals?
4. Act: Execute the plan.

Coordinating an Organization's Metrics

It is important to have comprehensive performance measures for all parts of an organization, but simply having them is not enough. They need to be actively coordinated such that the measurement system encourages integration across the organization and drives everyone to achieve common goals. Integration of this type has to start with the strategic intent and with top management's translating the strategy into goals, which can be cascaded down the organization.

Siebel Systems, before its acquisition by Oracle, serves as an interesting example of the coordination of goal setting and performance measurement. Siebel had a very clear strategy that emphasized sticking to its core software competency and establishing a strong focus on its customers. The firm's number one goal was customer satisfaction. It recognized that the behavior of its employees was the key determinant of customer satisfaction. Siebel therefore used an employee relationship management software system that, among other things, focused on customer satisfaction.

Here is how the Siebel system worked. During the first week of each quarter, Siebel's executive committee met and established the objectives for the next three months. By the seventh day of the month following the meeting, the objectives of the CEO were posted on the company's intranet, which was accessible by all the employees in the organization. By the fifteenth, the CEO's objectives were translated into objectives for the various functions and business units that reported to the vice presidents. By the twenty-first of the month, every employee was expected to have posted and received feedback on his or her objectives.

The net result of this approach was that by early in each quarter, all employees had produced performance objectives that were the result of a downward-cascading process, and all the objectives had metrics associated with them. Through the employee management software, anyone could view the objectives of any other employee, including those of the CEO and the members of the executive committee. Because customer satisfaction was a key focus of the committee, all employees had a customer satisfaction goal in their personal objectives.

The evaluation of individual performance at Siebel was directly tied to and subject to the same process. Each manager was responsible for evaluating his or her reports by the fifteenth of the first month of each quarter. The results of the review were posted on the Siebel performance module and were visible to the managers to whom the employee reports. This means that all managers could see the performance reviews of individuals at lower levels than theirs. The obvious advantage to the Siebel system is that employees gain insight into how their goals and targets follow from the company strategy. Because they also see company performance results, they can get a sense of how they contribute to the company's performance.

The Siebel approach exemplifies several of the features of the b2change organization: frequent goal setting (in this case quarterly), customer focus (which is in everyone's goals), and transparency (everyone can see each other's goals). Missing from the Siebel approach to performance management is an assessment of the organization's capabilities and core competencies. The company doesn't conduct a regular assessment (as InterContinental Hotels does, discussed earlier) that looks at how well its organizational capabilities are developing and performing. Adding this to the Siebel system would seem to be an important step. It would enable an organization to regularly set performance goals and review performance, and to systematically look at the *causes* of organizational performance.

Particularly for organizations that experience rapid environmental change, it makes sense to look at key capabilities at least annually, ask whether these are still the right ones, and assess how effective the organization has been in developing them. This approach both enables an organization to identify where change is needed and provides a potential incentive for change. In turn decisions based on this approach can drive the allocation of dollars, performance improvement efforts, and potentially a rethinking of the organization's strategic intent.

Decision Making

In the traditional hierarchical organization, there is little doubt that the key strategy and operational decisions are supposed to be made at the very highest levels. The reason for this is obvious—that is where the information exists and where the greatest decision-making and analytic expertise rests. For certain kinds of decisions, particularly major strategic decisions, we have little argument with the view that they are often best made at the top of a b2change organization. This is true even for flat, team-based organizations that believe in employee involvement and have pushed operational decision making down.

When it comes to formulating and executing a strategic intent, what differentiates b2change organizations from traditional ones is who is asked for input. Executives in b2change organizations need to seek broad-based input when they make major decisions. In fact, this practice is exactly what we see in studies of today's high-performance organizations.[10] It is critical for two reasons: employees often have a great deal of useful information that can improve the decision, and it promotes employees' accepting and acting on the decision throughout the organization. In other words, seeking employee input leads to better decisions and better implementation of those decisions.

As important as transparency is in measuring performance, it is even more important in decision making. Everyone in a b2change organization needs to understand who is making decisions, what the decisions are, and what the basis is for decisions. This kind of transparency is key for a number of reasons. It is needed to create accountability and to prevent the kind of accounting scandals that occurred at Enron, Tyco, and a long list of other well-known companies.

By combining transparency with structures that increase employee involvement, it is possible to move decisions to places in the organization where individuals have both the information and knowledge to make the best choices. For example, in a business unit organization, most of the major business decisions and change decisions need to be made in that business unit, not at the corporate level. The specific level of hierarchy where they should be made needs to reflect the reality of who has a line of sight with respect to the business, as well as who will implement the decisions.

Changes in the environment will cause the best locations for decision making to change over time. This is something that traditional organizations rarely think about; at best it comes up during reorganizations every few years. But in the b2change organization, discussing where certain decisions should be made occurs regularly and represents an important consideration when there is a strategy change. In general, however, b2change organizations try to move as many decisions as possible to lower levels.

Moving decisions to the lower levels of an organization needs to be done with care. It is not enough simply to move operational decision making down; the information needed to make those decisions, as well as the skills and knowledge needed to make good decisions, also must be located where decisions are being made.[11] Failure to do this is a prescription for major problems; doing it can produce a high-performance organization.

P&G, International Paper, General Mills, and PepsiCo are among the many companies that have successfully used high-involvement decision-making processes in their manufacturing operations. The process technologies they use fit particularly well with moving operational decision making into the hands of self-managing work teams. In the service sector, Nordstrom's, Whole Foods, Ritz-Carlton, and a host of other organizations have used the same principles to improve customer service.

At this point, there is a tremendous amount of evidence that testifies to the advantages of using self-managing work teams to improve operational effectiveness. Simply stated, they can usually make decisions more quickly and control processes better, which means they outperform traditional hierarchically managed organizations.

CONCLUSION

B2change organizations utilize information, measurement, and decision-making processes in line with the following points:

- Decisions about major strategic changes need to be grounded in input from broad-based metrics that reflect organizational performance capabilities and financial performance.

- Decisions about improving ongoing operations and existing processes are often best made at the level of the organization where these processes are centered and managed. In making these decisions, input from employees can improve decision quality and reduce resistance to change.

- Information, measurement, and decision-making processes must be closely coordinated, so that individuals who are making the decisions get information about the need for change, the capabilities in the organization, and, ultimately, the impact of the change on organizational performance. Involving individuals in the change process is a positive when they have the type of position, information, and knowledge needed to generate and assess change alternatives.

- Transparency and employee involvement in decision making are vital. They improve the quality of decisions and the likelihood that those decisions will be accepted and implemented. With transparency comes accountability, which decreases the likelihood of bad decisions and the use of false or misleading data.

Chapter 6

Acquiring the Right Talent

Built-to-Change Strategy:
Have a B2Change Employer Brand

Managing human capital is a critical part of the designing process in the B2Change Model. Human capital is so critical to the performance of b2change organizations that its management deserves as much or more attention as the management of financial and physical assets. Of course, it's one thing to say it deserves this level of attention; it is quite another to actually bestow this much attention on it and to develop the practices that lead to the effective management of human capital.

In this chapter, we look at the first half of the human capital management equation by discussing the process of acquiring the right talent. The increasing complexity and changing nature of work make this task doubly difficult. Often talent is needed that has a high level of skill and knowledge—a great C++ programmer won't necessarily be a great database analyst. Unfortunately, managers often underestimate the complexity and skill requirements of jobs. For example, managers in one call center organization—not a technology that normally would be listed as complex—estimated that it took 90 days for new employees to get up to speed; a research study showed that in fact it took 210 days.[1]

B2change organizations must recruit individuals who at a minimum meet current needs and, if the employment strategy calls for it, are willing and able to change themselves to keep up with the changing organization. How do you recruit the right individuals when future needs are difficult to know? It is not a matter to be left to chance or happenstance. It needs to be based on intelligent strategies and implemented through effective practices that identify the right people and attract them.

ADOPTING AN EMPLOYMENT STRATEGY

Any b2change organization's talent acquisition process must be guided by a human resource strategy that determines how much it depends on people to change as the organization's strategy changes. Two approaches are outlined here: commitment to development and travel light.

Commitment to Development

The *commitment to development* approach hires individuals who are skilled but who, above all else, are willing and able to change and develop along with the business. The advantage of this strategy is obvious: it allows organizations to make a stronger commitment to maintaining a stable workforce, and it avoids the high cost of turnover. But it has serious limitations.

The first limitation is that development is expensive and not always successful. It requires an organization to continually invest in the development of its workforce in order to keep up with change. The selection process must face the challenging task of identifying individuals who are willing and able to change.

A second limitation is that the commitment to development policy may slow change because of the time it takes for individuals to learn new skills and mind-sets. Although organizations may want to train and develop their people, often the only training programs they have time for are the ones clearly oriented toward solving immediate problems. Even when an organization wants to develop its employees, the rapid pace of today's business world may rule it out. All it takes is for one competitor to develop a new technology to make an organization realize that it simply doesn't have time to retrain an existing workforce. Unless it hires people who already have the skills it needs today, it will miss the market opportunity. Thus hiring talent with the right skills and knowledge may be the only way to survive.

Travel Light

Kodak's shift to digital imaging provides a good example of the second type of human resource policy and highlights the talent challenges involved in making a major change. Moving from chemical to electronic imaging required the development of a new core competency. This hasn't been an easy change for

Kodak, but it looks like the company will be successful. One key to Kodak's success is the decision not to retrain its chemical engineers; instead, the company went into the market and hired new ones, and in some cases it acquired companies that had the competencies it needed.

The essence of the *travel-light* approach is to acquire and discard talent as needed. In a turbulent world, this approach has some clear advantages over the commitment-to-development strategy. It gives b2change organizations great flexibility in recruiting and allows the organization to shift competencies relatively quickly.

The radical changes in today's business environment are altering the relative attractiveness of buying versus developing talent. Hiring someone who already has the new skills may be cheaper and less risky than trying to develop an existing employee. Further, most organizations have little room for redundancy in resources, particularly human capital. With the relentless pressure to improve shareholder value, it is unlikely that organizations in the future will ever have a great amount of slack.

Before we conclude that the travel-light approach is usually best, it is important to consider its very serious limitations. First, management and leadership skills are always in short supply, and how people are led is a key source of competitive advantage. So even a travel-light organization may have little choice but to have a core group of leaders who are there for the long term.

Second, travel-light organizations may simply not be able to find the talent they need because there are few people in the labor market who have the necessary skills. This is more likely to happen to organizations that are technology leaders, such as Intel and Applied Materials. These organizations often have no choice—they have to train and develop existing employees.

Finally, the travel light policy calls for employing people only as long as they can meet the current needs of the organization. It means there will be large recruiting and orientation costs as well as heavy workforce churn. It also leads to a workforce that is not loyal, and the very real possibility of a culture of "haves" and "have nots." Traveling light sounds like a "cool" approach until you encounter these very real problems.

What is the best approach, a commitment-to-development policy that emphasizes stability and learning in order to adapt to change, or a travel-light one that emphasizes employee mobility? The right approach depends very much on the rate of environmental change, the organization's identity, and its strategic intent. The more radical the expected changes, the more the organization should lean toward a travel-light strategy. The major rationale for this is the high cost and time commitment required to significantly reskill a workforce.

The Employment Contract

As we hope we have made clear, choosing an HR employment strategy for a b2change organization is an important strategic decision. It has many serious implications, and the whole organization, not just HR, needs to clearly understand what those implications are.

The approach or approaches to skill acquisition and development an organization takes must be stated in its employer brand and contract. An organization's approach to skill development very much shapes the way people look at their work situation and needs to be made clear at the time people join the organization. In all cases, the contract must make clear that change, either through development or hiring and firing, is part of the deal. They need to be "contingency" contracts that make continued employment dependent on performance and having the right skills.

The commitment-to-development contract needs to stress the organization's commitment to its people and conversely demands flexibility and even sacrifice on the part of the employees to keep changing with the organization. The travel-light contract will be similar to that given to a contract worker: "We have this work that needs to be done; this is the reward package, and if all goes well, there is a chance we'll have another project for you."

Employees also need to be told who is responsible for their careers, how they can develop their careers, and what rewards they can expect as a result of their work. Having an employment contract that expresses what rewards and treatment individuals can expect is critical to attracting employees who will be satisfied with and motivated by their work. It is the foundation on which the relationship between an organization and its employees should be built.

Most large b2change organizations won't be able to adopt just one employment contract; they will need two somewhat different contracts. The commitment-to-development organizations will find there are parts of the organization where they need the flexibility to rapidly hire and fire people to respond to change. For example, the IT staff may comprise independent contractors who come and go depending on the current needs of the firm.

The travel-light organizations will find that they need the stability of a core group of leaders, and the capability to develop skills when they cannot buy them in the labor market. In consulting firms, the junior consultants are often hired and fired in a classic travel-light strategy, but the partners are likely to stay and develop themselves to respond to ongoing change.

MOTIVATION AND RECRUITING

The establishment of a development strategy is an important first step in the recruiting process. The second is achieving a fit between it and the rewards that an organization offers. A good fit must exist in order for a b2change organization to attract and motivate effective performance.

The value of rewards is determined by a person's needs. Most people are familiar with Maslow's hierarchy of needs. According to Maslow, the needs of individuals arrange themselves into a hierarchy of importance. At the bottom are our needs for the means of fundamental physiological survival (food, water, shelter, security). They are followed by the needs for social interaction, respect from others, self-esteem, and finally for personal growth and development.

Maslow states that most of us have the same basic needs, but that we give these needs different levels of importance.[2] This is why it is so critical in the selection process to focus on how strong the needs of individuals are.

Employment Contracts and Rewards

Different employment contracts attract people with different needs and therefore require organizations to utilize different kinds of rewards. The rewards that satisfy lower-level needs are tangible, or extrinsic, rewards. They usually are given by someone or some system, either directly or indirectly. Maslow's higher-level needs remind us that people can also give themselves rewards in the form of self-esteem as well as feelings of achievement and growth. Individuals can literally reward themselves for certain kinds of behavior because they feel they have accomplished something worthwhile, achieved a personal goal, learned a new skill, or experienced excitement or intellectual stimulation.

The reward strategy of a b2change firm will depend very much on which employment strategy it follows. A travel-light organization needs to stress rewards that it can deliver in the short term, such as pay, interesting work, and fair treatment. A commitment-to-development organization can offer security, personal growth, promotions, community, and development.

The important thing is to be clear about the employment strategy and to match the reward strategy to it. Once an organization has chosen its employment strategy, it has bought into the corresponding reward system. You cannot get the payroll flexibility of a travel-light organization without weakening the value of promotions as an incentive.

Willingness to Change

Because of their needs, individuals differ greatly in their desire to experience change. Some people prefer stability, security, and predictability, and a situation where they are in control and feel a high sense of competency as a result of their mastery of that situation. These are people who do not fit a b2change organization. Fortunately, not everyone finds change threatening and disruptive. Some individuals prefer change and enjoy the learning opportunities it creates. They see it as exciting and find stability and predictability boring and stagnating. Individuals who prefer change thrive in b2change organizations. One obvious implication of this is that b2change organizations should recruit them.

There is no good research evidence on what percentage of the population prefers stability and what percentage prefers change. What evidence there is suggests that individuals are probably distributed along a continuum that is anchored on one end by individuals who fear change and resist it, and on the other by people who seek change at every opportunity. Our guess is that people are distributed along the continuum in somewhat of a normal distribution. That is, there are a small number of outliers who always prefer change and a small number who strongly prefer stability. In the middle is the largest group of individuals. Their reaction to change is very much a situational one—which is the critical point.

In the case of workplace change, one factor that influences how people respond to it is their own desire to experience change. Another, and, in the case of most people, the overriding one, is how the change will affect them. An organization can exert a lot of control over how change affects its members, so it's not essential that selection systems do a fabulous job of finding people on the extreme end of the "willingness to change" scale. By creating the right environment for change, an organization can greatly enhance it's employees' willingness to change.

If people perceive that change will have a positive impact on their future, they will not resist it—in fact, they will seek it out. If, in contrast, change appears to be disruptive and to cause the end of what is a good situation for them, they are most likely to resist it. In other words, most people take a rational approach to change and ask the self-interested question, "What's in it for me?" If what's in it for them is negative, they resist it (not surprisingly). If what's in it for them is positive, they welcome change and embrace it.

A commitment-to-development firm has to work particularly hard to ensure that no one who has a development deal suffers serious losses due to the ongoing changes in the organization. This means people must keep their jobs, their compensation, and their status—as long as they are willing to change. The extra effort this takes is an investment the organization makes in maintaining a change-ready workforce. It is an investment that is simply not an option.

Experienced managers will tell you there is a catch to this rational argument: people are frequently inaccurate in their judgments about whether a change is good for them or not. Their trust of the organization and their trust of management both strongly influence whether or not they believe that the change will be positive for them. Of course, their previous experiences with change also play a major role in determining what they expect the impact of the change will be on them.

If a person's previous experiences with similar changes were negative, they are going to be very prone to rejecting change. If, however, they have trust in management and have had good experiences with change in the past, they are likely to embrace it and, in fact, may advocate change. The b2change organization should note the implication: when it hires employees with whom it wants a long-term relationship, it must avoid hiring change-damaged individuals. People who have had a negative history when it comes to organizational change are particularly likely to resist change and mistrust management.

Performance Motivation

The third issue that needs to be considered when recruiting individuals relates to their motivation to perform. There is an overwhelming amount of evidence concerning what motivates individuals to perform well. As will be discussed further in Chapter Nine, the research establishes that individuals are motivated to perform well when they perceive that good performance leads to rewards they value.[3] When recruiting and selecting employees, a b2change organization needs to take into account the kinds of rewards it has available and whether or not these rewards can be tied to performance. If an organization cannot give out meaningful bonuses, it shouldn't focus on recruiting individuals who value money. If it can't offer performance-based promotions, it shouldn't focus on recruiting individuals who value promotions.

In addition to focusing on rewards and performance, a b2change organization must consider what rewards can be tied to change. Tying important rewards to change is one of the best ways to reduce resistance. From a motivational perspective, therefore, the ideal recruit for a b2change organization is an individual who values the kind of rewards that the organization uses to motivate performance *and* change. Stated another way, an organization needs to recruit individuals who value the type of rewards that it is able and committed to using to motivate performance and change.

The Development of Skills and Knowledge

Recruiting individuals with the right skills and knowledge is critical to an organization's ability to develop and execute its competencies and capabilities. It is difficult to state any generalizations about what skills and knowledge organizations should look for. Each organization needs to develop its own recruiting profiles, based on an analysis of the kinds of competencies and capabilities it needs. The one exception occurs when an organization hires individuals on the basis of a commitment-to-development contract. In these cases, its members need to have the ability to grow, develop, and learn.

The critical ability to learn new skills is not equally possessed by all people. It is related to the intelligence levels of individuals, but it is not the same as intelligence. Some individuals simply are more able than others, just as some are more willing, to continue to learn new things throughout their lives. Much like the willingness to change, ability to learn is a feature of individuals that can be thought of as existing along a continuum; that is, there are some individuals who are extremely good at developing new skills and performance capabilities, and others who are extremely poor. Between them are individuals with varying degrees of ability to learn and develop new skills. B2change organizations need to be sure that they offer commitment-to-development contracts only to individuals who are good at developing new skills.

ATTRACT THE RIGHT TALENT

B2change organizations can use a variety of specific practices to recruit people with the right knowledge, skills, and needs. The most powerful is to develop a strong employer brand.

Developing an Employer Brand

To attract the right individuals, organizations need an employer brand that fits their identity and strategic intent. In many respects, attracting the right employees is no different than attracting the right customers. Employees seek to work for organizations just as customers seek to do business with them: when they feel that the organization offers what they desire.

Part of the reason for developing an employer brand is to help employees make good decisions about whether there is a fit between them and the organization. Just as there are good and bad potential customers, there are good and bad applicants for jobs. Good applicants are ones who are the type of individual an organization can motivate; who can do, or learn to do, the work of the organization; and who fit the identity of the organization.

A number of organizations have done a good job of developing their brand as employers. Who, for example, doesn't know what it is like to be a U.S. Marine? Nordstrom's has a clear brand for its salespeople, with the result that they are called "Nordies" because of the distinct relationship they have with the department store. Abercrombie & Fitch, Starbucks, and, in California, In-N-Out Burger have all developed the distinct brand of being a "cool" place to work. This branding has given these businesses a competitive edge in attracting sales personnel.

Basic to having an accurate, and therefore effective, employer brand is a statement of the organization's employment contract or contracts. B2change organizations have written, visible employment contracts because they are powerful in establishing its brand and the relationship between the organization and its employees. An effective contract identifies both what the individual is expected to do and what the individual will get in return for being an effective employee.

Each organization needs to fine-tune its employment contract to fit the type of rewards it can offer and the type of skills it needs employees to have. Because of its focus on change, the employer brand of a b2change organization must be significantly different from that of traditional organizations; changing its employment contract, therefore, is one of the first things an organization needs to do when it adopts the b2change approach.

Let's begin our discussion of b2change employment contracts by specifying what the value proposition should *not* offer. It should not be a "loyalty" contract that offers job security and a career employment relationship (see the list that follows).

LOYALTY CONTRACT

If you:	*We'll provide:*
Are loyal	A secure job
Work hard	Steady pay increases
Do as you're told	Financial security
	A career

What should the employment value proposition of a b2change organization be? The answer is obvious: it should offer change and the opportunity to be a member of a virtuous spiral organization with its accompanying risks, rewards, and growth opportunities.

Table 6.1 presents data from a national survey of Fortune 1000 corporations.[4] It shows how these corporations describe their employment contract with respect to what individuals are

TABLE 6.1. Employment Contracts: Survey Responses of Fortune 1000 Companies

Individuals are responsible for:	*Percentage Saying "To a Great Extent"*
Their career	63
Managing their performance	36
Continued employment depends on:	
Performance	76
Skills	48
Rewards are for:	
Seniority	7
Loyalty	17
Individual performance	59
Group and organizational performance	51

Source: Lawler, Mohrman, and Benson, *Organizing for High Performance* (Jossey-Bass, 2001).

responsible for, what continued employment depends on, and what rewards are for. The data clearly show that individuals are expected to manage their own careers. They also show that continued employment depends on performance and skills rather than on loyalty and seniority.

Seniority plays very little role in determining any kind of rewards. In essence, what counts are individual, group, and organizational performance. It appears that many organizations are already operating on the basis of performance-focused employment contracts; this is a good step toward being a b2change organization.

The contract used by Allstate Insurance Company (see Exhibit 6.1) is an especially attractive commitment-to-development contract. It stresses the mutual commitment shared by the individual and the organization. It identifies both the

EXHIBIT 6.1. **Allstate Commitment-to-Development Contract**

You should expect Allstate to:

1. Offer work that is meaningful and challenging.

2. Promote an environment that encourages open and constructive dialogue.

3. Recognize you for your accomplishments.

4. Provide competitive pay and rewards based on your performance.

5. Advise you on your performance through regular feedback.

6. Create learning opportunities through education and job assignments.

7. Support you in defining career goals.

8. Provide you with information and resources to perform successfully.

9. Promote an environment that is inclusive and free from bias.

10. Foster dignity and respect in all interactions.

11. Establish an environment that promotes a balance of work and personal life.

Allstate expects you to:

1. Perform at levels that significantly increase our ability to outperform the competition.

2. Take on assignments critical to meeting business objectives.

3. Continually develop needed skills.

4. Willingly listen to and act upon feedback.

5. Demonstrate a high level of commitment to achieving company goals.

6. Exhibit no bias in interactions with colleagues and customers.

7. Behave consistently with Allstate's ethical standards.

8. Take personal responsibility for each transaction with our customers and for fostering their trust.

9. Continually improve processes to address customers' needs.

Source: Courtesy of Allstate Insurance Company.

responsibilities that the organization has to its employees and what employees are expected to contribute to Allstate. Notice that the contract is not a loyalty contract. It does not promise job security, only the opportunity to obtain certain rewards and to develop skills and knowledge. This is congruent with a commitment-to-development approach. In travel-light organizations this contract might apply to a core group of employees, but not most, because of its strong commitment to development.

Contracts aid in the recruitment process by reinforcing an organization's value proposition and thus contributing to a realistic job preview. And after people are hired, contracts establish the ground rules for performance and rewards and serve as a touchstone for the organization and the individual throughout their entire relationship.

Research shows that employment contracts can be a significant enabler of an organization's ability to change.[5] Organizations we have studied that clearly link skill development with employment security—and rewards with performance—execute change more effectively than others. They create "mobile" human capital, that is, people who realize that they must continue to learn, develop, and perform to maintain their positions and careers.

B2change organizations need mobile human capital because getting stuck with obsolete human capital is just as bad as getting stuck with outdated equipment—perhaps even worse. Whereas you can readily buy new equipment, you cannot always buy talented human capital. This is, of course, one of the reasons why some firms will choose to adopt the commitment-to-development approach, rather than just assuming they will be able to pick up the best talent on the open market.

Communicating the Employer Brand

Once an organization has established its employer brand (we say "brand" here because most organizations have one dominant brand, even though they may have two) through a clear and visible contract, the next challenge is to utilize it effectively. For an organization to recruit effectively, its brand needs to be known and understood. One way to ensure this is to feature it in all communications about job openings. In the case of some b2change companies, it makes sense to feature the brand in ads for products and services. Southwest Airlines does this in its TV commercials. The brand also should be featured on the company's website, with videos that show employees talking about what it is like to work for the organization and what the brand means to them.

When individuals actually apply for a job, either online or in person, they should be given an introduction to the company that emphasizes what life will be like if they join the organization. It should be a realistic preview that tells it like it is. This type of preview not only can help set realistic expectations but can drive away individuals who are not a good fit and if hired, would not stay long.

Google, as part of its effort to attract the right type of software engineer, has worked hard to establish its brand as an employer. One of the more interesting things it has done is place ads in a number of technology journals and magazines that feature its GLAT (Google Lab Aptitude Test).

The GLAT contains a number of questions that, over the years, Google has found useful in predicting who would be a good engineer for the company. By putting the GLAT into the public domain, Google allows individuals to self-assess and see whether they are a good fit for the organization. In essence, it is a different kind of realistic job preview and branding of Google as an employer. What kind of questions are on the GLAT? Here is a sample: *What number comes next in this sequence: 10, 9, 60, 90, 70, 66? . . .* Sorry—we don't know the answer, but if you do, contact Google. You may be right for them!

B2change organizations try to eliminate individuals who are not a good fit very early in the recruitment process. Organizations often spend far too much time interviewing and processing applications from people who are simply not a good fit. Much of this time can be saved if organizations develop a clear employer brand and make a stronger effort to acquaint individuals with it.

In addition to discouraging bad applicants, having a strong brand can serve to attract individuals who otherwise wouldn't apply for the job. Given an unclear image of what working for an organization is like, individuals who in fact would be a terrific fit may simply not be interested enough to go through the application process. A strong brand that makes it clear what working for the firm is like can significantly help in creating an applicant pool that is an excellent fit for the organization.

Identifying the Right Talent

The special challenge in picking individuals who fit a b2change organization concerns determining how they will respond to change. As we noted earlier in this chapter, only those individuals who respond favorably to change should receive a commitment-to-development contract. Organizations rarely try in their selection processes to assess how individuals respond to change, but there are ways to do this. Although an organization can make use of personality tests (for example, tests of authoritarianism, measures of flexibility versus rigidity, and of open versus closed attitudes), they are only very rough indicators. As a general rule, data that are gathered from interviews, an analysis of past behaviors, and, where possible, a temporary employment relationship with the recruit are preferable.

Use Interviews to Gather Objective and Subjective Data

Often the best way to determine how someone will respond to change is simply to ask him or her. Independent of its predictive value, asking is a worthwhile thing to do. It communicates the importance of a willingness to change and may indeed yield interesting information about the person. Individuals who clearly have trouble answering the question or indicate that they are not interested in change can be ruled out immediately.

The challenge for the b2change organization is in assessing the validity of applicants' claims that they like change and regularly seek out opportunities to learn new things. Individuals may say these things even though they are not true, for at least two reasons: either they simply don't know themselves very well or they may be consciously providing misinformation because they want the job and know the right things to say.

The key to assessing individuals is to go beyond simply asking them what they like by asking for behavioral examples from their past. Behavior-based examples provide revealing information, and they are much more difficult to fake than simple questions like "What kind of person are you?" and "What do you like?" For an applicant to fake examples of change-seeking behavior requires not just understanding what is desired but being able to come up with facts, figures, numbers, and behaviors to demonstrate that he or she has actually done it.

Most recruiting specialists are skilled at doing behaviorally based interviewing. The b2change organization needs to apply these skills to finding employees who can thrive in a change-oriented company. In the case of learning new skills, for example, asking how a job applicant responded the last time he had a chance to learn something new at work can be instructive; it is also useful to ask how many new jobs the applicant has taken on in the last several years. Other behavioral interview questions could include asking when the applicant last signed up for training courses or asking her to describe a time she was asked to change and didn't, and why that was. In short, any series of questions that asks people to provide behavioral examples of their reactions to change are likely to yield valid and useful information about their favorableness to change.

Look at Past Behavior

When it comes to predicting job behavior, remember that the best predictor of future behavior is past behavior. The implications of this for selecting individuals who are likely to be both good performers in their present job and willing and able to change are straightforward. It is very important to look at the past behaviors of individuals for evidence of change. It is also important to check their references and to test the validity of their resumes. All too often, individuals present false data; the accuracy of any information applicants give about past jobs, pay levels, and assignments needs to be confirmed.

A background analysis needs to go beyond a validity check—it needs to look at the individual's pattern of past behavior. A person with both positive performance reviews and a pattern of behavior that indicates a willingness to learn and take on new assignments is ideal for an organization that is trying to create a workforce that is able to change.

One note of caution here: in terms of looking at changes in jobs, a pattern of very rapid change is probably not desirable. Too frequent change can indicate poor performance in a job, or an employee's moving on so quickly that an organization never has a chance to recoup the time it has spent recruiting, developing, and preparing the individual to perform well. How rapid is too rapid varies somewhat by job type, but as a general rule, eighteen months to two years is a good minimum time in a job. On the other hand, an individual who has stayed in the same job year after year is hardly one that would be a desirable recruit for a b2change organization.

Use Temporary and Contract Employment Where Possible

Hiring individuals as temporary or contract employees can help an organization change its staffing as the work to be done changes. This is a good reason to use temporary and contract employees, but not the only one. Employing a person for days, weeks, or months can accomplish two other important purposes.

One purpose is to determine whether the individual can do the work and whether he or she fits the motivational profile that the organization is looking for in a regular employee. Although this may be seen as exploiting the person, it doesn't have to be if the employee is given a clear picture of what to expect and regular feedback on how things are going.

The other purpose of temporary employment is to give the person a realistic preview of what the organization is like— there is usually no better way to do this than to have him or her work as a temporary or contract employee. If the organization turns out to be a bad fit, the person avoids the embarrassment of being let go, and the organization avoids the cost of terminating a regular employee. Thus hiring someone as a temporary to see if the fit is good can benefit both the individual and the organization.

ACQUIRING COMPANIES AND HUMAN CAPITAL

Until recently, acquiring a company to garner its people was not high on the list of reasons for acquisitions. Much higher were some of the reasons we mentioned in our discussion on structure: increasing market share and entering new markets and businesses. A company's human capital was simply not seen as important enough to warrant the complexities and cost of an acquisition; it was easier to hire the people away from a company than it was to buy the entire company.

But as was mentioned in Chapter Four, acquiring corporations to obtain the knowledge and capabilities of their employees is gaining credibility, and is something b2change organizations need to consider. This is often a quick, relatively easy, and relatively inexpensive way to get valuable talent that is experienced in working together and therefore has valuable capabilities and core competencies. It is a particularly effective way for a b2change organization to quickly develop new organizational capabilities. The fact that the individuals have worked together increases the chance that they will bring their capability to the acquiring company, something that can never happen when individuals are hired.

The challenge in acquiring talent through an acquisition is retention, particularly when the people acquired have equity in their old company. If the terms of the acquisition make them wealthy, there is a danger they will leave. As was mentioned in Chapter Four, for just this reason it may be better to use an alliance. If a b2change organization decides to acquire talent this way, it is important to structure the deal in a way that locks in the desired talent. This can be done by delaying the payout of the stock or cash that comes to the equity holders and by making them valued and satisfied members of the acquiring organization.

Cisco has done an especially smart job in this regard. It acquires firms with no more than a few hundred employees, making it easier to assimilate them into Cisco swiftly. Cisco has a team that specifically focuses on the cultural integration process and Cisco's identity. It makes it clear that the acquired staff are now Cisco employees, entitled to Cisco's excellent benefits and HR practices. This strategy has allowed Cisco to retain most of the top talent it has acquired.

Marriott Corporation's acquisition of the Ritz-Carlton hotel chain serves as an interesting example of an acquisition that was driven by the desire of a corporation to develop an organizational capability. Before the acquisition, Ritz-Carlton had an outstanding reputation for customer service. It received a number of awards for its ability to anticipate and satisfy customer needs. Marriott, in contrast, had a number of great properties but not a particularly good reputation for customer service.

To jump-start its customer service capability, Marriott decided to purchase Ritz-Carlton to learn more about building an organizational capability in customer service, and ultimately to transfer the appropriate parts of the Ritz-Carlton approach to Marriott properties. Among the challenges the company faced was the price-point difference between the Ritz-Carlton and the Marriott properties, the former being much higher. Nevertheless, Marriott was convinced that there were some practices that could transfer, and history has proven the firm right. It has transferred a number of the Ritz-Carlton practices and concepts to itself and as a result has been able to improve its customer service ratings.

Rerecruiting the Best

With the death of the loyalty contract and the growth of a free-agent mentality, it is inevitable that good employees will leave even the best organizations, but this doesn't mean they should be forgotten. In many ways, former employees often make the best future employees of b2change organizations because they have already had a realistic preview of the work and the organization. They are already trained and tested as to whether they can do the work. If they were indeed outstanding performers when they worked for the organization, there is a tremendous advantage to rehiring them. This is particularly true for b2change organizations because they want individuals who are comfortable with change. What better evidence is there that an individual is willing to change than the fact that he or she has changed jobs?

The lesson is clear: it is to a b2change organization's advantage to treat its valued employees who leave as potential future employees. It should do everything possible to ensure that they leave with a favorable image of the company and to keep track of them. When and if the time is right, the firm should make an effort to rerecruit them.

Conclusion

Attracting and recruiting the right talent is a critical part of managing human capital and an integral element of the designing process in b2change organizations. But it is only the first step. As we will discuss in the next chapter, it needs to be followed seamlessly by development experiences that produce individuals with the skills and abilities that support the organization's strategic intent. These experiences need to be complemented by practices that ensure that an organization's human capital is retained for as long as it is needed.

Chapter 7

Managing Human Capital

Built-to-Change Strategy:
Make People Responsible for Their Careers

What should human capital management look like in a b2change organization? What is the single most important key to doing it right? Quite simply, it is senior executives spending as much time making decisions about the acquisition, allocation, development, and retention of human capital as they spend making decisions about other kinds of capital. All levels of a b2change organization must demonstrate unflinching commitment to the effective management and development of an organization's human capital, but it is particularly important to have it at the top. Senior executives need to show their commitment in ways that are visible to people throughout the organization, and they need to require that others in the organization be equally committed.

This chapter describes the second half of the attracting and managing human capital element of the designing process. Top management—and that includes the CEO—must be deeply involved in recruiting and developing the organization's managers by choosing a development policy, creating an employer brand, and identifying the right talent.

GE's Session C is an example of how senior management can demonstrate its commitment to human capital management and development. The CEO runs Session C annually beginning in April with a full-day review of all the major businesses. He follows up with a videoconference in July and finalizes the process in November. Session C focuses on evaluating the strengths and weaknesses of the organization and its business leaders, including the company's development needs and depth of talent. It looks at not only the business performance of key managers but also how they behave in their leadership roles.

In recent years, the Session C meetings have expanded to include reviews of accomplishments, presentations on business results, and a general summary of how the human capital of the organization is performing. As we argued in Chapter Five, information systems should generate data about the strength of a b2change organization's capabilities, as these are leading indicators of performance.

Meetings like Session C are one of the information-gathering systems that can answer the question, "Do we have the capability to adapt?" GE's process also reviews such organizational capabilities as Six Sigma, globalization, e-business, and diversity. So the question about the capability of human capital to adapt to change is not just an abstract one; it is asked in the context of strategic initiatives that are GE's response to a changing environment.

KEEPING THE RIGHT PEOPLE

Effective management of human capital needs to be based on keeping the right people. There is no question that turnover is expensive; that said, there is also no question that not all turnover is bad. In fact, when an organization needs to adapt to changes in the environment, some turnover may be quite desirable. It can make downsizing unnecessary and can reduce fringe-benefit costs for retirement.

The challenge every organization faces is determining the right amount and kind of turnover. It then needs to put into place practices to achieve it. The first things a b2change organization needs to decide are who its core employees are and whether it is a travel-light organization or a commitment-to-development organization.

Before we look at what kind of turnover is functional and what kind is dysfunctional, we need to briefly consider why individuals choose to leave organizations voluntarily. There is a great deal of research on turnover, most of it focusing on its relationship to employee satisfaction. There is a clear relationship between how satisfied employees are with their work situations and whether or not they search for other jobs.[1]

Rewards and Satisfaction

When it comes to rewards, quantity and mix are the key factors in determining whether people are satisfied. As you might imagine, the general rule is that the more rewards people receive, the more satisfied they are. However, some quirks of human nature come into play here. People's degree of satisfaction can change rapidly. For example, a basketball player who signs a record-setting contract of x million dollars may be very satisfied until another player signs one for $x + y$ million dollars.

On the few occasions when a reward amount exceeds what individuals think is fair, they can even feel guilty about being overrewarded. However, it appears that feelings of being over-rewarded are short lived. Most people quickly rationalize the excess and decide that they are, in fact, fairly paid. This phenomenon is quite visible in CEOs who somehow get over the guilt of multimillion-dollar bonuses even when their company is losing money. In contrast, when individuals feel underrewarded, they do not skillfully rationalize the shortfall and decide it is fair. Instead they complain and try to get more.

How can organizations understand the standards against which their people measure rewards? The answer comes from research indicating that people set up standards by comparing what they receive to what similar people are getting. Individuals determine who these "similar others" are according to a variety of factors: performance, type of work, training, background, and other characteristics.

For comparison purposes, people are likely to look at those characteristics that they think are their strengths. For example, if they are well educated, they compare themselves to other people with a similar level of education, and they think that education should be a major criterion in determining reward levels. If they perceive themselves to be high performers, as most do, they tend to compare their rewards with the rewards of other high performers and of course are strong advocates of basing rewards on performance.

The reward comparisons that individuals make can sometimes appear to be irrational. For example, executives who are highly paid compared to other executives within their firm sometimes look at other organizations in order to find people who are paid more. And if they are in the difficult position of not finding other executives who are paid more, they look elsewhere, comparing their reward level to that of star athletes and entertainers.

Time and time again, we have heard CEOs say, "Well, I'm worth at least as much as Shaquille O'Neal or Tom Cruise." A more valid comparison would be to compare their pay with that of Shaquille O'Neal's coach or with that of Tom Cruise's business manager. These would be much better comparisons from the perspectives of work content and skills. But CEOs compare themselves to O'Neal and Cruise not because of the similarity of their work or skills but because they are using high rates of compensation as their comparison factor.

Reward mix is important because individuals value a variety of intrinsic and extrinsic rewards. What is an attractive and satisfying package of rewards for one person may not be for another. A clear implication of this that was mentioned in Chapter Six is that b2change organizations need to be sure that the reward packages they provide fit the type of workforce they need to attract and retain. Offering job security and a rich retirement package, for example, is the wrong way for them to go.

Because organizations clearly can influence satisfaction, it is well within the reach of b2change organizations to satisfy most, if not all, of the employees they want to retain. "All" it takes is a reward system that fits the new rules. It is also very useful to have an information system that measures employee satisfaction and perceptions of fairness, thus enabling the organization to assess and adjust how well the reward system is working.

One of the great challenges in satisfying employees is achieving alignment between what they value and what the organization can offer. As was noted earlier, individuals differ in what they value. Even though a good selection process can help homogenize an organization's workforce, there are always going to be differences among employees. Further, individuals and their needs change over time; thus the diversity in what people want from work increases when some people stay in an organization for a long time and others enter.

"Cafeteria" or flexible reward systems that allow for choice can help with the diversity problem but cannot solve it completely. There will always be some dissatisfied employees, and there will usually be more in an organization that is changing. The way to judge whether dissatisfaction is a problem is to look at whether valuable employees are leaving and how the level of dissatisfaction compares to the level in other organizations.

Turnover and Satisfaction

Research on turnover suggests that when people search for another job, they go through a mostly rational decision process in which they compare what a new job might be like to their current situation.[2] However, they are not always accurate in assessing what a new situation will be like, nor are they necessarily accurate in assessing what their future might be like with their current employer. Nevertheless, they weigh the pluses and minuses of their options as they perceive them, and leave or stay on that basis.

The challenge every organization faces is creating an attractive work situation for the individuals that it wants to retain. The challenge is greater in a b2change organization, because it cannot guarantee the same kind of job security traditionally offered in career-oriented organizations. This is even true for core employees because they have to be willing and able to change to maintain their employment. Organizations that are designed to change must therefore rely on such things as interesting and challenging work, new opportunities, and financial rewards. This brings us right back to the importance of the selection process, as described in Chapter Six. Get the selection criteria wrong and you will not be able to offer what employees value, and you will end up with damaging levels of turnover.

Turnover Management

One of the defining characteristics of an organization that is ready and able to change is that it is able to alter the skill mix of its human capital. As we have already discussed, one way to do this is through training and development; the other is to replace existing employees with new ones. For either of these approaches to work effectively, organizations need to be able to measure the skill and performance levels of all their employees. As we discussed in Chapter Five, organizations need to develop performance management systems that do this. They then need to make good decisions about whom to keep and whom to let go in order to support dynamic alignment.

It is one thing to say that poor performers and individuals with obsolete skills should be terminated; it is quite another to do this effectively. But a high-performance b2change organization must do it. Keeping employees whose skills are irrelevant to the current mission is a poor use of corporate resources, just as is keeping poor performers. Both practices send the wrong message to other employees: that they don't need to perform.

Helen Handfield-Jones, one of the authors of *The War for Talent*, has argued that managers need to be given targets for how many employees to terminate.[3] She points out that without the discipline enforced by specific targets, managers will take the easy route and say, "All my guys are pretty good." It was this kind of thinking that led Jack Welch to enforce his infamous ranking system in which those in the bottom 10 percent are marked for termination.[4] This approach seems to have worked for GE, but as we noted in Chapter Five, we cannot recommend it.

What we recommend is that firms take very seriously the task of pruning their talent; experience shows that if they don't, it just won't happen. One approach is to force managers to answer the question, "If you did have to lay off some people, whom would you let go?" This makes managers focus their attention and leads naturally to the decision point, "Should we let any of those people go?"

Notice that there is a difference in flavor between how traditional firms and b2change firms think about terminations. In traditional firms, managers are looking to cut deadwood (which should always bring to mind the question, "Did you hire them dead, or did you kill them?"). In b2change firms, managers should be looking to see if the talent they have is still aligned with the changing needs of the firm. The discipline of enforcing appropriate levels of turnover is an important part of the discipline of revisiting and implementing strategy.

Measuring Human Capital

Strategies for retaining and developing human capital need to be built on a solid foundation of metrics. This is true for both traditional and b2change firms, but it is especially true for b2change organizations. There are two obvious reasons why metrics are fundamental to having a strategy-driven approach to managing human capital. First, without measures it is almost impossible to make strategic judgments about how to allocate and develop talent. Second, what is measured tends to take on a greater importance than what is not.

Particularly if human capital metrics are used to evaluate performance and determine rewards, they tend to become very important. Individuals worry about the accuracy of the measures as well as how their own performance is reflected in those metrics. When the condition of human capital is not measured, it almost inevitably ends up as a secondary consideration relative to those things that are measured and rewarded. Even if the condition of human capital is recognized as an important influence on other metrics, such as profits or sales, the failure to measure it is a negative. It creates a situation where human capital management is seen as a nice to do, rather than as critical to organizational effectiveness.

Human capital management must begin with measures of the condition of individual employees. Measurement at this level is the foundation that is required in order for an organization to develop overall indicators of the condition of its human capital. We began our discussion of performance management systems in Chapter Five; at this point we need to return to it.

Managing Skills and Competencies

There are three main reasons that b2change organizations should have an effective performance management system.

As will be discussed in Chapters Nine and Ten, it should be the foundation of the organization's reward system. It also is critical to the validation of selection systems—recruiters need to know how their hires have worked out. The third and perhaps most important reason is that it is a building block for managing human capital.

As we noted in Chapter Five, everyone has seen dysfunctional performance management systems. They become dysfunctional because they are complex systems to design and operate, and they require skilled managers and employees to operate effectively. Nevertheless, an effective performance management system is vital to the management of human capital in a b2change organization.

Effective measurement of the skills and competencies of individuals is fundamental to the kind of task assignments that we discussed in Chapter Four. Good assignments are tougher to achieve in a b2change firm because there is a lot more movement of tasks and people. Traditional firms can put someone in a job and if after a year or two it isn't working out, they can consider moving the person. B2change organizations cannot waste that kind of time. They need to continually assign people to tasks at which they will perform well. It's not about putting people in the right job; it's about putting them on the right teams and the right projects.

Measuring skills and competencies is also fundamental to assessing the strategic capability of an organization and to making decisions about what strategies to pursue. B2change organizations should have a skill and competency profile for each individual. Obviously this requires the type of IT-based HR system that is offered by Oracle and SAP.

Developing Person Descriptions

To manage the development and management of individuals in most knowledge-work roles and managerial roles, b2change organizations need to develop a *person description* for every employee. It needs to specify what knowledge and skills the individual has and should develop. It should be combined with and based on a role description that specifies the tasks to be performed by the individual and the performance level required. (This role description should be a living document updated by the individual and his or her manager, not HR.)

The person description should be used as the basis for determining whether the individual has the necessary work-related skills and knowledge to fill a role, and as the fundamental building block of development and staffing activities. All organizations can improve their talent management by having person descriptions, but in b2change organizations they are not just nice to have—they are a necessity. Without them it is impossible to make good data-based decisions about change. Recognizing this, SAS, the statistical software company, uses person descriptions as the foundation of a program that enables their managers to determine the gap between the skills they currently have in their departments and the skills they need in the future.

The person description must capture the specific behaviors a person needs to master and not just deal in generalities. For example, instead of saying merely that the person needs to have communication skills, the person description should specify exactly what kind of communication the individual needs to engage in, as well as what level of mastery is required.

The person description should establish measures that distinguish between successful and unsuccessful mastery so that individuals can be certified as having the necessary communication skills. A version of these same measures should be used to assess ongoing job performance, but that is not what we are talking about here. In a person description, the focus is on what a person *can* do rather than on how well he or she actually performs on a day-to-day basis.

As a general rule, there are three areas of skill and knowledge on which each person description should focus. The first is the set of technical skills that are needed to do the role they are assigned. The skills for someone in HR are likely to be radically different from those for someone in engineering. In both cases certain functional or discipline-specific knowledge must be mastered; the needed level of expertise depends on the kind of work the individual is likely to be assigned. Knowledge is often best identified and assessed by specialists in the area of expertise and is often very specific to the core competencies of the organization.

The second area of knowledge pertains to the business model of the organization—that is, its financial measures and business strategy and how these relate to the work that employees do. To master this area of knowledge, employees in b2change organizations need to understand things about the marketplace, competitors, and, of course, the organization's financial model and measures. Again, the depth and kind of knowledge needed will vary from one work role to another.

The third area in which employees need specific knowledge and skills involves organizing, leading, and managing. The content of this area is shaped by the management approach and design of the organization. B2change organizations that use teams, for example, need individuals to develop good team skills and communication skills. As we will discuss in the next chapter, those who are expected to lead the organization clearly need to be evaluated on their leadership skills and their ability to communicate a sense of mission and vision.

A good example of an organization that has developed person descriptions is Fiat. The company has defined three types of knowledge that everyone in the organization needs to master, as well as seven types that are specific to the fundamental professional areas and business processes in which an individual works. The three general knowledge areas are (1) the company and its business, (2) the management practices of the company, and (3) the operations and economics of the business. The seven types of basic professional knowledge are defined in detail by each business unit and the functional areas in Fiat and are based on the area of professional knowledge that is the focus of each individual's work. For example, in marketing and sales, Fiat identifies knowledge concerning sales networks and channels, competitive market structure, and three other general areas as being important parts of the knowledge base.

Hallmark is another company that has spent considerable time and effort developing person descriptions. It has composed success profiles, which it uses to identify each individual's knowledge and skills, focusing on the specific skills needed for that person's position. The company uses a competency assessment worksheet to establish development objectives, which are ultimately used for performance appraisals as well.

Perhaps the best way to demonstrate what a person description contains is to show one. Exhibit 7.1 illustrates an example from a publishing company of the development part of the

EXHIBIT 7.1.   **Person Description: Development Section**

Potential

Short Term/Level:	Hold in Position
Mid Term/Level:	SVP, Operations
Long Term/Level:	SVP of Operations
Highest Attainable:	Business Unit President
Long-Term Career Goal:	CEO

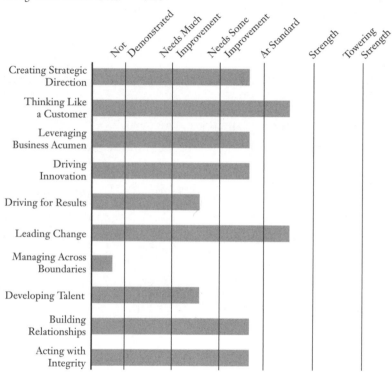

Leadership Strengths/Summary
- Excellent knowledge of the industry and competitors
- Holds informal but regularly scheduled calls with peers to build relationships and open lines of communications
- Tests thinking with peers and colleagues to gain input and build support
- Extremely high integrity and commitment to the success of his team

Specific Development Needs
- Mentor candidates for the position of VP of Operations
- Knowing the team
- Knowing the marketplace/customer
- Increase knowledge of best practices

description for a manager. It is backed up by definitions and the identification of specific behaviors and results.

Using Human Capital Metrics

What kind of summary human capital metrics should b2change organizations collect and use for the purposes of development, work assignment, and strategy development? There is no definitive list, but a number of basic measures have been identified in the literature on balanced scorecards and human capital.[5]

The measurement of human capital should start with metrics that focus on the skills and competencies of the workforce. A good example of the power of metrics is provided by Six Sigma programs. They measure and report on the skill level of the workforce in terms of quality (for example, the number of "black belts"). This serves to measure how far along an organization is toward having a quality capability and to motivate individuals to become quality experts. A b2change organization might do well to borrow the concept of karate belts and to identify the critical abilities of change-ready managers: rapid relationship building, quick learning, and strategic focus.

Metrics also need to be developed to measure the presence of technical skills that support core competencies. These metrics can help guide strategy development as well as indicate what is needed for an organization to execute its strategy.

Turnover is an obvious measure because the cost of turnover is anywhere from two times monthly pay up to twenty or more times, depending on the scarcity of the skill in the labor market and the learning time to become proficient. Because the b2change firm may actively pursue a certain level of turnover, this measure should distinguish between wanted and unwanted turnover.

Of course, once good people have left, it is too late to do anything about it, so, as was mentioned earlier, human capital metrics in b2change organizations should include measures of employee attitudes. Most good-quality attitude surveys ask employees not only how satisfied they are with their job but also whether they intend to leave. Clearly these measures, particularly the measure of intention to leave, tend to be highly correlated with later turnover behavior. By collecting attitude data, it is possible to intervene in situations where undesirable turnover is likely to occur. It is also important to measure motivation, involvement, and identity. They are good indicators of future performance and a good way to test how the organization design is affecting individuals.

Other human capital metrics that are frequently used include success in hiring and the amount of time required to fill open positions. These are obviously critical metrics and ones that make sense for b2change organizations.

Although metrics in the area of staff development require subjective judgments, they are very important in a b2change organization. Measures are needed that focus on how many individuals are in development positions and how many backups are available for critical positions.

Looking at development metrics is particularly important for b2change organizations that are committed to developing their existing employees. They must emphasize and measure career movement and continued development. If they don't provide development opportunities, they will find it very difficult to retain individuals who enjoy learning, developing, and changing their work and skills.

Finally, b2change organizations need to measure their investment in training. At the most basic level, they need to measure the number of days of training, the cost of training, and the type of training, but this often is not enough. Where possible, it is desirable to look at the impact of training on individual and organizational performance. This is particularly critical in an organization that is changing, because information about the impact of training can be very useful in making decisions about whether to travel light and buy employees who already have skills or to make the investment in training and developing existing employees.

Even though there is not yet a standard list of "must-have" human capital metrics, b2change organizations can and in most cases should develop a human capital report or scorecard. This human capital report should use a mix of the kinds of measures we have just discussed and display data for the organization's major units, parts, and groups. Creating these scorecards enables an organization to assess not only its current performance capabilities but also its readiness to develop new and different organizational capabilities and core competencies.

Targeting Critical Work and Individuals

It is inevitable that some kinds of work and some individuals will have a disproportionate impact on the success of an organization. The most important are usually those activities and individuals who are critical to the organization's core competencies and organizational capabilities. B2change organizations clearly need to put in place practices that ensure the retention and development of individuals who do a critical kind of work or have critical skills.[6]

Retention Strategies

Retaining the right individuals requires being in close touch with the external labor market and being able to change the amount and perhaps the type of rewards for individuals as the market changes. It also requires a clear focus on the strategic needs of the business and attending to the satisfaction, development, and rewards—financial and otherwise of key employees.

With respect to core employees, promising a "soft landing" in the event of future layoffs can facilitate retention. In today's environment, individuals take a considerable risk when they stay at a particular organization for a long time. Thus they need to be assured that the organization will support their transition to a new situation if they no longer fit where they are.

In many cases, retaining and motivating core employees in a b2change organization requires developing in them an organizational ownership mentality. They are the ones who must make the extra effort to see that the organization is doing well and adapting to important changes in the environment. At times they need to put their own interests aside to further organizational performance and change. In the absence of a loyalty contract, an organization cannot reasonably expect this kind of behavior from individuals who do not share in its long-term financial success. Thus, as will be discussed further in Chapter Ten, it is particularly important that core employees own stock and have stock options. It may also make sense to give them formal employment contracts.

The career path of high-potential individuals warrants special attention. P&G has done this by identifying certain "crucible" jobs that provide excellent development opportunities for individuals targeted to develop into general managers. The company pays careful attention to how these jobs are filled and to the development of the individuals who hold them. Why? Because crucible jobs are scarce commodities, and the firm needs to pay careful attention to them to see that they are used effectively to develop the critical human capital of the firm.

Notice how much this approach differs from traditional thinking, which calls for programs aimed at the whole employee population or at different levels of management. B2change organizations need to be keenly aware of what activities and competencies are critical to the execution of the present strategy, and also need to think one or two steps ahead. That is, b2change organizations need to create programs that will prepare the organization for a strategy change.

Critical Skills

What determines which individuals should be considered core and receive special attention? Clearly labor supply and demand are critical factors. When labor is scarce, it makes particular sense to focus on the retention of individuals who are in scarce supply. Losing them is particularly painful because the replacement costs are high, and continued churn in a technical specialty or business unit can lead to poor organizational performance.

The second consideration is the relationship between how well a set of activities is performed and the performance of the organization. There are some areas in most organizations where the performance of the individual is strongly related to the overall performance of the organization. This is clearly true of many of an organization's senior management positions, but it may not be limited to just those roles. For example, individuals in an R&D lab can come up with breakthroughs that have an enormous impact on the corporation; at a more mundane level, a particular person may deliver a critical service to a customer.

Our colleague John Boudreau points to the example of Federal Express. Analysis there shows that the performance of FedEx route drivers is particularly critical to organizational performance. Drivers are the primary interface with customers, and the decisions they make about waiting for packages and servicing a customer are strongly related to customer retention. In addition, their ability to arrive at airports and distribution points on time is critical to the timely delivery of packages and to customer satisfaction.

Less strongly related to customer satisfaction and organizational results is the performance of FedEx pilots. Although they are skilled and certainly valued professionals, there is little variance in the job performance of pilots. All of them are able to perform within very narrow parameters of effective behavior; therefore improving their performance will have relatively little impact on the overall effectiveness of the organization. This suggests that focusing on the development and retention of route drivers is likely to have a much bigger payoff than focusing on pilot performance.

Changes in Criticality

One of the more challenging aspects of managing human capital is that when organizations or their environments change, individuals and jobs may move into and out of a position of criticality. The toy manufacturing business is a good example. A number of years ago, a sales position in a toy company was an important position, but not necessarily a critical one. The salespeople dealt with a number of different retailers, and although the retailers were demanding, each retailer had relatively little impact on the effectiveness of the company overall.

Today the situation is dramatically different. A few large chains, most notably Wal-Mart and Target, dominate the toy business in the United States. Individuals in toy companies like Mattel and Hasbro who manage the relationships with these big chains are now in critical positions. If they make an error in their relationships, it can have a devastating effect on their company's performance. The implication of this change is obvious. The sales position needs to be much more of a focus with respect to human capital development and retention.

Creating Career Opportunities

One of the best ways to retain individuals who seek out change and like to develop their skills is to provide them with internal development opportunities. This can help a b2change organization fill critical vacancies, and functions as a retention and motivating device for just the kind of employees that a b2change organization needs. A b2change organization that is committed to development therefore needs to have internal systems that support individuals who want to make development moves.

We have studied many organizations where employees complain that it is easier to get a job with another company than it is to move internally within their own company. There are a number of reasons for this, including poor information about where job openings are and all the political issues that are involved with internal moves.

All too often, managers want to retain all their employees, because that reduces their need to train and develop people.

Internal moves have costs associated with them just as turnover has. Because of this, supervisors often don't nominate their employees for new jobs and may even keep their most effective employees a closely guarded secret.

One obvious answer to the problem of supervisors' hoarding good employees is to reward managers for developing their employees. More and more organizations have adopted this policy, but it is still relatively rare. It should not be rare in a b2change organization. Supporting the internal movement of people is just the kind of practice that is necessary to build a workforce that is ready to change.

The information problem, with respect to employee movement, can be solved relatively easily with the development of a company-based eHR system. In the best systems, individuals throughout an organization can use the intranet to quickly identify the openings that are available and also the kinds of skills and competencies that are required for these positions.

BP is one of a growing number of large companies that have an HR system that posts their job openings on their intranet. BP's system was developed as a part of their outsourcing HR to Hewitt. It allows employees to see job openings worldwide and goes into great detail about the employment conditions associated with the jobs.

With a good competency-based HR system, employees can compare the competency mix that is required in an open position to their skill mix and decide whether it is worth their while to apply for the it. With more advanced eHR systems, such as BP's, individuals can look at any special conditions that are associated with the move; for example, if it is an international move, they can look at how it will affect their pay, benefits, and a host of other issues that might be on their mind. If they decide to apply for the position, they can do it online and open communications with the person who is in charge of filling the position.

IBM is another company that has created an impressive intranet set of HR tools, the On-Demand Workplace, to help individuals manage their careers. One tool, called the Opportunity Marketplace, helps IBM employees find jobs that fit them. It contains a series of self-assessment tools accessible through the company's HR portal.

By using the Opportunity Marketplace, workers can establish their skills, competencies, work preferences, and educational backgrounds. They can then look at more than five hundred specific jobs in IBM and see how their skills and competencies match these jobs. The system can automatically match a skilled employee with the needs of a hiring manager. If employees so desire, they can request a notification via email of the openings that correspond with their skill sets, and the system can alert managers as to key individuals at IBM who fit the skill set needed to fill an opening in their area.

IBM's human capital database also allows managers seeking employees to search by keywords. For example, if a manager needs to find somebody with expertise in a certain kind of business who is located in a particular country and can speak a particular language, all he or she needs to do is enter three or four keywords and hit the search button, and a list of all the possible people across IBM comes up. Data about each of the individuals include contact information as well as the person's complete qualifications, background, and career history within IBM.

The Opportunity Marketplace tool also helps IBM assess the human capital balances and imbalances in various parts of the company. It lets managers know if they lack employees with a particular skill or have a surplus. A possible next step for

IBM's system would be to make it available to external job applicants. This could greatly improve the recruiting process. External job candidates could evaluate their skills and discover what openings at IBM exist that fit their skills.

The IBM system doesn't stop with assessment. It also includes a learning tool that can create customized learning paths for employees based on their career aspirations and gaps in their skills. The system automatically recommends courses and learning opportunities; a side benefit is that employees are regularly reminded of the importance of learning. Many of these courses are delivered by e-learning; currently more than half of all of IBM's training is done through e-learning. The IBM system is just what b2change organizations that take a commitment-to-development approach need because it speeds up changes in the skills of the workforce and ensures that the workforce's existing skills are utilized. Indeed, the availability of this type of system should make it possible for more b2change organizations to take a development approach.

Overall, having an effective means of managing the internal movement and development of people is critical to attracting and retaining the kind of change-oriented individuals b2change organizations need. Without it, people who enjoy change, learning, and development will inevitably migrate to other organizations. Individuals who like change usually prefer to actively manage their own careers. Organizations that want to be change-ready don't need to take over the management of these people's careers. Quite to the contrary—these individuals might find the loss of control oppressive.

What organizations do need to do is support an individual's development of his or her career within the organization. To truly develop, the person ultimately may have to leave the organization, but that should be because the organization is no longer a good fit, not because he or she did not receive support for development.

Managing Layoffs and Downsizing

Reducing staff is a high-risk action for an organization, but some b2change organizations need to do it, particularly those that are built to travel light. When carelessly decided on or indiscriminately managed, layoffs and downsizing can ruin a company's brand, damage its culture in ways that make the people who remain less productive, result in the loss of significant knowledge and social capital, and be major triggers of death spirals. In many ways, layoffs are more crucial to an organization's reputation for treating people right than initial hiring decisions.

Many organizations simply overreact to downturns in their business. A growing body of evidence says that organizations tend to eliminate too many people in times of economic distress, incurring long-term costs that are often far greater than the short-term savings.[7] These costs include losing people who are not easily rehired when the economic downturn is over; losing people who are critical to important organizational capabilities and core competencies; losing social capital, which is found in the relationships and implicit knowledge that former employees have; and causing existing employees to lose faith in the company and its management, resulting in turnover among the remaining employees when the labor market improves.

Most organizations see downsizing as a cost-cutting measure. In a b2change firm, downsizing is about adjusting capabilities—something that should be done with a clear sense of identity, strategic intent, and knowledge of one's existing capabilities. All the points we made in earlier chapters about building strategy and using information systems to learn about human capital come into play here. Strategy and information should guide any major human capital decision, downsizing being a particularly poignant example.

Clearly it is foolish to argue against all staff reductions in a b2change organization. Sometimes layoffs and downsizing are necessary for a variety of good reasons: when strategy changes, a restructuring may be needed to bring in different skills; an economic downturn can force reductions; sometimes building a new core competency can be accomplished only by recruiting new employees.

But there are significant advantages to not downsizing or doing only a little of it. For example, in an economic downturn, it may be possible to grab market share from competitors who overreduce their staff. This is particularly true if competitors lose their ability to serve their customers well or if they are in a poor position to recover when the downturn is over. B2change organizations that have a commitment-to-development strategy can also use a period of downturn to develop new products or to improve employees' skills and knowledge.

Overall, staff reductions should be used by b2change organizations only as a last resort, after weighing the many other less disruptive options that can be used to reduce labor costs, including the following:

- Voluntary leaves
- Shorter working hours
- Pay reductions
- Delayed start dates for new hires

- Cutting back on the use of temporary employees
- Shortened workweeks
- Reduced bonus and variable pay amounts
- Reduced benefits and extras

If involuntary reductions are necessary, it is critical that the senior management of a b2change organization make a strong case for them as the only practical alternative under the prevailing business conditions. This should not be difficult if management and employees have a good understanding of the nature of the business, the economic condition of the industry, and the status of the organization. All of these should exist in a b2change organization if it has a history of transparency and communication. Needless to say, this understanding should be built *before* downsizing or any other major change is needed.

A b2change organization must handle downsizing in ways that fully support its existing identity and employment brand. Many companies follow the traditional method of selecting individuals for layoffs based on seniority, but this does not fit the b2change approach. Seniority-based layoffs often mean that some of the best employees will be lost, thus diminishing the organization's ability to perform.

As specified in a b2change organization's contingency employment contract (see Chapter Six), staff reductions should be based on performance and skills. Here we have yet one more reason why b2change organizations need to have well-functioning talent management and performance management systems. Without them it is impossible to make good staff reduction decisions.

Some of the best practices we have seen in managing lay-offs occurred in technology firms during the dot-com down-turn. For example, Cisco paid employees part of their salaries if they went to work for volunteer organizations or contributed their time to public service. Other organizations paid tuition for laid-off employees so that they could improve their knowl-edge and be ready to reenter the organization at a later date with better skills and a positive attitude toward the company.

DEVELOPING A TRAINING STRATEGY

When traditional organizations do training and development, it usually is based on looking at existing jobs and analyzing the skills people need to do them. It is assumed that a person's job and perhaps career path should dictate the kinds of skills and knowledge the person needs to learn. Thus most of the train-ing and development done by organizations is focused on preparing people to do their current jobs and possibly their next one or two. Often organizations mandate training and put peo-ple on predetermined career paths. This approach to training works well when organizations can predict what jobs will be like, but this approach does not fit b2change organizations that are committed to development.

Does change mean that companies should not invest in the development of their people? No, that would be an overreac-tion, but it does suggest that b2change organizations need to take a very different approach toward training—an approach that is founded on two premises.

The first is that a b2change organization is simply not in a position to make many decisions about what people should learn and how they can be optimally positioned for employment in the future. The best that a b2change firm can do is provide its employees with information about what is happening within its walls, what its business strategy is, and what kind of technical areas and core competencies it anticipates it will need in the future.

As a general rule, a b2change organization should not direct individuals to learn certain skills and competencies. Yes, there may be some instances where an organization should require people to learn essential skills the company knows it requires (for example, how to use an intranet HR system), but in general a b2change organization should not take responsibility for the long-term development of most or all of its people. This is obvious in a travel-light organization but also true of a commitment-to-development organization.

This first premise gives rise to a second. People in a b2change organization need to be responsible for making their own decisions about what they learn and how they develop their careers. A b2change organization is responsible for providing them with information about what new skills are likely to be needed in the future and perhaps a chance to learn those skills, but for the most part, people must make their own choices about what skills to develop and how to develop them. They need to be responsible for their own careers and employability.

When all is said and done, people are usually in a better position to manage their careers than are the organizations they work for. If they are not in a better position, they need to get there. In our view, career self-management will increasingly become the model on which all organizations—not just b2change organizations—and people fashion relationships in the future.

A b2change organization cannot employ people simply because they are loyal. It needs people whose skills and abilities fit the firm's ever-changing strategies. Mobility needs to be more than a buzzword; it needs to be a new reality. Given this reality, the b2change organization needs to do what it can to support its employees' being employable, but as a general rule it should not promise something it cannot deliver—namely, a career.

Use Just-in-Time Training

Even b2change organizations that travel light need to use targeted "just-in-time" training. This type of training is focused on content that people need to do their current job and that is delivered when they need the skills. In today's world, just-in-time training is often needed for new hires as part of their on-boarding process, as well as for current employees, who may need to update their skills when a new approach to technology, customer service, budgets, or some other management system affects the area in which they work. One major advantage of just-in-time training is that it fits well with when adults learn best—that is, when they need to solve a problem and when the training they receive addresses a specific issue on which they need to work.

The best performance management systems build training in. They provide every employee with a recommended training curriculum. In one company we worked with the vast majority of the recommended courses are available on the intranet and can be taken when they are needed. They include a training program that focuses on using the performance management system. This program contains online testing, which certifies employees as capable of using the system. In the case of the performance management system, employees are required to pass a test on how the system operates.

Reward Learning

Rewards are a great motivator that can inspire people to learn and to accept change. As will be discussed further in Chapter Ten, developing a skill-based pay system that rewards employees for learning new skills can motivate them to learn more quickly and thus enable b2change organizations to change more quickly. It is a particularly good fit for b2change organizations that adopt a commitment-to-development approach. Rewarding specific learning also helps retain employees; it shows people that the organization is committed to their development and also raises their compensation level so that they are less likely to be attracted to another job.

Rewarding general learning, as opposed to job-specific skills, is difficult to justify in many situations. However, if a b2change organization takes a commitment-to-development approach, it may be a good practice.

United Technologies Corporation (UTC) has a program that supports its approach. UTC wants to establish a culture of learning and education and to create the best-educated workforce in the world. To accomplish this objective, UTC has created an employee-scholar program that encourages employees to get a university degree—associate, bachelor's, or advanced. UTC pays for tuition, books, and academic fees and gives employees time off to study. When employees obtain their degree, they are given UTC stock as a graduation reward. One hundred shares of stock are awarded to every employee who achieves a bachelor's, master's, or doctoral degree; fifty shares are awarded to everyone who receives an associate degree.

One unusual feature of the UTC program is that it rewards employees even though the courses they take are not related to the work they do or the work of the organization. The rationale for this is that UTC wants to create a knowledgeable, learning-oriented workforce, so its program is designed to do this rather than to develop specific job skills. Given that many of the company's businesses are in high-tech fields (such as the design of jet engines) that are changing rapidly, it is easy to see the rationale for this strategy.

One can raise legitimate questions, however, as to whether or not the UTC program would be even more effective if it targeted the specific skills individuals need either to do their work or to build the organization's capabilities. This is particularly true when you take into account the cost of the program, $60 million a year.

Two rationales justify spending money to support general skill development in a b2change organization. First, offering a significant reward for completing a degree can be an effective approach to retention. At the very minimum, people will stay with the company until they complete their degree—and often longer out of a feeling of wanting to pay back the company that helped them. This practice may also help the company retain the right kind of employees: learning-oriented individuals.

Second, supporting general learning can reinforce a learning culture throughout the organization. This is especially important in technology companies whose workers must constantly update their skills and abilities. UTC, for example, profits from the halo effect created by rewarding employees who earn degrees for general skill development; their learning tends to create a companywide culture that values and appreciates learning and change in all its forms.

Admittedly, many organizations do not accept the arguments in favor of general learning. For example, SAS, the software firm that is often mentioned as one of the best places to work, takes a narrow approach to development, rewarding people only for learning skills directly applicable to SAS work. SAS does not reward its employees for earning an M.B.A. It regards an M.B.A. as a mobility degree that often leads to posteducation turnover. This policy is consistent with the company's employment contract, which is based on a long-term, somewhat paternalistic relationship with its employees.

Conclusion

The management of human capital is a complicated task, even in an organization that faces a stable environment. It is much more complex when the environment changes and the organization then needs to change its strategy, competencies, and capabilities. There is no substitute for systems that effectively manage staffing and the development of employees; they are critical to the success of all b2change organizations. Effective systems can be developed only if senior management assigns a top priority to the ongoing management of human capital.

There are no magic bullets that can ensure that a b2change organization has the right approach to managing its human capital. There are, however, some practices that are generally effective. These include careful attention to the satisfaction level of employees, because it has a strong impact on turnover; careful analysis of which individuals and jobs are critical to the organization; and the strategic, at times almost surgical, use of training and development opportunities.

Chapter 8

Meeting the
Leadership Challenge

Built-to-Change Strategy:
Make Leadership a Team Sport

What does it take to be an effective leader in a b2change organization? This chapter addresses the fourth element of the designing process in the B2Change Model. It describes what type of leadership is needed in a b2change organization. Leadership is an important contributor to dynamic alignment because it is the glue that holds structure, information systems, talent, and reward systems together.

EFFECTIVE LEADERSHIP REDEFINED

Popular thinking distinguishes between leaders and managers. For at least the last twenty years, most books on management have glorified the types of behaviors that are associated with leadership and have paid little or no attention to those associated with being an effective manager.

According to this thinking, effective leaders create compelling visions of the future, make clear the rewards of contributing to that future, model the right behaviors, and inspire the workforce through their communication skills. Effective leadership is said to be particularly critical when change is needed. The more significant the change, the more charismatic the leadership needs to be.

Managers are usually pictured as doing the nuts and bolts of organizing and supervising work. They structure jobs and set goals, appraise performance and support the development of their subordinates. They also make tough decisions about rewards. Finally, they pass business information downward and gather new information, which they communicate upward.

The implicit and sometimes explicit suggestion is that it is necessary to make a choice: be a leader or be a manager—and by the way, being a leader is the high road. As we noted in Chapter One, this attitude is harmful, because it encourages corporate boards to search for saviors who can transform a failing organization. The research evidence shows that this is often a fool's errand.[1] Even the most effective leaders are rarely successful in changing organizations that are not designed to change. They are particularly unlikely to be successful if they lack managerial skills, because these are critical to executing successful change.

B2change organizations take a different perspective. Numerous research studies dating all the way back to the 1950s have highlighted the importance of excelling at both managerial and leadership behaviors.[2] Rather than finding that inspiring leadership and a focus on results are somehow conflicting, studies found that skillful managers combine the two focuses in ways that create a win-win situation for individuals and for organizations.

What was true half a century ago is even truer today. All organizations, and especially b2change organizations, need individuals who are both good managers and good leaders, not one or the other. The b2change firm can make use of the distinction between leadership competencies and managerial competencies, but it must make clear that it expects to find both sets of abilities in its managers.

Great leaders who are also great managers have two characteristics in common. They adjust to the business environment and leverage a shared leadership model.

Importance of the Business Environment

In most years, more than six hundred new books on leadership are published, and almost all make the same mistake: they make the assumption that one leadership style and one set of managerial behaviors fit all environments. This is simply not true; organizations in different business environments have different identities and require different leadership and management behaviors.

Growth situations require different behaviors than do recessionary environments. Technology firms require a different style and behaviors than do capital-intensive companies, such as ExxonMobil or Chevron. Single-product service companies, such as Southwest Airlines, require a different style and behaviors than do investment banks.

Many CEOs in the 1990s overreacted to the argument that corporations are overmanaged and underled. They became so carried away with emphasizing the leadership side of their role that the managerial side slipped out of focus. This failing hurt them when a slowing economy demanded different behaviors. It is not surprising that CEO turnover increased dramatically in this period, as it is not easy for leaders to adjust their styles.

B2change companies must contend with the fact that one management style does not fit all situations. Clearly, any approach intended to produce a particular type of leader is extremely risky. Such an approach, if it does anything at all, may well produce leaders who fit yesterday's business environment but not today's or tomorrow's.

B2change firms can use two tactics to deal with change: one is to employ managers who can change styles, the other is to replace managers whose styles go out of alignment. We will look at these options in more detail later in this chapter. The critical idea to hold on to at this point is that b2change organizations need to be able to change their managers' behaviors. This represents an enormous adjustment for companies, which have invested in selecting and developing one right type of manager—a very popular approach that makes sense only when you assume the world is stable.

Shared Leadership

Much of the popular writing on leadership focuses on the behaviors of senior management. There is a good reason for this—they are the most visible and, in many respects, the most important leaders in an organization. However, if they are the *only* effective leaders in an organization, it will not operate or manage change effectively.

Good leaders who are also good managers believe in the power of shared leadership. As Mark Hurd, who replaced Carly Fiorina as CEO of HP, noted in a *Wall Street Journal* interview, leadership should be a "team sport."[3] He went on to note that management is a dynamic process, that managers need to understand the business, and that everyone has to have the same script.

It is easy to get swept up in the belief that hero-leaders are critical to an organization's success and to be deceived by hero-leaders who are masters at self-marketing. For example, in 1999, the book *Lessons from the Top* identified America's best business leaders.[4] Its authors said that they used a rigorous methodology that enabled them to identify the very best business leaders in America. Since its publication, nine of those leaders, including Ken Lay of Enron, Dennis Kozlowski of Tyco, and Bernard Ebbers of WorldCom, have watched their companies become subject to criminal prosecution, regulatory rebukes, or shareholder revolts—or all three.

There are obviously a lot of lessons to be learned from the failure of these apparently successful CEOs, but we would like to focus on just one: organizations that are led by hero-leaders often are fragile entities. If the CEO messes up, the organization suffers. They are unlikely to be able to navigate a rapidly changing environment and all too often, cannot survive the leader's personality defects or the loss of their leader. They can't live with their hero-leaders, but they can't live without them either.

Sometimes corporations are viewed as big ships with the CEO at the helm ordering changes in direction. This is not a helpful metaphor. It may fit traditional hierarchical organizations, but it doesn't fit today's knowledge-centered businesses. A better metaphor is to think of a corporation as a community of people spread out over miles and miles of hills, fields, and forests. To get the community moving in a new direction, competent leaders need to be dispersed across the countryside. It's a far bigger job than simply moving the tiller.

There are three advantages to shared leadership. First, shared leadership can very effectively replace hierarchy. Hierarchy and rigid levels of management are, in effect, control devices that substitute for having a workforce that performs effectively because they understand the mission and vision and are motivated to make the organization effective. Viewing leadership as a team sport allows b2change organizations to spread decision making and dealing with uncertainty across a lot of knowledgeable people.

Second, a shared leadership approach has the advantage of building a deep cadre of leadership talent. Given the turbulence in individuals' careers and the changing demands of environment, it is reasonable to expect increasingly high levels of turnover among managers. Thus an organization needs either to recruit individuals who can fill leadership positions or to develop a surplus of leaders. If it faces a great deal of change, it probably needs to do both.

Finally, and most important, a shared leadership approach supports more effective change management. Multiple leaders at all levels of an organization who understand the external environment and the internal capabilities of the organization often see trends that call for organizational change before senior management does.

Even in b2change organizations, when organizations change their strategic intents or how they create value, individuals need to have the change explained and supported by someone who is close to them, whom they respect, and to whom they can talk about the change. The best person usually is their boss or someone in their work group, not just a few senior managers who may be several levels removed. Thus, the more an organization needs to change its strategy, the more leaders it needs.

Organizations need to make the choice between looking for hero-leaders or building leadership at all levels; they cannot coexist. The right choice for the b2change firm is clearly the latter. Not every manager needs to be a great leader, but it is an enormous plus for an organization to have a lot of effective managers, many of whom are also effective leaders. An organization that has a broadly shared leadership capability is likely to be effective at enrolling people in its strategy and, as a result, to be able to change.

LEADERSHIP TALENT

How difficult is it for an organization to manage leadership talent effectively? At this point, the answer should be obvious—it is very difficult. Even in a stable environment, managerial positions are difficult to fill because they require a mix of managerial and leadership skills. The difficulty increases under the shared leadership model because it requires organizations to have talented leaders in managerial and some nonmanagerial positions, throughout the organization. In a changing, unstable environment, the challenge is even greater; an organization needs to have managers who are able to change their managerial and leadership behaviors as the environment changes. Alternatively it needs to have multiple individuals available who have different leadership and managerial capabilities.

There are a number of approaches that b2change organizations use to build a leadership capability. Some of them are the same talent management practices that we discussed in the previous chapter. But there are enough unique issues involved in developing leaders that it warrants being treated separately. As we will emphasize in our discussion, successful leadership development is not just a matter of picking the right practices; organizations must develop systems that combine compatible practices.

Establish the Leadership Brand

Just as it is useful to brand an organization's value proposition, products, and employment policy, branding its leadership style is an effective way to distinguish the organization in the marketplace. Having a clearly identified leadership brand can be a powerful factor in helping attract, retain, and motivate the right leaders and employees. A positive leadership brand that permeates the organization can also serve as a touchstone for all current employees who are managers or who desire to be managers, guiding them toward an organization's "true north" with respect to the leadership behaviors and skills expected of them.

Every organization needs to develop its own leadership brand; no formula exists to indicate what is right. However, there are three essential characteristics we can identify that are critical to strengthening the leadership brand of a b2change organization and making it effective.

First, the leadership brand must reflect the organization's identity. If an organization views itself as a product-driven company, its leadership brand must reflect innovative practices, maintenance of technical expertise, and creative problem solving. A leadership brand that does not honor the firm's identity can create cynicism in the workplace because what the organization believes is different from how people are led.

Second, it must commit leaders to communicating truthfully and openly with their employees about what is going on in the business. Managers quickly lose credibility when they withhold critical information from employees or, worse yet, give them inaccurate information. Sometimes the best answer is "I don't know"; at other times, it is letting employees honestly know that conditions are worsening and changes will need to be made. And whenever bad news about the company must be delivered, it is best to frame it in terms of what is happening in the external environment and how this requires the organization to make changes.

Third, the most important characteristic is that a leadership brand must apply across the entire organization and at all times; it should not involve what is often called "situational leadership." Some leadership gurus have suggested that the most effective managers consider each work situation and then decide how to behave. They argue that managers should take into account such things as the experience of employees, the time available to make a decision, and the type of work that is to be done. We agree that these should have some influence on how a manager behaves, but we believe that all too often, situational leadership results in confusion and alienates people. Employees don't want to be uncertain about how they will be treated or unable to count on being involved in decisions or informed by their manager.

At this point you may be wondering about what we said earlier concerning the importance of the external environment in driving appropriate leadership and managerial behaviors. Although we criticized the idea of situational leadership, we are not abandoning the idea that leaders have to take the environment into account. What we are arguing is that there needs to be a set of givens—including honesty, integrity, providing business information, and helping people understand the implications of organizational strategies and decisions—that simply aren't optional. They need to be the foundation of a b2change organization's leadership brand and relevant in all environments.

A brand is a promise, and in a b2change organization the leadership brand is likely to contain promises about being focused on the environment, not internal politics; about never settling into a status quo; and about always communicating. These kinds of promises can and should be kept, even as some behaviors change due to the nature of the business situation. Like the organization's identity, its leadership brand must be stable, something that people can trust.

Effective leaders do need to adjust their leadership and managerial behaviors to the economic times. What should be situational are many of the management behaviors—for example, what is looked at in evaluating performance, what the consequences of negative performance reviews are, what kind of goals are set, and so forth. These all need to be contingent upon the environment and the organization's business strategy.

In an adverse economic environment, what our colleague Jim O'Toole calls "yellow-light leadership" is appropriate.[5] Managers need to make tough analytic decisions about cost controls, investments in new products and services, and especially the treatment of their human capital. If they have to downsize, it must be done in a way that remains respectful of their staff, with a positive long-term vision.

In short, organizations need to maintain their leadership brand regardless of the economic conditions they face. What they need to change when the business environment changes are their tactics, business practices, and business models.

If leaders can't change their managerial behaviors to fit the organization's strategy and environment, then they clearly will be leaders for only one season. This may not be a severe limitation on the careers of managers whose organizations encounter only one season, but for managers in b2change organizations, a season can be short. They need to be warned that if there is a change of seasons, they may no longer be effective and, therefore, no longer needed by the organization. In other words, they, like other employees, need to know that their continued employment is contingent on the relationship between their skills and the organization's strategy.

Plan for Leadership Change

Maintaining a leadership brand is an important cornerstone of leadership development, but sometimes organization change requires leadership change. When this occurs, b2change organizations must determine the best way to make a leadership style change.

Sometimes it is so difficult for managers to change that an organization making a major transition will do best by simply hiring a new group of managers. Many organizations that went through deregulation in the telecommunications business, for example, found they had to change their brand and recruit a large number of new managers. Similarly, fast-growing small companies often need a fresh management team when they discover they are no longer small.

GE, which is often identified as one of the best developers of leadership talent, has recently hired a number of senior managers from other companies, breaking a long-standing GE tradition of promotion from within. Why did CEO Jeff Immelt decide to look outside for talent? He wanted to quickly increase the degree to which GE is focused on growth from existing businesses. To do this, he needed managers who were not just good leaders; he needed managers with deep expertise in a single business. GE was short of this type of leader because its frequent movement of managers prevented them from developing deep expertise in particular technologies and industries.

One alternative to recruiting new managers when change is needed is for an organization to have a diverse pool of leaders with different styles. This can enable it to draw on the talent it needs from within rather than having to go outside. Thus, odd as it may be, b2change organizations may find it advisable to develop some leaders who don't fit the current environment. Before doing this, systematic thinking is required about the different types of change that are likely to be needed and which managerial behavior may be appropriate if the changes occur. It also requires a tolerance for a diversity of leadership styles.

To produce a diversity of leaders, it is not enough simply to train for it and advocate it. The reward and evaluation processes of the organization must reflect this goal. Individuals must be rewarded for demonstrating a diversity of managerial behaviors. B2change organizations shouldn't just ask, "What have you done for me lately?" They should also ask, "What will you be able to do for me when the world changes?"

Immelt has taken steps to increase the diversity of leaders that GE develops. Some are being asked to stay about five years in positions that provide good development experiences. They are being well rewarded despite their not being promoted every two years.

It is difficult to develop a diversity of leaders, but we believe that b2change organizations can develop leaders who have a range of management styles. To do it, they need to pay particular attention to the kinds of jobs in which they place individuals and to the kinds of coaching and career opportunities they offer. If they have a systematic program to develop a diversity of managerial behaviors, we believe it is possible to develop leaders who can respond effectively to strategy changes.

A COMPANY OF LEADERS

B2change organizations profit from having leadership at all levels. Without it, shared leadership is impossible. Building leadership depth and breadth calls for a development approach that moves away from the traditional focus on growing senior leaders. Shared leadership doesn't rule out giving high-potential executives special courses, competency training, and developmental assignments, but it does argue that following this model is not good enough. Building a company of leaders requires a leadership development approach that touches all levels. It must encourage people throughout the organization to develop the skills needed to take on leadership roles and responsibilities. For a stable organization, shared leadership is a luxury; for b2change firms, it is an essential part of their infrastructure.

The shared leadership approach operates best from the bottom up. Rather than just identifying and grooming a select group of potential leaders, an organization needs to use its structure, work designs, and development programs to open the way for the emergence of leaders at all levels. Doing so requires making leadership training and development programs available to people throughout the organization and opening up information about business results and business strategy to create a shared sense of mission and direction.

In P&G's 2002 annual report, CEO A. G. Lafley describes his view of what has made and will continue to make P&G a successful company. Sounding very much like the leader of a b2change organization, he argues that the secret to P&G's success lies in developing leaders at all levels and creating a culture that values and embraces leadership. According to him, this leads employees to feel a "passionate sense of ownership" of the business.

Leadership Opportunities

The shared leadership approach requires a commitment to innovation and creative thinking from everyone. Emerging leaders need to be able to propose new projects and get the budget authorization and support required to make those projects happen. For example, 3M has a well-developed process that allows people who want to take on a leadership role to get support for projects they initiate. It has special budgets for such new projects so that aspiring leaders can apply for money outside the normal hierarchy of approval.

The last critical element of a shared leadership approach is that it must include sufficient rewards for those who are successful in becoming leaders. As we will see in the next two chapters, rewards motivate people to take risks and achieve goals. Without rewards, the best potential leaders may not emerge, or they may look to move to another company that will reward them for their skills.

W.L. Gore is an excellent example of an organization designed to support the emergence of broad-based leadership and product innovation. Gore, which has a staff of six thousand produces textiles for manufacturers of a variety of products; their Gore-Tex fabric is well known by consumers. Bill Gore, the founder of W.L. Gore, intentionally built an organization that relies on teams and emergent leaders rather than on hierarchical bureaucratic management. It is a b2change organization that supports change based on new applications of its core competency in fabrics.

Everyone at Gore is considered an associate, and there are no hierarchical titles. Becoming a leader is a matter of finding a new business opportunity and convincing others to pursue the venture. Gore does not make the process easy; all emerging leaders must compete for the talent and resources that are needed to get their new product to market.

People are rarely assigned leadership responsibilities or singled out by senior managers for leadership. Instead, everyone takes a one-week course on how the company operates and is assigned a sponsor. Emerging leaders get a great deal of feedback about how effectively they are contributing to the company. They are rated by their peers and given regular feedback on their leadership skills and their development as leaders, but it is up to them to actually become leaders.

Gore's emerging leaders must show they can overcome challenges to earn their stripes as true leaders, and the company makes the rewards for doing so worthwhile. Any associate at Gore who succeeds in growing a business opportunity can end up running his or her own mini-enterprise within the company. Admittedly, the Gore model is an extreme case of structuring an organization to encourage emergent leaders and change. Nevertheless, most organizations can use parts, if not all, of Gore's approach.

Leadership Development

B2change organizations need to develop leaders who not only are willing to change but also have shown competence in getting others to buy in to change. As part of the selection process, candidates for leadership development programs should be asked to "Tell about a time when you led a change effort" and to "Describe how you got others to change."

Leader development needs to start early in someone's career and continue well beyond his or her initial year or two in a management job. If an organization wants to create shared leadership, it must make development experiences available to a broad range of employees within the organization, not just a select few who have been chosen as candidates for senior management positions.

B2change organizations recognize that classroom training is important in leadership development, but that the right experiences are even more powerful. Emerging leaders learn most from taking on challenging job assignments that force them to examine their capabilities and improve their leadership skills. As mentioned in Chapter Seven, b2change companies identify "crucible" jobs that provide good learning experiences for emerging leaders. For example, to learn about making trade-offs among the demands of customers, employees, and financial markets, emerging leaders should fill a crucible job (for example a general management job) for a while and then have a chance to reflect on their experiences in the job. This reflecting can be done with the help of a coach or through an educational experience that focuses on making trade-offs. Overall, the best leadership development efforts are those that combine classroom education, coaching, and strategically timed job changes.[6]

There is one big mistake many companies make: in their eagerness to give people a wide range of leadership experiences, they move them too quickly. As the earlier GE example showed, this can create managers who lack a deep knowledge of a business. It can also reinforce bad habits, such as quick-fix mentalities. In many pivotal positions, such as that of division manager, it often takes at least two years to see the impact of a person's managerial and leadership behaviors. The more senior the position, the longer this will be. Usually senior managers have a good sense of what the right period of time is; they simply must have the discipline to follow that good sense rather than to rush someone's development.

Ideally, as part of its talent management program, an organization should specify the critical leadership and management skills that everyone needs and how they are going to develop them. Capital One, for example, has done an excellent job of identifying key leadership and management competencies and alternative ways to learn those competencies.

One last point to emphasize about leadership development is that in b2change organizations it is crucial to have leaders at the top who are role models and can educate and communicate well. It is very difficult—and in fact may be impossible—to get managers throughout an organization to adhere to a leadership brand if senior managers do not follow it and teach it to others. Both the development of the leadership brand and a consistent leadership style need to start at the very top.

Top-level managers in particular need to be excellent communicators and educators who never miss an opportunity to teach everyone in the organization about the company's business and to engage in dialogue with employees about how the company is doing. At the very minimum, senior managers must be able to articulate the organization's leadership brand in an "elevator speech."

Two CEOs we have worked with are models for how top leaders need to behave. Rich Teerlink, the now-retired CEO of Harley-Davidson, took every opportunity to talk with employees about what they were learning and how the company was performing. Bob Eckert of Mattel is cut from the same cloth. He is always ready and able to talk with employees about the toy business and to learn about new developments in management. Given the major changes that these leaders orchestrated for their companies, both have clearly demonstrated that a commitment to communication and education can produce important benefits.

Transparency

Too many organizations shroud many features of their leadership development program in secrecy. As many as 60 percent of managers in large companies do not know whether they are explicitly part of their company's succession plan, and many more don't know what their position is in it. When we ask organizations why they keep such information as who is being developed secret, we get a variety of answers. The most frequent one is that they fear that if everyone knows who is on the "fast track" for leadership development, others will be jealous and may lose their motivation. Another common one is that they don't want to make an implied promise that they may not be able to fulfill.

Secrecy may indeed fit well in a world of paternalistic management and top-down moves. But it doesn't make sense in a b2change organization where the need for leadership behaviors is changing, leadership performance is regularly assessed, and shared leadership is the predominant mode.

A major advantage of transparency and openness policies in b2change organizations is that they allow individuals to self-manage their careers. As was noted in Chapters Six and Seven, this should be an important part of the employment contract in b2change organizations. It goes along with the idea that rapidly changing organizations often can't do a good job of managing individuals' careers, and individuals shouldn't count on them doing it.

When career management isn't a major responsibility of their organization, individuals need to act. To take on the responsibility, individuals need to know what opportunities exist and how to take advantage of those opportunities. Job openings should be visible to all candidates, and information should be available about the learning opportunities the jobs offer and, of course, what skills they require.

Many organizations rate each individual on the level of management that they think he or she is capable of reaching. (As you may remember, the person description in Exhibit 7.1 contained this information.) This is a useful planning device and should play strongly into the career planning and opportunities that are offered to individuals. There is a key question here, however, about whether the individual should be aware of this assessment.

Although doing so may be a bit uncomfortable at times, we think that b2change organizations should provide just this kind of information to individuals. Having the information can allow them to challenge the perception that others have of them and, one hopes, stimulate a positive dialogue that will lead to a change in either the organization's assessment or in the individual's self-assessment. Admittedly, at times it may lead to the departure of the individual, but that is not necessarily a bad thing.

Transparent career development systems allow employees to reasonably assess their future in the organization and make good decisions around how they pursue career opportunities. They can place their bets on how the environment will change and what new skills they will need, and make a realistic assessment of how likely the organization is to meet their needs. In a world where the organization is not responsible for their career and doesn't guarantee them job security, the ability to access career information is an important feature. Access to it supports an employment contract that is based on mutual understanding and a fair exchange of data. Particularly if an organization's development programs allow most individuals to develop their leadership skills, it can be highly consistent with the model of making every employee a leader, if not a manager.

Finally, when a major change in the firm does occur, transparency can be a tremendous aid to change management. It can help identify people within the organization who are the best candidates to fill new positions, and it can help individuals sense how well they will fit after the changes occur. If they see a relationship, they can take advantage of it. If the organization is moving away from the kind of things that they want to do, then transparency can enable them to receive an early warning that they need to look elsewhere. Clearly, self-managed departures are much better than organization-managed departures, for both the individual and the organization.

Regular Assessment of Managerial Performance and Behavior

B2change organizations regularly assess managers against leadership, managerial, and business performance criteria. Fortunately, the growth of assessment software packages makes it increasingly easy for organizations to gather information about the leadership behaviors of their managers. By using intranet-based systems, such as those at IBM and Capital One, much of the paperwork and forms associated with appraisals can now be eliminated.

Without referring to it by name, we mentioned one potentially useful leadership assessment technique, the 360-degree appraisal, when we discussed Michael Dell in Chapter Five. When an organization assesses its leadership, it should ask customers, employees, peers, and bosses to offer their views of a manager's performance. This breadth of feedback creates a far more useful appraisal of someone's leadership behaviors and skills than can be derived from a single boss's appraisal. All too often, managers develop the ability to manage upward and thus to receive good performance reviews from their bosses, even though their ability to manage downward or laterally is poor.

But 360-degree feedback tools are not perfect. They can be biased by competition among raters, the relationship between the rater and the ratee, and inaccurate or incomplete data. As a result, 360-degree processes in a b2change organization are most useful as a source of development feedback to managers who want to improve their skills.[7] As a general rule, a 360 should not be used for evaluation purposes as part of a regular performance appraisal. It should be a separate activity that is for development purposes only. One way to ensure that this is the case is to have the results go only to the person being appraised and, if there is a coach involved, to the coach.

Figure 8.1 presents a way to think about evaluating leadership performance in a b2change organization. It shows that good results alone are insufficient. Those results must be achieved in the right way; in other words, the organization must also evaluate how well the leader adhered to its leadership model.

Behaviors

	Incorrect	Correct
Good	At risk	Star
Bad	Fire	At risk

Results (vertical axis label)

FIGURE 8.1. **Leadership Performance Matrix**

CONCLUSION

Leaders are a key component of their organization's human capital. They contribute significantly to the intangible value of all corporations. They are particularly important in b2change organizations, where they are needed to lead change as well as to produce good operating results. Leaders need to play a key role in gluing the elements of the designing process together to create dynamic alignment. B2change organizations need to focus specifically on the development of leaders—not just a few, but rather an entire organization of leaders. This is what we mean when we say that a b2change organization must develop a leadership capability.

Fortunately, there are things an organization can do to be sure it will have the leaders it needs. The most important is having senior management focus on the development of leadership in the organization. Neither of us has ever seen an organization develop a leadership capability without the strong support of senior management. Companies that have a strong leadership capability, such as IBM, PepsiCo, and GE, all have had CEOs who see developing effective leaders as one of the most, if not the most, important part of their job. They teach leadership classes, conduct talent reviews (for example, GE's Session C), and in many other ways show their commitment to developing leaders in their companies. This kind of support is not optional: it *must* exist if an organization is to meet the leadership challenge that change creates.

Following a shared leadership model is not only a powerful force toward improving current organizational performance; it helps guarantee that an organization will have a reserve of leaders and, in many cases, a diversity of leaders. As a result, the company will be well positioned to cope with change.

Chapter 9

Designing
Reward Systems

Built-to-Change Strategy:
Make Reward Practices Transparent

Organizations have the ability to reward individuals in a multitude of ways. Because they can vary both the kinds of rewards they give and the reasons for which they give them, there is an almost infinite number of approaches that organizations can take to rewarding individuals. The challenge for b2change organizations, and it is a tough and important one, is to develop an approach to rewards that improves organizational effectiveness and facilitates change.

Fortunately, there is a great deal of research that shows how reward systems affect organizational behavior and performance.[1] Before we begin looking at the specific reward systems that b2change organizations need to use, let's look more generally at the impact of rewards on individual and organizational performance.

Motivation and Rewards

The determinants of people's performance are captured by the equation

$$PERFORMANCE = MOTIVATION \times ABILITY$$

Of course, this equation oversimplifies some very complex issues, but it reinforces a fundamental truth that performance depends on two factors, not one. People need both motivation and ability. Highly motivated individuals will not achieve results if they do not have the skills, expertise, and personality the organization needs. This, of course, is why we discussed human capital management in previous chapters. Similarly, expertise, knowledge, and skills will not produce great results if individuals are not motivated.

People don't automatically come to work, continue to work for an organization, or work hard. They need to be motivated to take a job with a company, to come to work on a daily basis, to continue to work there, to learn, to perform efficiently, and to accept change. Thus, in focusing on motivation, we need to look at both an individual's immediate job performance and the entire relationship between individuals and organizations.

Expectancy Theory

The most widely accepted explanation of why people are motivated to work, perform, learn, and change is rooted in what psychologists call expectancy theory. Expectancy theory argues that people are mostly rational decision makers who think about their actions, and act in ways that satisfy their needs and help them reach their goals.[2] The theory recognizes that we sometimes have misperceptions about reality, make mistakes in our assessment of the likelihood that something might happen, and badly misread situations. But overall the theory assumes, and research evidence confirms, that people generally try to deal rationally with the world as they see it. It views people as proactive, future oriented, and motivated to behave in ways that they believe will lead to valued rewards.

Expectancy theory is popular because it is useful for understanding how people are motivated in many aspects of their lives, including social relationships, family, and work. In fact, we earlier introduced some of its most important principles when we discussed satisfaction and turnover. The theory accepts Maslow's view that there are large differences among people in their needs and, as a result, in the importance they attach to rewards. As the name implies, expectancy theory points to the fact that people are motivated by the promise of rewards. Simply stated, it assumes that people behave in ways they believe will lead to rewards they value.

Reward Attractiveness

The rewards offered by organizations are truly diverse and at times downright amusing. In addition to the usual ho-hum rewards of interesting work, recognition, fringe benefits, cash, stock options, and big offices, some corporations give out private rodeos with mechanical bulls, fly fishing on western ranches, flights in a fighter plane, river rafting, sabbaticals, forty-two kinds of free drinks, and a lifetime supply of Ben and Jerry's ice cream. Any of these rewards can be effective motivators if they are valued by individuals.

The attractiveness of a reward depends on at least two determinants: (1) how much of it is being offered and (2) how much the individual values the particular type of reward being offered. The more an individual values the type of reward and the more of it that it is offered, the more motivational potential it has.

If you live in a state with a lottery, you can readily see that the amount of reward is a significant factor. Think about what happens when your state lottery prize goes up. A $100 million payoff attracts many more players than a $1 million payoff. When the prize is big enough, a surprising number of people are willing to endure traffic jams and standing in line for hours just for a miniscule chance of being the next big winner.

Individuals vary significantly in terms of what they consider valuable, attaching different degrees of importance to such rewards as money, recognition from a supervisor, and a ride on a mechanical bull. This variation is the result of their needs, environment, culture, age, generation, and a host of other factors.

In Chapter Six we pointed out that b2change organizations need to give serious consideration to individual differences when they acquire talent. The talent must fit the reward system. The implication of this for the design of the reward system in a b2change organization is clear: as we stressed earlier, it needs to be coordinated with the talent acquisition strategy so that it offers rewards that the employees value.

REWARDS AND PERFORMANCE

The purpose of an organization's reward system should be to motivate people to behave in ways that support its strategic intent and performance requirements. Expectancy theory tells us that people are motivated by the promise of future rewards; therefore, a critical need in developing a motivating reward system is to establish a clear connection between the reception of a reward and the behavior required to obtain it. This is often referred to as a line of sight, although calling it the line of influence is probably more accurate. Using the word *influence* highlights the fact that to be motivated in a work situation, people must see how their behavior influences a performance measure that, in turn, drives the receipt of a reward they value.

Whichever term is used, the concept is the same: if people see valued rewards as being tied to a particular performance or behavior, the organization is likely to get more of that behavior. The complement is equally true: if a particular behavior is not rewarded, the organization is likely to get less of it.

Establishing a line of sight requires a combination of trust and transparency. Individuals have to trust what they are told by their managers about how the reward system operates and what they will be rewarded for. To some degree, trust can substitute for transparency, but in today's world it is rare that individuals will trust what they are told about how rewards are managed without being allowed to see what is actually happening. We are clearly in a "show me" era. Thus trust develops only when transparency is present. Employees must be told what their organization's policies and practices are and then have the chance to see and experience a system operate as they were told it will.

Having transparency and establishing trust is particularly important in b2change organizations. To support change they often have to modify their reward systems. When they make reward changes it is important that employees believe what they are told about how the new system will operate. If they have to see it operate before they believe it has changed, there is a good chance changes in their behavior will be too late and the change effort will fair.

A high level of openness and visibility also creates a high level of accountability. Decision makers are much less likely to "bend the rules" if they know that their decisions will be visible. The bottom line, therefore, is that transparency contributes to the effectiveness of reward systems.

In many organizations, pay amounts and pay decisions are closely guarded secrets. Not surprisingly, this often leads to confusion about how the compensation system works—and to the loss of a potentially powerful motivator of performance and change.

The Impact of Goals on Motivation

Motivation theory strongly emphasizes the importance of goals in motivating people. Research backs this up by showing that when individuals commit themselves to a goal, they are highly motivated to achieve it.[3] One reason often is that their self-esteem and sense of self-worth are tied to accomplishing the goal. When they achieve the goal, they experience feelings of achievement and success, or what in psychology are called intrinsic rewards. People may also be motivated to achieve goals because there are financial or other extrinsic rewards tied to them.

As we mentioned earlier, a perennial debate exists about how difficult goals should be: Can goals be set too high and become too difficult for people to meet? Can they be too easy? Expectancy theory provides an interesting way of thinking about this. It argues that if the goal seems too difficult, people may see a low probability of achieving it. This in turn destroys their motivation to work toward the goal, because receipt of the reward becomes very unlikely.

This is not to suggest, however, that people never try to achieve very hard goals and as a result they cannot motivate change. As long as two conditions exist, people may be motivated to reach for a difficult goal. First, the connection between achieving the goal and receiving the reward must be strong; in other words, the line of sight or line of influence must be clear. Second, the amount of reward associated with accomplishing the goal needs to be very large (remember the lottery example). Conversely, if there is a low probability of achieving a goal and the rewards for achieving it are small, people are highly unlikely to put forth the effort required.

The research on goal difficulty leads to a somewhat contradictory and paradoxical conclusion related to the impact of intrinsic rewards on motivation. Some evidence suggests that as goal difficulty rises, people feel a greater sense of accomplishment when they achieve it. As a result, they become more motivated to achieve difficult rather than easy goals, even though the probability of achieving them is low. In essence, what may be happening is that the intrinsic rewards associated with accomplishing something difficult become so large that people are willing to put out extraordinary effort to achieve them.

As a final point, we need to once again raise a caution flag about very difficult goals. When very difficult goals are combined with very large rewards for achieving them, some people will do whatever it takes to reach them. Unfortunately, "whatever it takes" sometimes includes cheating, unethical behaviors, and falsifying performance measures.

Consider the scandals that enveloped Enron, WorldCom, Adelphi, and other companies in which corporate fraud has occurred. In these companies, the executives had extraordinarily large stock option grants whose worth depended on their producing ever higher levels of corporate performance. When for a number of reasons these levels became unachievable, executives chose not to forgo the rewards but instead to falsify the books, cash in their stock options, and reap millions of dollars. Obviously organizations need to be particularly vigilant when they set difficult goals, and high rewards are at stake. They also need to ask whether the goals are too high.

Job Satisfaction, Performance, and Change

Many managers believe that job satisfaction is an important determinant of motivation and performance. This is more a myth than a truth. In fact, the opposite may be true.[4]

In the view of expectancy theory, motivation is based on anticipated rewards and future satisfaction, not on present satisfaction. Anticipated satisfaction causes people to view a reward as important and thus is a potential source of motivation. Job satisfaction may be the *result* of performance when performance leads to rewards, but job satisfaction does not *cause* performance.

Job satisfaction can influence the ability of organizations to change in part because it is an important determinant of retention. Over time, people tend to gravitate to work situations that meet their needs, and as a result their overall job satisfaction goes up. This bodes well for organizations that try to retain their people and develop a virtuous spiral relationship. On the negative side, satisfaction with the status quo is also a major reason why it is difficult to change older successful organizations. Simply put, most people are satisfied with their situation; otherwise they wouldn't be there.

244 Built to Change

To motivate change in an organization, it is necessary to have some dissatisfaction with how things are. In the case of a b2change organization, there doesn't have to be a high level of dissatisfaction, but there does need to be the belief that change is desirable because it will lead to a better future. Thus, increasing job satisfaction is unlikely to have a positive effect on either performance or the willingness to change. In fact, it may have a negative effect because, at least temporarily, people will cease to seek additional rewards and focus on maintaining their current rewards.

Satisfaction and Organizational Performance

Even though satisfaction does not drive individual motivation and performance, it does not mean that satisfaction does not influence *organizational* performance. When employees are dissatisfied with their jobs, they are saying that they do not see positive consequences associated with remaining part of the organization as it presently operates. It is therefore hardly surprising that, as we discussed in Chapter Seven, dissatisfied employees typically begin to look elsewhere for employment and leave if they find a situation that offers a better mix of rewards.

If dissatisfied employees do not leave, they become disgruntled employees who often seek to change their current situation by organizing and voting for a union, becoming activists, filing lawsuits, or engaging in other actions that they think will improve their lot. In b2change organizations it is critical to focus the desire for change that results from dissatisfaction on organizational performance improvements that will create a virtuous spiral. This is why b2change organizations are designed to make strategy adjustments and strategy-driven change easy to accomplish. It is also why b2change organizations strive to become companies of leaders.

ORGANIZATION STRUCTURE AND REWARDS

A b2change organization needs to link and coordinate reward practices to its structure. There are essentially two issues when it comes to linking structure and rewards. The first involves how structure influences which reward system designs are effective. The second involves the impact of the reward system on how the structure operates and how effective the system is in supporting organizational performance and change. Let's first look at the issue of how structure influences reward system possibilities.

How Job Design and Structure Affect Rewards

We began our discussion of structure and rewards in Chapter Two, when we pointed out that in a b2change organization reward practices should be dynamically aligned with the other elements of the designing process. To complete that discussion, we need to consider the impact of structure on the intrinsic rewards that are available to individuals, and how structure influences the ability to deliver such extrinsic rewards as pay and promotions.

Research shows that how individual jobs and teams are designed plays a critical role in the degree to which an individual experiences intrinsic rewards as a result of good performance. Such rewards as feeling a sense of accomplishment when a task is successfully performed and a feeling of competency as one performs one's job well are highly dependent on the structure of the work itself.

As mentioned in Chapter Four, research on job design shows that individuals are motivated when they do work that involves meaningful tasks that require them to use abilities they value and provides them with feedback about how well they perform.[5] When these conditions exist, individuals experience a sense of intrinsic reward when they perform well. Not surprisingly, doing simple tasks well doesn't lead to feelings of accomplishment. How good can you feel about yourself when you do something everyone can easily do? Doing tasks that don't provide feedback doesn't lead to rewards either. How rewarding is it to bowl if you can't see the pins fall?

Originally much of the research on the relationship between an individual's work and motivation focused on the impact of enriching jobs. It led to change efforts that combined work activities or tasks so that individuals were responsible for an entire customer interaction, or, in some cases, for producing an entire product.

Following the research work on individual job enrichment, research on teams became popular. The same general principles were found to produce an intrinsically motivated team. This research showed that teams are motivated when they are given control over an entire product or customer relationship, perform a task that is meaningful, and get feedback about their performance.[6] This discovery has guided the design of numerous high-performance factories where teams are responsible for creating products, and the design of customer service operations where teams are responsible for servicing customers.

The research on teams has had a particularly strong impact on process production plants, such as paper mills, chemical plants, and food-processing operations. In process production plants, because of the nature of the technology, it is impossible to give an individual responsibility for a whole production process. It is not, however, impossible to give a team of up to twenty individuals such responsibility. When teams of this size are given responsibility, the results are very similar to those obtained when individuals are held responsible. These teams typically perform well and are motivated to improve their performance.

Assigning work to teams that are responsible for whole production processes is, of course, more complicated than assigning work to an individual. It requires a variety of selection and training processes that help develop the team as well as a continuing focus on the effectiveness of the relationships among the team members. Teams are the Ferrari of work design—expensive to build and maintain, but capable of very high levels of performance. And because some technologies simply don't allow for the creation of individually enriched or meaningful jobs, creating teams, complicated as the effort it is, can be the best (and sometimes only) option for b2change organizations. One way or another, they need to design work that is motivating and rewarding.

How Reward System Designs Affect Structure and Performance

B2change organizations need to consider several factors in the designing extrinsic reward systems to match work structures. We have already emphasized that for rewards to be motivating, they need to be tied to measures of performance. These measures can be measures of individual, team, or organizational performance. What they *can't* be are metrics that an employee can't understand or influence. These kinds of measures will not motivate either performance or change. The measures that an organization can collect and report to individuals are strongly determined by the organization's structure.

As noted in our discussion of structure in Chapter Four, organizations that are designed around their functions (for example, marketing, finance) are particularly poor when it comes to producing metrics that capture the performance of their parts. All too often, they must rely on budgets that capture only a small part of what determines organizational effectiveness and, in many cases, are badly out-of-date and inappropriate by the time the budget period is complete. Employees in these organizations have little feel for how their company is performing and experience little sense of their performance being rewarded. As a result, if their organization's performance declines, they are not motivated to make changes that will improve it.

Reward systems are best at motivating performance and change when organizations have designs that allow the development of metrics that validly capture the strategic performance of key units. In other words, a structure that features business units is generally best for b2change firms, not just for the reasons mentioned in Chapter Four but also because this structure makes it easier to align rewards. If metrics for business unit performance can't be created, then it is critical that the organization use metrics that are based on its overall performance (for example, profit) as the basis for rewards. To be effective, b2change organizations need to give individuals valid, understandable, and timely information about how they and their organization are performing and to reward them based on performance. It is basic to motivating them to perform and to change.

The Impact of Rewards on Structure

Extrinsic rewards can have a powerful impact on how individuals think about and react to the structure of an organization. This is particularly true when it comes to hierarchy. In traditional organizations, the rewards individuals get are strongly related to the position they occupy in the hierarchy—generally speaking, the higher up the hierarchy, the more financial and nonfinancial extrinsic rewards individuals receive.

Many of the nonfinancial rewards that go along with hierarchy are not only valuable but are also highly visible. For example, senior executives typically get company cars, prime parking spaces, large offices, and country club memberships. We could go on: in many cases, the perquisites include such highly visible rewards as private jets and helicopter service to and from company locations.

One impact of hierarchical rewards is to clearly differentiate individuals who are higher up in the organization from those at lower levels. Hierarchical rewards often have a strong impact on the desire of people to move up in the organization. Inevitably, success in the organization becomes defined as moving upward and obtaining the rewards that go along with promotions. One result is that employees will often resist structural changes that affect their upward mobility and the rewards associated with it. Another is that individuals will resist career moves that are not upward.

The more hierarchical an organization becomes, both in terms of structure and culture, the more likely it is that decisions will be made higher up in the organization. This, in turn, means that individuals lower down feel less personally responsible for the success, or for that matter the failure, of the organization. This can affect their motivation to perform and lead change because they do not feel that they have an influence on the organization's success. It also can lead to their resisting change because they are not motivated to improve the organization's performance.

The alternative to a hierarchical, perquisite-laden organizational environment is one that is egalitarian. Southwest Airlines, Jet Blue, Lincoln Electric, and Whole Foods are examples of companies that have few visible reward differences between the top members of the organization and the other members. Egalitarian treatment includes similar offices for management employees, similar dress, and an absence of the kind of eating, parking, and recreational perks that are associated with senior management in most organizations. In a few cases, it also includes less hierarchical pay levels. Whole Foods, for example, has about a 16-to-1 top-to-bottom pay ratio, whereas the average for Fortune 100 firms is over 500-to-1.

Having a low degree of hierarchical differentiation creates an egalitarian culture in which it is easier to move decision making to the most appropriate place. It also can send a message of shared leadership and shared responsibility for the success of an organization. This in turn can lead to high levels of motivation throughout the organization and to employees' identification with the mission of the organization, conditions that are essential to the success of a b2change organization.

Rewards can also affect the degree to which the parts of an organization are integrated, particularly the degree to which different business units and functions see themselves as separate entities. Separation and even some competition are created when parts of an organization have different reward systems.

For example, if two business units have different bonus plans, it most likely will lead to them act independently. This can be either a positive or a negative depending on the organization's strategy. If one business unit is new and the other is well established, this is most likely a positive, because success requires different behaviors. However, if the two units need to cooperate to serve a customer, separate reward systems can be very dysfunctional.

ORGANIZATIONAL IDENTITY AND REWARDS

Reward systems should be a powerful reflection of a b2change organization's identity. What is measured and rewarded has a strong effect on what people believe are the right things to do and the right way to do them, what the organization values, and what kind of people are the right ones for the organization to employ. For this reason, a critical issue for b2change firms is the degree to which their reward systems reflect and reinforce values, behaviors, performance levels, and change orientation that are consistent with their identity.

All too often, executives are better at describing what they would like their identity to be than they are at aligning reward systems to support it. In most situations, reward systems speak louder and more clearly than do senior executives because they affect people much more directly than do speeches about what the organization wants from its people. Clearly it is not easy to design a reward system that supports the high-performance, change-oriented identity of a b2change organization, but, as we will see in the next chapter, such designs are possible and critical to their success. An organization cannot maintain—or, in the case of a transformation, change—its identity without aligning its reward system to support that identity.

Teamwork is one of the key areas most powerfully influenced by an organization's reward system. Often the organization's work design and identity call for teams. Reinforcing an identity that includes teamwork, however, takes more than simply designing work for teams. Teamwork must be rewarded in a clear and visible manner. Individuals need to see a clear line of sight between their team-oriented behaviors and the rewards they receive.

One way to achieve a line of sight is to reward groups of individuals based on their collective performance. A second way is to reward individuals for team-oriented behaviors. The latter tends to produce and maintain a focus on individuals and is therefore less effective in producing cohesive, supportive teams, but even this approach takes a giant leap beyond a focus simply on individual performance.

The reward practices that an organization adopts early in its life cycle are particularly important in shaping its identity. They reinforce certain behavior patterns and signal how the organization values different individuals. They also attract and retain a certain type of employee and in a host of little ways indicate what the organization stands for and values.

Once an identity has been established, the reward system can be particularly difficult to change. This is one of the major reasons why identity change is difficult. People become married to existing reward practices and thus are hesitant to see change. Often they have been attracted to the organization because of the reward system and identity, and have stayed because of them. The idea of change thus becomes scary, and all too often employees end up resisting it. Unfortunately, there is no substitute for changing a reward system if it is not contributing to dynamic alignment and is out of synch with the identity of a b2change organization. Failure to revise the reward system will create a failure to change.

Strategic Intent and Rewards

The reward system should play a key role in implementing a b2change organization's strategic intent. Executives need to pay a great deal of attention to the key elements of their firm's strategy when they design its reward system.

First, the reward system must focus on the performance outcomes the organization needs in order to execute its strategy. Any number of metrics can indicate the success of the strategy—for example, new product introductions or revenue growth of certain customer segments. Once these metrics have been identified, the organization then needs to focus on the key issue: how to dynamically align the rewards that teams and individuals receive with the appropriate metrics. Individuals who can influence the indicators of success must have their rewards tied to those indicators. This is a key step in translating the strategic intent of a b2change organization into organizational performance.

Closely related to the practice of measuring and rewarding the outcomes that strategy calls for is that of focusing on the organizational capabilities and core competencies needed to execute strategy. Because competencies and capabilities evolve and change, linking rewards to the creating value process of a b2change organization is a great way to build dynamic alignment. As was mentioned in Chapter Five, b2change organizations need to measure and evaluate their capabilities and core competencies on a regular basis, as they are critical to the company's strategic performance.

But simply measuring and evaluating capabilities and competencies is not enough. Rewards for individuals and groups in b2change organizations need to be based on their ability to maintain and develop new competencies and capabilities. For example, if quality is a key capability, it must be measured as a capability, and rewards must be tied to its level of development. In a b2change organization, it is particularly important to reward the development of new competencies and capabilities that support changes in strategic intent.

Conclusion

Overall, a reward system needs to attract, retain, and motivate individuals who are capable of developing and implementing a strategic intent. One implication of this is that if strategy changes, the reward system needs to be examined and most likely will have to be altered. It also means that if the reward system can be adjusted to encourage behaviors that support a new strategy, it can serve as a lever for change. It can create an organization that is motivated to change and can push the skills and capabilities of the organization in a direction that supports change.

Because rewards have such a strong impact on motivation and satisfaction, they are a key design element of every organization. Failure to have a well-designed reward system can create an organization that is poorly staffed, that fails to change in the face of a strong need to change, and that over time becomes a corporate dinosaur. The implication of this for b2change organizations is clear: they must have reward systems that support change. We will see in the next chapter that, not surprisingly, the reward systems of b2change organizations need to look different, operate differently, and drive different behaviors than those of traditional organizations.

Chapter 10

Rewarding Performance and Change

Built-to-Change Strategy:
Link Rewards to Skills,
Knowledge, and Organizational Performance

Organizations get the behaviors they reward. Organizations that wish to perform well and change effectively need to create reward systems that emphasize both performance and change. Sounds simple, but it is not easy to do. It is also not what most organizations do. All too often they reward stability more than change, seniority more than performance, and job size more than skill development. B2change organizations must do it differently.

Seniority-Based Rewards

When it comes to creating a b2change organization, it is hard to think of a more dysfunctional practice than basing rewards on seniority. Despite this, the array of rewards that many organizations tie to seniority is vast. Some of the rewards are relatively trivial and minor, others quite valuable and important.

In the case of our employer, the University of Southern California, seniority determines seating at football games (an important reward to some). It determines parking space eligibility (an important reward to many), and it determines the level of benefit coverage, including free tuition. However, USC does not have the practice, common in many organizations, of giving formal rewards for key employment anniversary dates: no lunches, certificates, or other recognition awards.

Although we have not seen any studies of how common seniority-based rewards are today versus ten or fifteen years ago, our guess is that they are much less popular today. They fit well in a world where organizations try to build loyalty, and individuals spend their entire careers with the same organization. They fit very poorly in a b2change organization.

Seniority-based rewards make it hard to reward current performance, but more than that, they make it hard to motivate individuals to change. They also run counter to the reality that organizations may need to have layoffs, make staffing changes to develop new capabilities, or remove poor performers. It simply is not consistent to reward people for the length of time they have been with an organization while also downsizing and churning the employee population in order to create new competencies and capabilities. Most important, there is the inconsistency of rewarding something that the organization probably does not want—namely, a long-term employment relationship with *all* its employees. As we have noted earlier, a b2change organization may want this arrangement with some employees, but rarely with all.

One other problem with seniority-based rewards is that often they don't lead to the retention of the right people. Individuals with valuable skills usually are not persuaded to stay to earn a seniority reward. There are exceptions, of course; seniority rewards may retain even good performers if the rewards are large enough.

One of us was made very aware of this when giving a talk at a large engineering firm. He made the point that seniority rewards rarely retain anyone, particularly good performers. He then asked the audience if, in fact, rewards for seniority were effective in retaining them—and a surprisingly large number of employees raised their hands. Astonished, he asked the audience what the rewards for seniority were. It turns out that one of them was rather valuable: a gold Rolex watch (worth approximately $25,000!) for twenty-five years of service. This is, of course, a far cry from the typical wall clock or plaque most organizations award for long service.

Just to be clear here, we are not arguing that b2change organizations shouldn't reward people with greater seniority more than individuals with less seniority. What we are arguing is that rewards should not be given for seniority. They should be given because individuals are performing well or are core employees who are particularly valuable to an organization and, therefore, need to be rewarded so that they are inclined to remain. This can be done through performance-based reward systems and, as we discuss next, through rewards for the skills and competencies that individuals have.

Retirement plans are an example of a seniority-based system that b2change organizations can easily adapt to suit their purposes. Instead of defined-benefit plans that guarantee increases in retirement pay for each year of service, b2change organizations can utilize a cash balance program in which individuals and their organization make annual contributions to a plan that pays out based on the dollar amount in the plan at the end of the person's employment. These plans can be structured to encourage individuals to stay, but they don't have to be structured that way. They can vest early and be made portable. Remember, in a b2change organization, voluntary turnover can be a positive. People should leave when what they can do doesn't fit the strategy. Thus a good b2change reward system makes it easy for the "right" people to leave.

IBM, AT&T, and Owens Corning are among the many corporations that have dropped their traditional retirement plans in favor of cash balance plans. A number of technology firms, including Apple, have no employer-funded retirement plans. They allow employees to contribute to their own plans, but they make no company contributions to a plan that serves to "lock in" everyone. The rationale for this is simple. They are not sure they want to encourage employees to stay around long enough to retire. They have a travel-light strategy of churning the workforce to get the best young technology talent for whatever technology is hot at the moment. The idea of building loyalty through rewarding seniority just doesn't fit the b2change approach.

Merit-Pay Plans

Merit-pay plans are the most frequently used way to reward individuals for performance. Given their popularity, merit-pay systems must be effective—right? Wrong! The evidence is clear that in most cases merit-pay plans do little to motivate performance and often do not even help retain the right employees.[1]

The many different merit-pay plans that organizations use follow the same general model: individual performance is appraised, usually by a supervisor, and as a result of that appraisal an adjustment (almost always upward) is made to the employee's salary. How large that adjustment is depends on the favorableness of the appraisal and the size of the budget for salary increases. The latter is usually strongly influenced by the labor market and inflation. (Generally, the higher the rate of inflation, the higher the budget.)

In addition, the size of raises is often influenced by how well employees are already being paid compared to others doing the same kind of work. If they are highly paid relative to others and to the market, they are likely to get a relatively small raise, even if they are good performers and retaining them is a high priority. If they are paid less than others and below the market rate, they are likely to get a relatively large raise, even if they are not outstanding performers. The rationale for this approach is that good performers only need to be paid so much in order to retain them; therefore a large raise isn't necessary if they are already highly paid. On the other hand, good performers who are poorly paid relative to the market do need large raises if they are to be retained. This rationale is often true, but what about pay for performance and motivation?

Pay cannot be much of a motivator if, in order for an employee to get a "large" raise, inflation has to be high and the employee must be both poorly paid and an outstanding performer. Talk about a weak line of sight for most employees!

There is no ultimate scientific answer to the question of how large a pay change needs to be to motivate performance. Sometimes very small changes in pay can be powerful motivators if they are seen as a form of recognition. The same can be said for some nonfinancial rewards that have a low monetary value. For example, public ceremonies, certificates, and letters may be valued highly by some individuals, even though such forms of recognition are relatively inexpensive. That said, a good guess is that to be meaningful from an economic point of view, merit-pay increases must be at least 5 percent and probably must exceed 10 percent to be truly motivating.[2]

Merit-based salary increases typically become a permanent part of an individual's pay. The hope is that this will lead, over a number of years, to a pay level that reflects performance. This can happen if an individual's performance is stable from year to year, and for some it is. But individual performance often varies considerably over a person's working life. As a result of performance changes, poor performers can end up with very high pay and outstanding performers with very low pay. This often occurs when a new employee performs outstandingly well and a longer-term employee performs poorly.

To justify their merit-pay amounts, organizations often end up delivering a very confusing message. In essence, they tell their highly paid good performers that continuing good performance will not result in particularly large merit increases because they are already paid well. To make this message palatable, firms tell their good performers to look at their total compensation level, not their merit increases, to see the relationship between their pay and their performance.

Conversely, high-performing new employees are told that they should not look at their total compensation but at their merit increase because it indicates how well they are performing. Obviously, at this point the simple idea of rewarding better performers with bigger merit increases has been lost.

The bottom line is that merit-pay plans rarely encourage individuals to change their skills or performance. There is not enough incentive in the system to encourage individuals to make a major change in their behavior, particularly for people who have been in their job for several years and are approaching the top of their pay grade. Even if new goals are set and new challenges are presented, they may not result in a significant change in the individual's behavior.

Furthermore, there is little the organization can do to change someone's reward level if that person is unwilling to support a change effort. It can withhold a merit increase, but this hardly has a major financial impact on an individual. Ultimately, a merit raise pay plan creates a situation in which the only way to punish people who are not supporting a change is to fire them.

One final comment on the effects of merit-pay plans: they tend to enhance the importance of promotion. Typically, the only way for an employee to get a large pay increase in a merit-pay system is to get a promotion, because there is a separate budget for promotion increases. From the employees' perspective, promotion also has a second desirable effect; it moves them into the lower end of a new, higher pay range, thus making them eligible for larger merit increases if they perform well in their new job.

There is nothing inherently wrong with the idea of promotion as a positively rewarded and motivating event. It is a limited tool, however, in b2change organizations, as they are flatter and there are fewer promotion opportunities available. In addition, change often requires individuals to make lateral career moves and to learn new skills, two things that a promotion-based reward system doesn't support.

Despite the fact that merit pay plans are not effective, most companies continue to spend large amounts of time every year deciding how to distribute merit increases. For many companies, the annual merit-pay plan process has become a corporate rain dance, accompanied by great ceremony, noise, and activity. B2change organizations can put their managers' time to much better use than administering merit-pay plans. They simply aren't worth the time and effort they take.

BONUSES

B2change organizations that want to motivate performance with cash rewards must use bonuses. An increasingly popular form of variable pay uses the results of a performance appraisal to determine the amount of bonus that is paid to an employee. This approach eliminates one of the major failings of merit pay: not enough money being available to motivate individuals. It does this by eliminating the annuity feature of merit pay, thus freeing up dollars to be used for variable pay.

The Impact of Bonuses

B2change organizations can use bonus pay to reward individual performance as well as to retain excellent performers. It is particularly effective at retaining new employees because they can almost immediately be paid at a high level if they perform well; they do not have to wait for a series of merit increases. It also has the advantage of providing a way to quickly reduce the total compensation of poor performers. Finally, it can make very clear the relationship between a performance appraisal judgment and the amount of someone's pay. There is no need to explain how a person's pay history affects his or her bonus.

Bonus plans are useful in b2change organizations, especially during reorientation and transformation. Individual plans that offer relatively large bonus opportunities can provide a powerful incentive for individuals to perform well and to change their behavior when a new strategic intent calls for it.

A bonus system that ties bonus amounts to change goals can be a particularly powerful driver of change. In some situations it makes sense to have one-time bonuses awarded at the completion of a strategic change. Using short-cycle bonus periods (for example, three months) that target change implementation can speed up the installation of major changes.

When an organization bases bonuses on such organizational performance measures as profit and market share, it creates not only a reason to perform but also a reason to embrace strategic and operational change. Our research shows that the implementation of change efforts that are directed at building capability— for example, total quality management, knowledge management, and employee involvement—are more effective when pay is based on organizational performance.[3] Bonus plans that are funded based on organizational performance relative to competitors and market conditions are an effective way to alert employees when the organization needs to change. Failure to change means deteriorating performance and thus fewer financial rewards, so it is not a surprise that individuals are more focused on how to improve performance and are more willing to accept change when they are paid based on the performance of their organization.

The supermarket chain Whole Foods is a prime example of a company that effectively uses bonus pay. Their philosophy starts with the belief that there should be "no secrets." In addition to releasing a flood of financial data to its employees, it releases pay data for every employee, including executives. This provides transparency and accountability with respect to all pay decisions.

Whole Foods combines public pay information with a distinctive bonus plan. Every four weeks, individual work teams (there are usually ten in every store) are assessed for productivity, and bonuses are awarded to them. This practice establishes a clear connection between the store's performance and the rewards that the teams in the store receive. In addition to receiving bonus checks, employees are eligible for stock options. The company says 94 percent of its options go to its nonexecutive staff.

Design Keys

It's easy to see how and why bonus-pay systems can be effective in b2change organizations. The hard part is figuring out how they should be designed. Critical decisions include deciding on the degree to which bonuses should be based on individual, group, unit, and organizational performance, what specific metrics to use, and how much of a bonus to award. These decisions can be quite complex, because they need to support the dynamic alignment among strategic intent, talent, information systems, and shared leadership. We cannot specify an "ideal" approach; however, we can provide several general guidelines to keep in mind when designing bonus programs for a b2change organization.[4]

First, remember that individual bonus plans are the most effective way to drive individual behavior because they provide the clearest line of sight between performance and reward. For them to be effective, however, they must be combined with the kind of well-designed performance management system we described in Chapter Five. Unfortunately, individual plans do a very poor job of integrating the behavior of individuals. If an organization uses teams and has a highly interdependent work environment, it should have a bonus plan that primarily rewards collective performance.

Second, if a line of sight can be established between what an individual does and the performance of the entire business or business unit, then basing part or all of any bonus payments on organizational performance makes sense. In general, a bonus plan based on the performance of an entire business has many advantages. It both motivates individual performance and causes people to integrate themselves into a high-performing unit—a key step in creating the kind of virtuous spiral that every organization would like to have. It also can stimulate change if an organization's performance drops. Individuals get smaller bonuses and, as a result, want to know what happened and what needs to change.

In the best of all worlds, business-based bonus plans lead to pay well above market rates because the organization's performance is above average. This occurs as a result of the plan's effectively motivating everyone's performance as well as attracting and retaining top-performing people—a true virtuous spiral situation.

Third, operating an effective business-based bonus plan requires that people be thoroughly educated in the bonus plan. They need to know how their performance is measured, how their behavior affects the entire organization's performance, how the performance of the business is measured, and how they will be rewarded if different parts of the organization perform at different levels. When everyone's bonuses are determined, employees need to see how the decisions were made and what the amounts are.

One final point about bonus systems: often the best way to reward individual behavior and organizational performance is to tie the size of the bonus pool for individual rewards to the performance of a business unit or the total organization. The performance metrics that are used at the organizational level can be traditional accounting measures, operational measures, or a change target. The advantage of creating a bonus pool based on organizational performance measures is that it reinforces both individual and collective performance. And, as we mentioned earlier, it can also help focus the attention of individuals on the external environment and on how the company is performing relative to that market.

PROFIT SHARING

Profit sharing is the oldest and most commonly used bonus-based approach to rewarding organizational performance. In 2002, fully 69 percent of the Fortune 1000 companies operated profit-sharing plans.[5]

Most profit-sharing plans use the company's publicly reported earnings to determine the bonus payment made to employees. To create a line of sight for employees, sometimes certain costs are excluded from the earnings calculation. For example, interest and taxes are sometimes not considered; similarly, one-time extraordinary costs and write-offs are sometimes ignored.

Usually a firm has to achieve some minimum level of earnings to have a payout; earnings above this level fund a bonus pool that is divided among the eligible employees. The payouts to employees may come in the form of a cash bonus, or they may be used to fund a retirement account. The amount individuals receive is usually based on a standard percentage of their salary—although an individual's payout may be modified based on his or her performance. This, of course, represents an effort to increase the line of sight for employees by adding an individual pay-for-performance component to the profit-sharing plan.

Profit-sharing plans have a number of significant strengths and weaknesses. Perhaps their greatest weakness involves their ability to motivate employees. In large and medium-size companies, it is extremely difficult to establish a line of sight between employee behavior and corporate profitability. As a result, profit-sharing plans typically do not have a significant impact on organizational performance.[6]

Simplifying and taking out uncontrollable factors when measuring earnings can help a little bit. However, in a company as large as Ford, or for that matter Hewlett-Packard, which for years had a profit-sharing plan, this is not likely to make a significant difference in employees' line of sight. In contrast, profit-sharing plans can be significant motivators in companies with fewer than five hundred employees, because they can establish a line of sight.

Profit sharing, like any other variable-pay plan, is not universally attractive to all employees. It does introduce risk in an individual's compensation package and therefore is unlikely to be attractive to someone who cannot tolerate risk or is suspicious of how business organizations deal with employees. That profit sharing is differentially attractive to individuals may not be a major problem for b2change organizations. Indeed, it may be an advantage because it can help attract the kind of employees they need.

The major reason why profit-sharing plans should be used by b2change organizations is their impact on the way people think about their firm. When a profit-sharing plan covers most members of an organization, it can stimulate interest in the company's financial results and create an identity that is focused on performance.

Although profit sharing may not be terribly motivating in the sense of driving people to work harder, it may motivate them to pay attention to financial results and to try to understand the business. This effect occurs because employees want to understand what their bonus is likely to be, where it comes from, and how it is computed. This in turn contributes to employees' having a better understanding of the organization's business model and to more knowledgeable and profit-focused decision-making behavior.

Companywide profit-sharing plans also can have the effect of integrating the members of a b2change organization. When people have a "common fate," they are much more likely to cooperate and support each other. When change clearly will benefit everyone through higher profits, people are less resistant to change—there may even be peer pressure to change.

Generally speaking, profit-sharing plans are not a must for a b2change organization, but they can be useful, particularly for smaller organizations, for organizations that want to use a bonus pool to reward teams and individuals, and for companies that for some reason cannot award stock to employees.

STOCK OWNERSHIP

Two basic methods of creating broad-based employee stock ownership can be used by b2change organizations. The first is for employees to own stock through a company-supported program, and the second is to award them stock options. B2change organizations can use either method, but because they deliver somewhat different results that in several ways complement each other, there is a strong argument for using both.

The Impact of Stock

The effect of stock plans on the motivation to perform is likely to be less than the effect of profit sharing because the line-of-sight problem is even more severe. Stock prices depend on more than just the somewhat controllable financial performance of the company. They depend on the economy and on how the stock market evaluates the corporation's earnings, intangibles, and future prospects. These factors are less subject to the company's control than the company's earnings are. Thus, even for senior executives, the line of sight in relation to the value of their company's stock may be weak.

Corporations differ dramatically in how much of their workforces they cover with stock ownership plans. One study found that over half of U.S. companies that had stock option plans covered only senior executives.[7] In the case of some of companies, the size of the stock option grants to senior executives is truly astounding. Millions of options are granted to senior executives, whereas none are given to most of the employees. This practice is not one that fits a b2change organization because it does not motivate individuals throughout an organization to perform at a high level and to support change.

The strength of stock as a motivator relates to the amount of reward that people can receive. Potential gains from stock programs as a result of improvement in an organization's stock price are virtually unlimited. The amount of money earned by a number of CEOs during the 1990s and early 2000s puts the payouts from the major U.S. lotteries to shame. Literally hundreds of millions of dollars have been made by some CEOs as a result of their stock options.

As we noted earlier, if extremely large rewards are available, even a weak line of sight can have a definite effect on motivation. Thus there is a real possibility that at the very senior levels of management, stock options are an effective motivator. The same is unlikely to be true for the rest of the employees because they often have significantly fewer shares of stock and a much weaker line of sight.

Although it is not a particularly good motivator, what broad-based employee stock ownership can do is create a culture of ownership and cause people to focus on the strategic, business, and financial objectives of the organization. As a result, it can be a powerful integrator of behavior. As is true of broad profit-sharing plans, it can create a "common fate" culture that supports performance and needed change.

Broad-based stock ownership may be a better motivator of change than profit sharing. The company's stock price often is a better indicator of future prospects than earnings. In fact, the stock price often goes down before earnings decrease. This in turn has the potential to stimulate change before performance actually declines.

Stock plans that offer employees the opportunity to profit substantially from stock ownership can be powerful retention devices for at least as long as employees are required to stay with the organization in order for them to exercise stock options or own stock. Once these dates are reached, the retention power of the stock plan disappears, often necessitating the creation of a new stock grant.

B2change organizations that have decided to retain and develop a core group of employees should be sure that these individuals get enough stock so that they have the incentive to remain with the company. One way to do this is to give them larger than typical grants of restricted stock.

The use of stock options and stock ownership is particularly interesting with respect to attraction. High-tech companies commonly offer stock options or restricted stock when trying to attract knowledge workers. In many ways this can create a win-win situation. When the company's stock is performing well, there is good reason to believe that employees will value stock options at a level that is greater than the options' actual value. Thus stock options are a cost-effective way to attract employees.

Now that companies in the United States are required to reduce their reported earnings when they make option grants, stock options are being used less frequently, but they still have some advantages, particularly for new organizations.

Support for Change

Broad-based stock ownership can be particularly useful in b2change organizations. When it comes to leading change, options give the leaders of a b2change organization a platform on which to stand and talk about the advantages employees will experience with a successful change effort. They can go beyond saying that change is good for the organization and say, "Change will be good for you because it will lead to improved organizational performance and an increase in your personal wealth." It also eliminates the possibility of employees' sitting back and saying, "Sure, it's all right for him to argue for change because he's a senior executive. He has an enormous amount of stock, but I don't, so why should I listen to his call for change when it really is only going to benefit him?"

Broad-based stock ownership can also be a real positive in encouraging people throughout the organization to take on leadership roles in support of change. Being an owner carries with it a certain role and image that can encourage individuals to demonstrate leadership behaviors that support organizational performance. It is only when members of the organization develop the attitude of shared fate and shared responsibility that a company can truly be said to have a culture of shared leadership.

Even though W.L. Gore is privately owned, it is a good example of an organization that uses stock as a major feature of its reward system. Everyone who has worked there for at least one year receives the equivalent of 15 percent of their salary in stock that they can cash out when they leave. Because the firm is private and there is no market price for its stock, independent consultants evaluate its "phantom" stock and determine its price. Gore uses the stock and its potential increase in value as a way to build a virtuous spiral and encourage individuals to continue to reinvent the business.

Overall, the impact of broad-based stock plans on organizational effectiveness and change can be an important positive.

Stock plans can encourage employees to learn more about the business and reinforce an identity of ownership.

PERSON-BASED PAY

The distribution of financial and status rewards in most organizations is primarily based on the jobs people do. Indeed, with the exception of bonuses and perhaps merit pay, the standard policy in most organizations is to assess the size of the job, not the size of person, and then set the reward level. Big jobs—that is, those with high levels of responsibility—get big paychecks; small jobs get small paychecks. This definitely is not the best system to use in a b2change organization. To begin with, b2change organizations don't have traditional jobs. Further, focusing on what a person does motivates individuals to develop their jobs rather than themselves and to resist change that threatens the worth of what they do.

A reward system that focuses on jobs does little to produce an understanding of the new skills and knowledge individuals need or, for that matter, an understanding of what new individuals the organization needs to develop new competencies and capabilities. It also typically offers little or no incentive to develop the new skills and knowledge that will help the organization change. As a result, when organizations with job-based systems need to change their capabilities and competencies, they usually end up either failing to change or having to replace most of their existing workforce.

When an organization is constantly changing, job-based pay systems are particularly likely to create problems. In the old steady-state organization, employees and management could come to a reasonable consensus as to what various jobs were worth. In the b2change organization, there are no traditional jobs, only clusters of tasks and activities, and these are always changing. As a result, it is hard to decide what is fair and to adjust pay accordingly. In addition, paying the job runs the risk of mispricing employees in the labor market, because the tasks they are doing at the moment may not represent their total capabilities and as a result may not reflect their market value or their value to their organization.

The solution requires a radical shift. Organizations need to pay individuals for their skills and knowledge, not for their jobs. In a work situation in which people have changing task assignments, paying the person is much more effective than paying the job. When all is said and done, it is people that have a market value, not jobs. People change companies for higher pay, not jobs.

A number of organizations, including PepsiCo and P&G, have adopted person-based pay. This system involves developing the type of person descriptions we discussed in Chapter Six and using them to determine pay. Person-based pay will not necessarily produce pay rates that are dramatically different from those produced in a job-based system. The skills people have usually do match reasonably well with the jobs they are doing. It will, however, result in some employees' being paid more or less than they would have been paid under a job-based system, depending on their skills.

Perhaps the most important changes that person-based pay can effect are to organizational identity and employee motivation. Instead of being rewarded for moving up the hierarchy, people are rewarded for increasing their skills and developing themselves. This can reinforce an identity in which personal development and a highly talented workforce are receptive to change. It can be especially helpful when an organization needs to improve its competencies and capabilities, because the company can use rewards to encourage individuals to develop the appropriate skills.

In one respect, paying employees for skills, knowledge, and competencies is not a new idea; organizations have done it for decades. For example, most technical ladders in organizations and most faculty pay structures in universities are based on this concept. What is new is the idea of paying individuals *throughout the organization*—not just a few technical experts—according to their skills and knowledge in order to create a b2change organization.

One way of looking at pay based on skills and knowledge is that it uses the same money that would otherwise have been spent to reward employees for promotions and greater seniority. Typically, these pay increases are automatic and do little to improve performance.

A focus on the skills of individuals is highly consistent with a b2change management approach and a strategic intent in which individuals are a key source of competitive advantage. When people are an organization's key resource, it is logical to focus on them and what they are worth. It also makes sense to focus on their growth and development so that they can add more value to the organization's products and services.

Egalitarian Perquisites

The absence of hierarchical perquisites makes b2change organizations easier to change. Perquisites, like pay programs that are tied to jobs and management levels, strongly reinforce a hierarchical orientation and a career mentality of upward mobility.

Hierarchical perquisites are symbols of power and as such often make it difficult to move decision making to the lower levels of an organization when they belong there.

Does being a b2change organization mean having no perquisites? Not necessarily. What it does mean is that perquisites must support performance. Clearly, some people need offices and others don't. Clearly, some people have greater needs to travel than others and face risks in travel that might warrant special accommodations.

Perquisites make sense when they support the work someone is doing and when the process for allocating them is transparent. When perquisites are allocated based simply on hierarchy and position in the organization, they are dysfunctional and have no place in a b2change organization.

REWARDS FOR RISK TAKING AND INNOVATION

Earlier we noted that most organizations have great difficulty creating new businesses and capitalizing on new technology when it comes from their internal R&D processes. One of the major causes of this problem is that organizations find it extremely difficult to reward risk taking.

We remember interviewing a senior manager at a company that was having trouble getting a new business model going. It involved combining several new products with a traditional product. In essence, it promised to revolutionize the company's stores and brand. When the manager was asked why he was having trouble getting the new concept in place, he said that most employees enjoyed long-term employment and steadily growing rewards. For them there was no reason to take a risk by championing a new strategy.

Rewarding risk taking and innovation requires companies to treat people who are taking risks very differently from other members of the organization, which in turn inevitably leads to issues of fairness. But that doesn't mean it can't be done. Senior leaders need to insist that risk taking and innovation be rewarded, and they must defend the practice as critical to the survival of a b2change organization.

In the post–Jack Welch years at GE, Jeff Immelt has had to work hard to introduce more risk taking to GE. Under Welch, GE developed capabilities focused on quality, costs, and deal making. Immelt wants to develop capabilities that lead to internal growth. To change the focus at GE, bonuses are now tied to coming up with new ideas that support growth and customers' needs.

Google is one company that acts on its belief in the importance of rewarding innovation and change. It gives out large amounts of stock to employees who complete innovative projects. The first two of these "Founders' Awards" consisted of giving out restricted stock that was worth $12 million in late 2004 when the awards were made. The stock went to two teams of a dozen or more employees each. Both of the teams had done an outstanding job of coming up with an innovative new product. The stock vests gradually over four years, thus acting not only as an incentive for innovation but also as a targeted retention device that rewards Google's most valuable employees for staying on board.

Sergey Brin, Google's cofounder, says that Google created the Founders' Award to motivate its employees to be innovative and to encourage people to join Google. Now that the dot-com era is over, it is hard for innovative individuals to come up with new business ideas that will be funded by venture capitalists and make them millionaires. Google sees this as an opportunity. It hopes that it will continue to be organization that attracts innovative, entrepreneurial individuals by offering the potential to become millionaires. It recognizes that individuals want to be rewarded for the success of their projects and that rewards can both attract the right people to work for Google and motivate their performance once they get there.

Google has always offered bonuses and options to employees, and indeed many have gotten quite rich as a result. But the Founders' Award raises the potential for wealth to a completely different level; employees can make the kind of money that is comparable to what might be gained from succeeding with a start-up. Clearly Google has recognized that the impact of a reward is partially a function of its size. The company can't be accused of putting very little on the line to encourage employees to innovate.

As we mentioned when we discussed new ventures in Chapter Four, they need special systems that tie large rewards to the success of the business. Often the right reward systems can be created only by having separate business units. In this way, organizations create units that are not handicapped by the obstacles that typically hold back the entrepreneurial spirit in the existing organization.

It is hard to overstate how difficult it is for many organizations to start entrepreneurial units that truly are given the freedom to reward individuals highly for developing new businesses. We worked with a new business unit created by a large paper company to commercialize a new technology that it had developed. The company gave the managers of the unit considerable flexibility when it came to work practices and a number of other issues. When it came to the reward system, however, the firm failed to create the kind of entrepreneurial reward system that compensates high risk with high reward.

Virtually all the employees were kept on the company payroll, and it was made clear to the individuals that if the new venture failed, they would be welcomed back to the existing organization. It is easy to understand why the organization made this decision, but it had a negative impact on the motivation of the individuals in the new unit. They did not develop the kind of fire and commitment to the unit's success they would have had if they were truly owners of the business and had their future tightly tied to its performance.

Dealing with Failure

A key reward issue in almost every major organizational change is the consequences of failure. All too often, organizations don't distinguish between good failures and bad failures. They treat all failures as though they were the same and learn few lessons. If an organization continues to experience failures that it does not treat as opportunities for learning, the company becomes increasingly unwilling to take "good" risks and does not operate as a b2change organization.

The solution is easy to state but often difficult to put in place: reward good failures and learn from all failures. Doing so usually takes strong leadership and reward systems that are designed to reward learning and change.

Earlier we made the point that organizations starting new businesses need to establish specific goals and tie bonuses to the achievements of those goals. It is often useful to add another dimension to the reward plans of b2change organizations: a separate reward that is contingent on sharing the learnings from every new business regardless of whether or not it is successful.

The negative consequences of failure are the major reason why individuals don't take good risks. If the punishment for failure is certain and fatal, it's unrealistic to expect individuals to share what they learned from the failure, much less to champion major change efforts.

There is no question that bad failures need to have appropriate consequences, but sometimes failure occurs simply because of an unpredictable change in the business environment or a strategic change in the organization's direction that could not have been anticipated. In these cases, b2change organizations need to reward the individuals who championed the change if they performed well in implementing it. This is particularly true, for example, when new products are introduced and for various reasons abandoned. A classic example of this is the pharmaceutical industry, in which many, many compounds are developed but only a few ultimately reach the market. In businesses like this, it is particularly important to reward individuals who do good research and develop knowledge even if the products ultimately never reach the market.

CONCLUSION

We began our discussion of rewards by pointing out that organizations get the behaviors they reward. We noted that traditional reward systems support stability and reinforce a traditional hierarchical organization structure. What traditional reward systems do *not* lead to is a b2change organization. The inescapable conclusion, therefore, is that organizations that wish to be high performance and b2change need to employ significantly different reward systems than the ones commonly used.

B2change organizations need reward systems that motivate performance, reward change, and encourage the development of individual and organizational capabilities and competencies. Paying the person instead of the job and using variable pay and stock are the most powerful changes an organization can make in moving its reward system toward one that supports performance and change. Decreasing the rewards for seniority and hierarchical position are important and desirable positives, but they are not likely to be as powerful as redesigning the system to reward individuals for their skills and their performance.

Of all the changes we have discussed, the most important is the shift away from the job and toward the individual as a basic building block of an organization's design. Getting rid of job descriptions, which we advocated earlier in the book, is one step toward reducing the importance of fixed jobs. However, when organizations make the leap to rewarding individuals for their skills and knowledge, they have done something even more significant. They have reinforced the b2change approach and focused organization development efforts on an organization's competencies and capabilities.

Chapter 11

Creating a
Built-to-Change
Organization

Built-to-Change Insight:
Making the Transition to a B2Change Organization
Is Harder Than Operating One

The need for a new way of competing and organizing is compelling. Who among us can support a way of thinking about organization design that argues, "The world is changing faster and faster every day—I think we should make a long-term commitment to doing one thing really well"? In an increasingly complex world, organizations built on traditional assumptions of stability, equilibrium, alignment, and predictability will, more and more, be out of touch and ineffective. Pursuing the latest management fad that is sold as a way to make organizations more efficient, more agile, more reengineered, or more whatever doesn't address the fundamental need for organizations to change more quickly and effectively. We can put lipstick on the pig, but it's still a pig.

The heady objective of this book is to define a new way of thinking about organizations, one that assumes change is normal and that leverages our understanding of individuals and organizational effectiveness. We have outlined the key processes and components of the b2change approach. They include ways of looking at strategic intent, adding value, and organizing that build firms that are constantly changing, but still productive and effective.

Each of the processes in the B2Change Model—Strategizing, Creating Value, and Designing—is more changeable and flexible than the prior one. For example, as part of the strategizing process, the company recognizes its identity—the most stable aspect of a b2change organization—and within a set of potential environmental scenarios, crafts a robust strategic intent that describes how the company expects to achieve its business objectives.

Identity and intent work together to bring an organization into proximity with an unfolding set of environmental demands. Proximity is an important concept for us. It sums up in one word that effectiveness is primarily a function of how "close" an organization's products and services are to what is demanded by the environment. Because the environment is always changing, firms always need to change to stay in close proximity to it.

Strategizing, in turn, must be orchestrated with the creating value and designing processes. The creating value process determines what an organization can do and is a function of the competencies and capabilities of the firm. Competencies and capabilities must evolve and change in response to new strategies and as a result of organization learning.

The designing process—the way structures, information and decision-making systems, talent management, shared leadership, and rewards are created, configured, and changed—is the most changeable part of a b2change organization. As environmental demands change and new strategic intents emerge, the design of the organization needs to change.

The designing process is the key to developing the competencies and capabilities that are needed to implement a strategic intent. The relationships among strategizing, creating value, and designing over time must remain in a dynamic alignment. Sustained effectiveness in the b2change approach results in a virtuous spiral in which higher and higher levels of performance occur because an organization is better and better able to match the demands of the environment.

In Chapters Four through Ten, we identified the design principles and practices b2change organizations need to adopt. The ultimate question, of course, is "How do you create a b2change organization?" Or, for most executives, "How can you change a traditional organization into a b2change organization?"

The answer is complex, but there is one! Before we provide the answer, we need to establish that not all organizations can or should become b2change organizations. Some may not need to because the rate of change they are likely to experience is not sufficient to warrant investing heavily in a change capability. For example, an energy company or a public utility might want to think carefully about adopting too many b2change principles; the assets in these businesses are long lived and require a long-term commitment to their efficient utilization. Even so, there is a good chance that they can benefit from using some b2change principles. Royal Dutch Shell, for example, successfully employs a world-class scenario planning process—but it may not need to commit to being a b2change organization.

We are realistic about the necessity and ability of many organizations to adopt all of the principles of the b2change approach. Even though they *need* to adapt to survive, the reality is that many traditional organizations (for example, General Motors, ExxonMobil, and Kroger), simply are not going to become b2change organizations. Their identities are too entrenched. For them, the best alternative is to identify some b2change principles they can use, implement them slowly, and over time hope they become somewhat more flexible. For many other organizations, the b2change approach is exactly what they need, and they can implement it.

In this chapter, we address the most important issues in managing the transition to a b2change organization. Our objective is to describe how to replace traditional assumptions and practices with new beliefs about change and new practices that support change. We recommend a sequence of initiatives that will accomplish two important objectives. First, they will cause an organization to be more focused on achieving critical configurations, proximity, and dynamic alignment. Second, they will set the stage for moving fully to a b2change approach.

THE TRANSITION PROCESS

Managing the transition to a b2change organization is more like a traditional change management process than engaging in the dynamic processes that characterize change in a fully developed b2change organization.[1] And if you think about it, this makes sense. If an organization is built for stability, it is important to challenge that stability, address resistance, make a business case, and develop action plans to transform it into a b2change organization.

In the transition to a b2change organization there is no "end state" in the traditional sense of the term. Change management models and prescriptions that recommend the creation of a vision or end state reinforce the belief that change is an infrequent and unusual event. We offer no change management gimmicks; we are not encouraging an organization to set "big, hairy, audacious goals" or outrageous stretch targets for achievement as if an optimal organization design could be obtained.

The only end state in a b2change transformation is an organization that is ready to make strategic adjustments—in other words, one that is easier to change. To get there, traditional organizations must engage in a transformation, the riskiest type of change. Becoming a b2change company requires an organization to shift its identity, reconfigure its intent, acquire and develop new capabilities, and redesign itself.

An organization needs to coordinate five key initiatives on the road to becoming built to change. We will discuss them in the order we think they need to be implemented:

1. Create a change-friendly identity.
2. Pursue proximity.
3. Build an orchestration capability.
4. Establish strategic adjustment as a normal condition.
5. Create a virtuous spiral.

Pursuing these initiatives is a little like embracing the Dark Side of the Force in *Star Wars*—forever will it guide your destiny. These are real commitments to very different ways of doing things and (unlike the Dark Side) are aimed at achieving and maintaining a virtuous spiral.

CREATE A CHANGE-FRIENDLY IDENTITY

Identity occupies a unique place in the b2change approach. It is the most stable part of a company and can be the number one enemy in making the transition to a b2change organization. Companies that have grown up with traditional organization design and management assumptions usually have an identity that resonates with the concepts of alignment, congruence, stability, and predictability. They are built on the notion that organizations need to be controlled by a hierarchical structure, led by omniscient senior managers, and managed according to some strategic "plan" in which growth is the only acceptable goal. Their identity is an important driver and maintainer of the status quo; recommendations for change that don't fall within a fairly narrow "zone of acceptance" are rejected.

The same characteristics that make identity the biggest barrier to change can make it an organization's number one asset—if that identity is change friendly. Although it seems paradoxical, identity's stability makes it a potential enabler of change. Knowing that the firm's culture and ideology support growth, development, and change enable members of the organization to craft robust strategic intents, develop new capabilities and competencies, and continually redesign the firm. If an organization can develop a change-friendly identity, it sends continuous signals to organization members that they can count on support for their change efforts, and members know how they will be treated when change occurs.

An obvious prerequisite to having a change-friendly identity is knowing the current identity. In some organizations, identity is clear and well known—for example, as we mentioned earlier, Southwest Airlines (freedom), Microsoft (persistence), 3M (innovation), and Wal-Mart (low costs) all have well-established identities. But many organizations do not understand their identity and how it constrains change. These organizations must go through the difficult process of understanding their identity.

Espoused values and beliefs often have little to do with the ones the organization really holds and follows. Often people are reluctant to admit this. For example, we worked with an Internet company that said it valued teamwork, but in fact rewarded only individual effort. This same organization said that it valued innovation, but punished failure.

Somehow an organization must discover the real values and images of its identity. Because they generally are taken for granted, these values and images may be difficult to articulate and can be threatening. For example, it's often difficult for an organization to admit that its real identity is about "getting work done no matter what" or "shipping it on time and worrying about quality later."

As we discussed in Chapter Three, one way to understand an organization's identity is to debate questions about the driving force in the organization. Another excellent, if not profound, way to get at identity is to uncover the basic assumptions underlying the company's culture. This can be done by gathering diverse groups of organization members—executives, staff, supervisors, and hourly workers; newcomers and long-tenured employees; and representatives from different functions or businesses—to discuss the culture. Adding customers, regulators, suppliers, analysts, and other external stakeholders to this process can enrich it.[2]

The groups first brainstorm a large number of artifacts, such as behaviors, symbols, language, physical space arrangements, logos, and advertising messages. Participants then use this list to deduce the values and norms that produced the artifacts. For example, many companies have rituals around retirement or stories of how people gave great customer service. These artifacts can be explained by an inferred value of recognizing loyalty and individual achievement.

The groups can also create a list of the values espoused in mission or vision statements, credos, or other formal planning documents. For example, many organizations espouse values of teamwork, collaboration, integrity, customer focus, and corporate responsibility.

In the final step, the groups attempt to identify and explain any contradictions between espoused and inferred values. This is a difficult conversation, and a great deal of facilitation skill may be required to help organization members see the contradictions. The discovery process should be repeated several times with different groups until a pattern of identity emerges. The output of this process is a statement, metaphor, or short list of core values that define the organization's identity.

The central issue in becoming a b2change firm is whether the identity is change friendly. When an identity is based on stability, it needs to be "reframed" to include at least one of two features: (1) a focus on the environment and (2) the view that change is natural and necessary.

Before and during the deregulation of the U.S. telephone industry, AT&T and GTE could be characterized by an identity of "We need to meet the numbers our regulators look at." The regulatory agencies, not the consumer, had become the customer. Years of monopoly regulation had produced a culture in which service excellence was defined by "We'll be there for a service call sometime between 1:00 and 5:00 P.M." With deregulation, the identity of AT&T and GTE needed to be reframed to focus on the competitive environment and the changing needs of the consumer.

The best place to start the reframing process is by noting the reasons for the existing perspective. In the case of AT&T and GTE, these cultures existed because regulation protected the business from competition and also because the technology was relatively stable and well understood. When a customer picked up the phone, more than 99 percent of the time there was a dial tone, and a correctly entered number resulted in a placed call. Because the regulators were not concerned about introducing new technology, companies could delay technology changes until they were ready to implement them.

By recognizing the sources of identity, in a sense honoring the past, it is often possible to reframe the existing identity to be one that is accepted by organization members and not seen as marketing jargon or "spin." The best way to do this is to tie the reframed identity to important changes in the external environment and to how these changes influence the organization's effectiveness.

An important adjunct to affirming that an organization's identity is focused on the external environment is ensuring that the organization's design reinforces an external focus. Each of the chapters on designing mention a number of practices that can help focus the organization on the external environment. Installing some of them is a significant way to establish that the organization's identity includes a strong external focus.

The following are key elements that support an organization's focus on the external environment:

- Information systems that feature the organization's performance relative to that of its competitors
- Information about customer satisfaction and performance levels
- Information about economic and business changes in the external environment
- Organization structures that give a large number of employees direct contact with the external environment
- Reward systems that focus on the performance of the organization (for example, profit sharing or stock ownership)

The second characteristic of a change-friendly identity is that employees perceive change to be a natural and ongoing process in the organization. Again, it is one thing to give this idea lip service; it is entirely another to do what it takes to make the idea a reality. An organization that wants to be change friendly must have in place practices and designs that reinforce its identity as a company committed to change. Adopting the following elements will ensure that individuals see change as a natural process in the organization:

- Organization designs that do not include jobs but that instead focus on tasks being assigned to individuals or teams on a changing basis

- An employer brand and image stressing that continued employment depends on the need for an individual's skills

- Pay systems that reward individuals for the development of new skills, performance, and an understanding of the business

- Talent management systems that emphasize the opportunities individuals have to apply for new jobs and to learn new skills

Creating a change-friendly identity is a fundamental step in becoming a b2change organization. When the organization sees itself as rooted in changeability and there is an understanding of change as a normal state, organization members are free to pursue changes in strategic intent, capabilities, and design.

Pursue Proximity

Because the performance of an organization depends on how effectively its strategic intent addresses current and future environmental demands, it must have the ability to identify likely future demands. It must also be able to develop an appropriate strategic intent in light of those environmental demands. Without a scenario-planning capability that links strategic intent to environmental change, no organization can respond effectively to a rapidly changing environment.

Despite the practical tools available to help them, most organizations do not utilize scenario planning. We think this is a curious and unfortunate situation. Nobody we know of is publishing books or articles concluding that the business environment will remain stable and increase in predictability. In fact, every statement filed with the financial markets routinely disavows their accuracy.

Every "forward-looking statement" essentially says, "We really don't know what's going to happen." With that kind of uncertainty, it makes all the sense in the world for an organization to immerse itself in the world of scenario planning. Organizations that want to improve their ability to pursue proximity must commit to spending time thinking about the future. Doing so needs to be a major focus of the senior management team, especially the CEO.

When it comes to focusing on the future, we think Bill Gates is a good role model for executives. Several times a year for the last ten years, Gates has gone off, usually alone, to read about trends in the industry and think about the future of technology. He reads industry reports, "white papers" prepared by Microsoft employees, and articles related to Microsoft's business. (After getting snubbed by the Chinese government over the way an early version of Windows was localized, he spent a week reading up on Chinese history, culture, and government.) Out of these retreats come notes, comments, and meetings that shape future products and services; more important, Gates's obvious focus on change, the future, and proximity reinforces Microsoft's identity as a b2change organization.

CEO Jeff Immelt is another good role model. He has split GE's strategizing process into two components. The first half consists entirely of conversations among senior executives about future trends that could affect specific businesses. These future-oriented conversations are driven by data about trends in technology, globalization, and competition as well as their interaction. For example, how will trends in oil prices interact with terrorism, global warming, emerging market growth rates, and competitor strategies? GE business unit managers read about regulatory, technical, and other issues, make comments on their readings, develop their own thoughts and perspectives, and put all this information on an intranet portal that is available to the top executives of the company.

After reviewing the material, the management team meets for several days to discuss the information, hear from outsiders about their views of the future, and debate the likely paths their markets and industries might follow. Only then do they proceed to the second component of the process, which focuses on formulating business strategies for each of GE's businesses.

In b2change organizations, structured conversations like those at GE and Microsoft are major contributors to thinking about the future. But they are not enough. B2change organizations also need to find time to "play" with the future. Unfortunately, most organizations are too focused on current performance to think about doing this. Wall Street, shareholders, customers, and activists conspire to force them into short-term behaviors and thinking. It is hard to break out of the short-term mold, but it must be done even if only incrementally at first. There is no question who has to lead this break-out: it is senior management.

Futurists unanimously recommend against predicting the future; they instead suggest picturing and creating a wide range of possible environmental success paths. These activities should be informed by the use of seemingly unrelated inputs. This process of purposeful playfulness is a source of innovation and new ideas.[3] Applied to scenario planning, it involves expanding conversations about the organization's possible futures by incorporating information that at first glance is unrelated. It's a little bit like going onto the Internet to find out about European vacation spots and getting totally sidetracked by a pop-up ad that leads to a call to your stockbroker because of a "hot" product you discover.

A software development company, for example, might ask, "What would be the likely impact on our business if the price of oil went to $100 per barrel?" A playful conversation could yield the suggestion that if oil were at $100 per barrel, more people would be encouraged to work at home. As a result, there would be an increased demand for software that monitors at-home workers, allows at-home workers to safely access corporate databases, or allows at-home workers to contact customers. Conversations like this, combined with others, create a variety of alternative, but possible, future scenarios. Some possible futures will be preferred over others because of the firm's resources and capabilities. An important role of strategic intent is to envision actions for today that will increase the probability that markets and other environmental elements move in the desired directions.

Our belief is that a b2change organization needs to commit to *a set of preferred* futures, not to *the* future. When an organization doesn't play with the future, it can get locked into trying to predict what will happen or attempting to create the one vision of its future that seems most desirable. Too often, it will then construct strategic intents that are narrow and short-sighted, addressing current but fleeting pressures from global financial markets, regulatory threats, or consumer groups. These pressures are real, but they should be addressed tactically, not strategically.

A b2change strategic intent needs to be concerned with identifying the core competencies and capabilities that are likely to lead to success in the future. Playing with and picturing alternative futures is a most practical way to enhance the probability of doing this well, and robust strategic intents are the vehicle. By considering a range of potential futures, an organization can develop strategic intents that will succeed in a number of environments.

Several years ago, the Steinway piano company faced an increasingly competitive international market. Foreign piano manufacturers used production technologies and definitions of quality that were different from Steinway. By considering various levels of domination by foreign manufacturers, various levels of market and customer sophistication, and multiple segments demanding grand or upright pianos, Steinway formulated a variety of possible scenarios.

The company had to decide how broad a product line to offer (grand pianos only or some combination of grand and upright pianos), what price points to adopt, and what manufacturing processes to use. In the end, Steinway concluded that maintaining its focus on the top end of the market with its unique, handcrafted grand pianos was the most robust choice. If the market for concert grand pianos and other high-end instruments grew, Steinway would obviously be well positioned to maintain its dominance. If the high-end market contracted, the company would be well positioned to move into the higher volume, lower-quality market segments using its brand as an important differentiator.

Attacking the foreign players in the middle markets would have committed Steinway to "the" future of a broad range of offerings. It would have to compete on the basis of productivity (something the company did not have the capability to do) or by defending its share of the upright (middle) market. By maintaining its existing strategic intent and staying true to its identity, Steinway has successfully weathered the industry's consolidation and maintained its preeminence as the world's leading manufacturer of concert grand pianos.

BUILD AN ORCHESTRATION CAPABILITY

Compared to developing a b2change identity and pursuing proximity, the third initiative, building an orchestration capability, is a more complex operational challenge. It requires both financial and psychological investments, and it must be conducted according to the beliefs inherent in a b2change approach. Executives must commit to the belief—and it is a radical one—that the ability to change is the key to competitive advantage. There is little sense in investing in an orchestration capability if senior management believes that pursuing stability and execution is the path to success.

Orchestration is both an element of strategic intent and a capability. Its role in strategic intent is to develop and specify the sequence of events and decisions necessary to implement a particular strategy. This can involve specifying such actions as launching a new product, developing a new performance management system, restructuring the organization, or making an acquisition. The orchestration process may also specify how new capabilities and core competencies will be developed. Because organizations and environments can change at different rates and in different directions, orchestration represents a plan for maintaining proximity.

Orchestration is also a capability. Dynamic capabilities have received a great deal of press and researcher attention recently—and deservedly so.[4] Such capabilities as new product development and service processes that consistently exceed customer expectations are important. But the one dynamic capability a b2change organization must have is the ability to execute planned organizational changes.

Orchestration is not only about the plan; it is about the ability to carry out the plan. I may have detailed directions on how to get from one place to another, but I still have to actually get in the car and navigate traffic, look out for pedestrians, and make the correct turns. Similarly, it is not enough that an organization can identify what has to change and how it can be changed; it must also have the capability to execute those changes.

Forward-looking organizations, such as PepsiCo, Intel, GE, and Microsoft, have built their capability to manage change. In light of the environmental signals that having a change capability will be even more important in the future, this is a wise investment.

Building an orchestration capability is not easy. For organizations who want to invest in an orchestration capability, we have a short "must do" list of three items:

1. Develop change management skills.
2. Create an organization effectiveness function.
3. Engage in and learn from change.

Develop Change Management Skills

Any capability requires resources. To build a strong orchestration capability, an organization must develop the change management skills of its people. Today a typical organization's intellectual capital is mostly made up of skills and knowledge in technical, financial, logistical, and other operational competencies. Knowledge and skills related to change management account for only a small proportion of its intellectual capital.

A workforce that can continually renew itself and deftly orchestrate organizational changes is rare, valuable, and difficult to imitate. As a result, a strong human capital base with change-related knowledge and skills is a major source of competitive advantage.

Hiring professionals with skills in change management and organization development is the most direct way of developing change skills, and doing so sends a clear signal to the organization of the importance of this effort. The second most direct way is to train and develop existing managers and employees. Training courses, like those developed at GE, BP, and Capital One, should focus on diagnostic models and processes, internal consulting skills, intervention design, visioning and consensus-building processes, project management, action planning, conflict management, and organizational effectiveness.

Create an Organization Effectiveness Function

The second step in creating an orchestration capability is to create a center of excellence in organization effectiveness. Traditionally, competencies in change management and organization design have been located in the HR, training, or organization development functions. Strategic management competencies have been located in the planning function.

When change is a rare event and strategizing an annual process, differentiating change and strategy development may make sense. But when strategizing and designing are ongoing routine activities, it is best to have the skills and knowledge associated with orchestration in a single integrated center of excellence.

A fully developed orchestration capability requires merging the strategic planning and HR functions into an organization effectiveness function. In some organizations, this label has been used to identify a group of internal change agents or organization development professionals. But we are proposing a much broader mandate for organization effectiveness than this.

The organization effectiveness function should provide expert advice and execution help in the areas of HR management, change management, organization design, and organization development. All too often, expert advice in these areas is missing from the strategic management process. For historical and now obsolete reasons, most organizations have viewed strategic planning as the "hard" side of business, where financial analysis, quantification, and operations thinking should dominate. We believe, however, that it is time for that to change.

Organization development, change management, and organizational capabilities not only need to be at the strategic planning table; they need to "set" the table. The first order of business is to reorient and focus change competencies into a new function. Simply restructuring the resources, however, will not be sufficient to drive the strategizing and designing processes in the right direction. In addition, executives in this new function need to lobby for the importance of these processes and for making the function a high-visibility C-level activity.

The new organizational effectiveness function does not own the organization's strategy and design. Executives and line managers must be held accountable and responsible for the development and execution of their strategic intents. What the new function *should* own are the processes for developing future scenarios, helping line managers and executives conduct strategic reviews, facilitating decisions about strategic change (reorientation or transformation), crafting and clarifying strategic intents, structuring the organization, managing talent, and designing reward systems—in short, orchestrating the firm's moves.

The second order of business for the organization effectiveness function is to adapt existing change management and planning systems or set up entirely new ones. Some existing processes, such as capital and operational expense budgeting, may suffice as they are. In general, however, the organization effectiveness function needs to develop and refine the strategizing and designing processes so that they support the b2change approach.

The new function needs to train its members in strategy, business analysis, organization design, and change management. It also needs to develop the tools to be used during the processes of change and negotiate its relationship to other organizational units, the budgeting process, and other key processes.

If an organization truly believes that the ability to change is the key to high performance now and in the future, then the competencies associated with that capability cannot be buried in the organization. Building an orchestration competence requires giving power and resources to people who understand and can help the organization manage change.

Engage In and Learn from Change

Capabilities and their development are partly a function of experience. An operations capability must have equipment, materials, and people, but having them is not enough. When those elements actually work together to produce something for the first time, the productivity is awful. Only through experience and learning does the capability become effective and valuable. By the same token, there cannot be an effective orchestration capability without change experience.

To build a change capability, an organization must embrace change and then reflect on its experience. Organizations that seek stability cannot learn to orchestrate change. Similarly, organizations that do not reflect on the change experience will not learn as much as they should. Thus, the organization effectiveness function must be involved in as many change efforts as practical. We are not talking about implementing change just for the sake of gaining practice. We are advocating frequent, planned strategizing and designing activities that involve the organization effectiveness function.

An orchestration capability is the *sine qua non* of a b2change organization. It allows organizations to reap the advantages of change as a competitive advantage. To purposely pursue change in order to learn from it and build the capability to change *is* a radical idea. It is to invite chaos, inefficiency, and ineffectiveness in the short run, but it can lead to adaptability, agility, and virtuous spirals in the long run; thus to pursue change is an investment well worth making.

Adopt Strategic Adjustment as a Normal Condition

If we randomly chose a time to observe an effective b2change organization, what would we see? The answer is clear and simple to state: we would see a firm engaged in strategic adjustment. The orchestration process would be working to create dynamic alignment—laying out the proper sequence of activities to bring strategy to fruition, developing existing capabilities or adding new ones to support the strategy, and mixing and remixing organization design elements in response to current and emerging environmental demands.

To become a b2change organization, a firm must shift its members' perceptions about the importance, frequency, ease, and desirability of change. Further, it must implement changeable forms of each organizational design feature. The key to making change a normal condition in an organization is to create structures, talent systems, and rewards that can be reconfigured to support new strategic intents and new opportunities.

A b2change organization knows that its ability to proactively change is the source of its effectiveness and an important competitive advantage. Therefore it is anxious about being caught unaware. It wants everyone, not just marketing and senior management, to be close to customers, regulators, technology providers, suppliers, financial analysts, and other stakeholders. Putting as many people as possible into contact with the external environment increases the amount of business intelligence available to the organization, giving it the potential to be more flexible and responsive.

Structures with maximum surface area not only put more people in touch with the environment but also encourage people to focus on what the organization can do (capability) and should do (intent). Small business units are good examples of such structures. They allow people to see more of a whole business; employees are not physically or psychologically "far away" from the organization's capabilities or its work. The result is that there is much more focus on getting work done.

Small business units with maximum surface area also support the "no job descriptions" principle. At a gut level, b2change organizations don't believe in jobs. Jobs and job descriptions imply predictability and assume stability; b2change organizations believe in teams and individuals taking on changing bundles of accountabilities and activities. There is a sense that people need to, and will, take on the collection of tasks that need to be done, that this collection changes all the time, and that when it does change it isn't a big deal.

Anyone familiar with the TV series *The West Wing* will have a sense of how a jobless structure can work. Each hourly episode depicts how the White House deals with a variety of planned and unplanned events while trying to move the country forward according to the president's agenda. Although people have titles and specialties, everyone is focused on getting work done. Task assignments vary, and anyone can bring an issue up for action.

Every week on the show, whenever a terrorist attack, new piece of legislation, visible case of domestic violence, or upcoming election emerges as the issue du jour, there's an immediate vetting of the event by an appropriate mix of people. What does it mean? Who will be, or needs to be, involved? Who will be affected? How does it fit with our agenda? Does it challenge our administration's goals or who we are as a country? At what level should this issue be addressed—should the president be involved, can it be handled by senior staff or delegated to interns? Where does it sit in the priority queue? What tactics should we employ? How should we bring about success?

From time to time, unplanned and highly visible events seem to push the White House staff off of their shared agenda. They find themselves reacting to events or issues instead of carrying their message to the Congress or the American people. At times like these, the White House staff finds a way, with the president but also often without him, to stop action and say, "Look, we aren't doing 'our' thing, we're doing somebody else's thing. Let's stop that and get our agenda moving forward again. Let's be the initiators of change." In other words, let's allow identity and intent to drive action.

Having structures with maximum surface area and work assignments based on activities that need to get done is not enough to create dynamic alignment. If organization members don't have access to information and can't perform the tasks that need accomplishing, the possibility for chaos exists. Dynamic alignment requires that all of the elements in the designing process be coordinated. In addition to the right structures, an organization must be populated with the right people and systems.

In the 1980s and 1990s, efforts to increase employee involvement and empowerment successfully tapped into a long-held value about the importance of people and an emerging belief that people are more adaptable than most organization designs.[5] It is time for organizations to leverage and apply the lessons from these efforts. To do so requires organizations to push down decision-making responsibility, look for leadership at all levels, share relevant information widely, give people the right skills and knowledge, and reward the right things. Throughout an organization, individuals must possess the willingness and ability to initiate strategic reviews, suggest new product ideas and ways to increase operational efficiency, and figure out what work needs to be done. They must have business information, and they need to feel recognized and rewarded for their initiative.

Nordstrom provides a provocative example of empowerment; it is not the easiest place in the world to work. The organization, formally and informally, differentiates between its best and worst performers. The people who succeed work extraordinary hours, seek out loyal customers, send thank-you notes, provide superior customer service, get large commission checks, and learn to influence and persuade colleagues, managers, and customers. People who can't live under the system don't last long.

Nordstrom consistently operates at high levels of effectiveness because many if not most of the individuals who work there have the necessary information, the knowledge and skills to process the information, the incentives to make things happen, and the power to make decisions. Information coming into the system in the form of customer requests and new fashion trends is processed by employees who understand the organization's identity and strategic intent. The information is acted on without an extensive senior management approval process. The "employee manual" consists of a single phrase: do what's right for the customer. Individual decisions—perhaps even more than management's strategic decisions—greatly influence and determine Nordstrom's performance.

The Nordstrom system is not without its detractors and provides ample evidence of the difficulty of operating a b2change organization. It puts enormous pressure on the clarity of the organization's purpose; the design of its structures and systems; the way people are hired, developed, and retained; and perhaps most important, the faith of management in the people of the organization. But it is also a powerful example of leveraging an involved workforce. Nordstrom pays for people and performance, not jobs. It puts many people in touch with the environment, gives them lots of relevant information, and gives them with authority to make decisions.

SEEK VIRTUOUS SPIRALS

The final initiative in becoming a b2change organization is to bring all of the prior processes together into a virtuous spiral. Virtuous spirals—periods in the life of an organization—are characterized by critical configuration, proximity, and dynamic alignment. They are built and sustained by a series of temporary competitive advantages. B2change organizations compete over time; they consciously balance the short and long runs.

To translate the b2change approach into performance, the economic logic of strategic intent must support the belief that change will yield a higher level of effectiveness over time than a single advantage. Pursuing virtuous spirals challenges the traditional economic logic of commitment and efficiency as sources of sustainable competitive advantage. Looking at that logic helps in understanding why and how a b2change organization will outperform one that focuses on stability and efficiency.

The logic of commitment and efficiency encourages the belief that slack is bad. For example, when traditional organizations consider investing in an orchestration capability, they run into a "logic trap" of important questions about efficiency and long-term effectiveness: How can we justify an investment in a capability that is not directly adding value? Aren't we committing to an investment in (not a reduction of) slack resources? These are good questions that cannot be satisfactorily answered using traditional business logic.

B2change organizations pursue a logic that calls for spending money on learning how to change. Although change is often neither efficient nor pretty, b2change organizations believe that the ability to change is more valuable than efficiency, or at least that effective change is much more valuable than the alternative. Every organization is going to spend money on change; the only questions are when, how much, and will there be anything to show for it.

B2change organizations employ a logic of entry and exit, or "hit and run." They expect that success will result from identifying future opportunities, organizing to gain the most revenue from them, and then changing to take advantage of the next opportunity.

In HP's early days, when it was in the "small instruments" business, there was a clear entry and exit logic that propelled the organization. Through their "bootstrapping" innovation process and the HP Way culture, they created products to meet important needs, manufactured and marketed those products at high prices to early adopters, and, when the market was recognized by others, reduced their participation as price competition emerged. Remember HP calculators?

Because b2change firms look for a series of temporary advantages, their paths can change frequently as they seek to maintain proximity with an unfolding environment. Organizations that obsessively pursue the logic of commitment and efficiency are likely to overinvest in a single advantage, leaving them vulnerable to obsolescence and the inability to change quickly. The research results on downsizing, reengineering, mergers and acquisitions, and other corporate restructuring is clear: the relentless pursuit of cost reduction, efficiency, and fewer slack resources frequently does not result in a virtuous spiral.[6]

CONCLUSION

Stringing together a series of temporary competitive advantages clearly distinguishes the b2change organization from the traditional firm. In combination with the other distinctive features of b2change organizations, virtuous spirals, critical configurations, and dynamic alignments support both short-term performance and long-term adaptability. Creating long-term virtuous spirals is supported by the following features:

- A clear and change-friendly identity that gives the organization a reason to learn and develop
- A sophisticated strategizing process that includes a strong focus on the external environment and the creation of alternative future scenarios
- The ability to craft robust strategic intents
- A strong orchestration capability that promotes a clear understanding of the strategy; provides information about relevant aspects of the environment and the organization; and develops the processes for keeping strategy, capabilities, and organization design elements in dynamic alignment
- A creating-value process that develops the core competencies and organizational capabilities that enable strategy implementation

- An organization design that maximizes the number of people who interact with the external environment and are held accountable for business results

- Information and decision-making processes that move decision making to the place in the organization where action can be taken and information is available

- A system of talent management that hires, develops, and retains people who thrive on change and seek out work assignments based on their understanding of strategy

- Reward systems that focus on skills rather than on positions

- Rewards tied to the right combination of individual, team, and business performance

- Constant strategizing and a simultaneous focus on short- and long-term performance

Taken together, these features form an approach to organizational effectiveness that establishes the ability to change as the foundation on which organizations can build a virtuous spiral. This b2change approach is a new way of competing that responds to the realities of today's rapidly changing world. While it is easy to say that demographic changes and global political trends will affect organizations in the future, it is hard to know *how* they will affect them. What is next is anybody's guess. What we do know is that the best way for an organization to prepare for whatever is next is to confront and abandon the assumption of stability and to embrace the principles that create b2change organizations.

Notes

CHAPTER ONE

1. Lawler, E. E., III, Mohrman, S. A., and Benson, G. S. *Organizing for High Performance: Employee Involvement, TQM, Reengineering, and Knowledge Management in Fortune 1000 Companies.* San Francisco: Jossey-Bass, 2001.

2. Becker, B., and Huselid, M. "High Performance Work Systems and Firm Performance: A Synthesis of Research and Managerial Implications." In G. Ferris (ed.), *Research in Personnel and Human Resources Management* (Vol. 16). Greenwich, Conn.: JAI Press, 1998. See also Huselid, M. A. "The Impact of Human Resource Management Practices on Turnover, Productivity, and Corporate Financial Performance." *Academy of Management Journal*, 1995, *38*(3), 635–672.

3. Lev, B. *Intangibles.* Washington, D.C.: Brookings Institution, 2001.

4. Christensen, C. *The Innovator's Dilemma: When New Technologies Cause Great Firms to Fail.* Boston: Harvard Business School Press, 1997.

5. Lewin, K. *Resolving Social Conflicts.* Washington, D.C.: American Psychological Association, 1997.

6. Foster, R., and Kaplan, S. *Creative Destruction: Why Companies That Are Built to Last Underperform the Market—and How to Successfully Transform Them.* New York: Currency/Doubleday, 2001.

7. Kotter, J. P. *Leading Change.* Boston: Harvard Business School Press, 1997.
   Tichy, N. M. *The Leadership Engine.* New York: HarperBusiness, 1997.

8. Greiner, L., Cummings, T., and Bhambri, A. "When New CEOs Succeed and Fail: 4-D Theory of Strategic Transformation." *Organizational Dynamics*, 2002, *32*(3), 1–17.

313

Khurana, R. *Searching for a Corporate Savior: The Irrational Quest for Charismatic CEOs*. Princeton, N.J.: Princeton University Press, 2002.

Zhang, Y., and Rajagopalan, N. "When the Known Devil Is Better Than an Unknown God: An Empirical Study of the Antecedents and Consequences of Relay CEO Succession." *Academy of Management Journal*, 2004, *47*(4), 483–500.

CHAPTER TWO

1. Porter, M. *Competitive Strategy*. New York: Free Press, 1980.
   Kay, J. *Foundations of Corporate Success: How Business Strategies Add Value*. Oxford: Oxford University Press, 1993.
   Ghemawat, P. *Commitment*. New York: Free Press, 1991.

2. Prahalad, C. K., and Hamel, G. "The Core Competence of the Corporation." *Harvard Business Review*, 1990, *68*(3), 79–91.

3. Ulrich, D., and Lake, D. *Organizational Capabilities*. New York: Wiley, 1990.

4. Lawler, E. E., III. *Treat People Right! How Organizations and Individuals Can Propel Each Other into a Virtuous Spiral of Success*. San Francisco: Jossey-Bass, 2003.

CHAPTER THREE

1. Hatch, M. J., and Schultz, M. "The Dynamics of Organizational Identity," *Human Relations*, 2002, *55*(8), 989–1018.

2. This process was first described by Michael Robert. Robert, M. *Strategy: Pure and Simple*. New York: McGraw-Hill, 1993.

3. Our model represents an integration of views from two primary sources: Carroll, G., and Hannan, M. *Organizations in Industry: Strategy, Structure and Selection*. New York: Oxford University Press, 1995; and Hambrick, D., and Fredrickson, J. "Are You Sure You Have a Strategy?" *Academy of Management Executive*, 2001, *15*(4), 48–59.

4. Gladwell, M. *The Tipping Point*. New York: Little, Brown, 2000.

CHAPTER FOUR

1. Galbraith, J. *The Customer-Centric Organization*. San Francisco: Jossey-Bass, 2005.

2. Hackman, J. R., and Oldham, G. *Work Redesign*. Reading, Mass.: Addison-Wesley, 1980.
   Hackman, J. R., and Lawler, E. E., III. "Employee Reactions to Job Characteristics." *Journal of Applied Psychology*, 1971, *55*, 259–286.

3. Lawler, E. E., III. *From the Ground Up: Six Principles for Creating New Logic Organizations*. San Francisco: Jossey-Bass, 1996.

4. Gibson, C. B., and Cohen, S. G. (eds.). *Virtual Teams That Work: Creating Conditions for Virtual Team Effectiveness.* San Francisco: Jossey-Bass, 2003.

5. Galbraith, J. R. *Designing the Customer-Centric Organization: A Guide to Strategy, Structure, and Process.* San Francisco: Jossey-Bass, 2005.

6. Lawler, E. E., III, Ulrich, D., Fitz-enz, J., Madden, J., and Maruca, R. *Human Resources Business Process Outsourcing: Transforming How HR Gets Its Work Done.* San Francisco: Jossey-Bass, 2004.

7. Bossidy, L., and Charan, R. *Execution: The Discipline of Getting Things Done.* New York: Crown Business, 2002.

CHAPTER FIVE

1. Lawler, E. E., III, Mohrman, S. A., and Benson, G. *Organizing for High Performance: Employee Involvement, TQM, Reengineering, and Knowledge Management in the Fortune 1000.* San Francisco: Jossey-Bass, 2001.

2. Lawler, E. E., III. *Rewarding Excellence: Pay Strategies for the New Economy.* San Francisco: Jossey-Bass, 2000.

3. Lawler, *Rewarding Excellence.*

4. Mohrman, A. M., Jr., Resnick-West, S. M., and Lawler, E. E., III. *Designing Performance Appraisal Systems: Aligning Appraisals and Organizational Realities.* San Francisco: Jossey-Bass, 1989.

5. Welch, J., with Welch, S. *Winning.* New York: HarperBusiness, 2005.

6. Ulrich, D., and Smallwood, N. "Capitalizing on Capabilities." *Harvard Business Review,* 2004, *82*(6), 119.

7. Kaplan, R. S., and Norton, D. P. *Strategy Maps.* Boston: Harvard Business School Press, 2004.

8. Lawler, E. E., III, Ulrich, D., Fitz-enz, J., Madden, J., and Maruca, R. *Human Resources Business Process Outsourcing: Transforming How HR Gets Its Work Done.* San Francisco: Jossey-Bass, 2004.

9. Hope, J., and Fraser, R. *Beyond Budgeting: How Managers Can Break Free from the Annual Performance Trap.* Boston: Harvard Business School Press, 2003.

10. Lawler, E. E., III. *From the Ground Up: Six Principles for Creating New Logic Organizations.* San Francisco: Jossey-Bass, 1996.

11. Lawler, *From the Ground Up.*

CHAPTER SIX

1. Human Capital Institute. *ROI in Talent and Talent Management Thought Leader Panel Session.* www.humancapitalinstitute.org. Oct. 5, 2004.

2. Maslow, A. H. *Motivation and Personality*. New York: HarperCollins, 1954.

   Maslow, A. H. *Toward a Psychology of Being*. New York: Wiley, 1968.

3. Lawler, E. E., III. *Motivation in Work Organizations*. Pacific Grove, Calif.: Brooks/Cole, 1973.

4. Lawler, E. E., III, Mohrman, S. A., and Benson, G. S. *Organizing for High Performance: Employee Involvement, TQM, Reengineering, and Knowledge Management in Fortune 1000 Companies*. San Francisco: Jossey-Bass, 2001.

5. Lawler, Mohrman, and Benson, *Organizing for High Performance*.

CHAPTER SEVEN

1. Mobley, W. H. "Intermediate Linkages in the Relationship Between Job Satisfaction and Employee Turnover." *Journal of Applied Psychology*, 1977, *62*, 237–240.

   Mobley, W. H., Griffeth, R. W., Hand, H. H., and Meglino, B. M. "Review and Conceptual Analysis of the Employee Turnover Process." *Psychological Bulletin*, 1979, *86*, 493–522.

   Mobley, W. H., Horner, S. O., and Hollingsworth, A. T. "An Evaluation of Precursors of Hospital Employee Turnover." *Journal of Applied Psychology*, 1978, *63*, 408–414.

   Mowday, R. T., Porter, L. W., and Sterrs, R. M. *Employee-Organization Linkages: The Psychology of Commitment, Absenteeism, and Turnover*. New York: Academic Press, 1982.

2. Steel, R. P., and Griffeth, R. W. "The Elusive Relationship Between Perceived Employment Opportunity and Turnover Behavior: A Methodological or Conceptual Artifact?" *Journal of Applied Psychology*, 1989, *74*, 846–854.

3. Michaels, E., Handfield-Jones, H., and Axelrod, B. *The War for Talent*. Boston: McKinsey, 2001.

4. Welch, J., with Welch, S. *Winning*. New York: HarperBusiness, 2005.

5. Huselid, M., Becker, B., and Beatty, R. *The Workforce Scorecard*. Boston: Harvard Business School Press, 2005.

6. Boudreau, J. W., and Ramstad, P. M. "Talentship and the Evolution of Human Resource Management. From 'Professional Practices' to 'Strategic Talent Decision Science.'" *Human Resource Talent Journal*, *44*(2), 129–136.

   Boudreau, J. W., Ramstad, P. M., and Dowling, P. J. "Global Talentship: Toward a Decision Science Connecting Talent to Global Strategic Success." In W. Mobley and P. Dorfman (eds.), *Advances in Global Leadership* (Vol. 3). Greenwich, Conn.: JAI Press/Elsevier Science, 2003.

7. Cascio, W. F. *Responsible Restructuring: Creative and Profitable Alternatives to Layoffs*. San Francisco: Berrett-Koehler, 2002.

CHAPTER EIGHT

1. Greiner, G., Cummings, T., and Bhambri, A. "When New CEOs Succeed and Fail: 4-D Theory of Strategic Transformation." *Organizational Dynamics*, 2002, *32*(3), 1–17.
   Khurana, R. *Searching for a Corporate Savior: The Irrational Quest for Charismatic CEOs*. Princeton, N.J.: Princeton University Press, 2002.

2. Stogdill, R. M., and Coons, A. E. (eds.). *Leader Behavior: Its Description and Measurement*. Columbus: Bureau of Business Research, Ohio State University, 1957.

3. Tam, P. W. "Boss Talk: Hitting the Ground Running; New CEO of HP Immerses Himself in Studying Company; 'Management Is a Team Sport.'" *Wall Street Journal*, Apr. 4, 2005, p. B1.

4. Neff, T. J., and Citrin, J. M. *Lessons from the Top: The Fifty Most Successful Business Leaders in America—and What You Can Learn from Them*. New York: Doubleday, 2001.

5. O'Toole, J., Pasternack, B., and Bennett, J. "Economically Correct Leadership." *Leader to Leader*, Winter 2001, *19*, 36–42.

6. McCall, M. W., Jr., Lombardo, M. M., and Morrison, A. M. *The Lessons of Experience: How Successful Executives Develop on the Job*. San Francisco: New Lexington Press, 1988.

7. Conger, J. A., and Toegel, G. "360-Degree Feedback: Time for Reinvention." *Academy of Management Learning and Education Journal*, 2003, *2*(3), 297–311.

CHAPTER NINE

1. Lawler, E. E., III. *Rewarding Excellence: Pay Strategies for the New Economy*. San Francisco: Jossey-Bass, 2000.

2. Lawler, E. E., III. *Motivation in Work Organizations*. Pacific Grove, Calif.: Brooks/Cole, 1973.
   Pinder, C. C. *Work Motivation in Organizational Behavior*. Upper Saddle River, N.J.: Prentice Hall, 1998.
   Jenkins, G. D., Jr., Mitra, A., Gupta, N., and Shaw, J. D. "Are Financial Incentives Related to Performance? A Meta-Analytic Review of Empirical Research." *Journal of Applied Research*, 1998, *83*, 777–787.

3. Locke, E. A., and Latham, P. G. *A Theory of Goal Setting and Task Performance*. Upper Saddle River, N.J.: Prentice Hall, 1990.

4. Lawler, *Motivation in Work Organizations*.

5. Hackman, J. R., and Oldham, G. *Work Redesign*. Reading, Mass.: Addison-Wesley, 1980.

6. Lawler, E. E., III. *From the Ground Up: Six Principles for Creating New Logic Organizations.* San Francisco: Jossey-Bass, 1996.

CHAPTER TEN

1. Heneman, R. L. *Merit Pay.* Reading, Mass.: Addison-Wesley, 1992.

2. Worley, C., Bowen, D., and Lawler, E. E., III. "On the Relationship Between Objective Increases in Pay and Employees' Subjective Reactions." *Journal of Organizational Behavior,* 1992, *13,* 559–571.

3. Lawler, E. E., III, Mohrman, S. A., and Benson, G. S. *Organizing for High Performance: Employee Involvement, TQM, Reengineering, and Knowledge Management in Fortune 1000 Companies.* San Francisco: Jossey-Bass, 2001.

4. Lawler, E. E., III. *Rewarding Excellence: Pay Strategies for the New Economy.* San Francisco: Jossey-Bass, 2000.

5. Lawler, E. E., III. "Pay Practices in Fortune 1000 Corporations." *WorldatWork Journal,* 2003, *12*(4), 45–54.

6. Lawler, *Rewarding Excellence.*

7. Biasi, J., Kruse, D., and Bernstein, A. *In the Company of Owners: The Truth About Stock Options (and Why Every Employee Should Have Them).* New York: Basic Books, 2003.

CHAPTER ELEVEN

1. Cummings, T., and Worley, C. *Organization Development and Change.* (8th ed.) Mason, Ohio: Southwestern College Publishing, 2005.

2. Schein, E. H. *Organizational Culture and Leadership.* San Francisco: Jossey-Bass, 1985.

3. Weick, K. E. *The Social Psychology of Organizing.* Reading, Mass.: Addison-Wesley, 1979.

4. Dosi, G., Nelson, R., and Winter, S. *The Nature and Dynamics of Organizational Capabilities.* New York: Oxford University Press, 2000.

5. Lawler, E. E., III. *High Involvement Management.* San Francisco: Jossey-Bass, 1986.

6. Druckman, D., Singer, J., and Van Cott, H. *Enhancing Organizational Performance.* Washington, D.C.: National Academy Press, 1997.

Acknowledgments

David Creelman worked closely with us on the final development of the manuscript. His analytical and writing skills were an enormous help to us, and his humorous prods at academia helped us stay practical. He asked the right questions and made our ideas sharper and more user friendly. Thank you, David.

We are also very grateful to Jerry Porras for writing the Foreword to our book.

Writing this book was greatly facilitated by the help we received from the members of the Center for Effective Organizations at the Marshall School. Special thanks to Dan Canning, Arienne McCracken, and Anjelica Wright for their help in preparing the manuscript and supporting our data-gathering activities.

Chris would like to honor and acknowledge his colleagues, friends, and family. Terri Egan, Ann Feyerherm, Miriam Lacey, Scott Sherman, and Ken Murrell have encouraged me to think differently about strategic change, and the "long gray line" of MSOD students helped shape my perspectives. My kids, Sarah, Hannah, and Sam, have been generous with their love, support, and patience while I wrote and rewrote, and I can hardly imagine my life without Debbie.

Ed would like to acknowledge the many colleagues and friends who have shared their thoughts and insights about organizational change with him. The list starts with Chris Argyris, who was the first to interest me in change, and includes so many others I will not mention them, with two exceptions. Jay Galbraith and Sue Mohrman have worked with me for over two decades and have greatly influenced my thinking. Finally, thank you, Patty, for your love, understanding, and support—you make it all worthwhile.

About the Authors

EDWARD E. LAWLER III is Distinguished Professor of Business and director of the Center for Effective Organizations in the Marshall School of Business at the University of Southern California (USC). He joined USC in 1978 and founded and became director of the university's Center for Effective Organizations in 1979. He has consulted with over one hundred organizations on employee involvement, organizational change, corporate board effectiveness, and compensation, and has been honored as a top contributor to the fields of organizational development, organizational behavior, and compensation.

Lawler has written over three hundred articles, and this is thirty-eighth book. His articles have appeared in leading academic journals as well as in *Fortune, Harvard Business Review*, and leading newspapers. His most recent books include *Rewarding Excellence* (Jossey-Bass, 2000), *Corporate Boards: New Strategies for Adding Value at the Top* (Jossey-Bass, 2001), *Organizing for High Performance* (Jossey-Bass, 2001), *Treat People Right!* (Jossey-Bass, 2003), *Creating a Strategic Human Resources Organization* (Stanford Press, 2003), and *Human Resources Business Process Outsourcing* (Jossey-Bass, 2004).

CHRISTOPHER G. WORLEY (Ph.D., University of Southern California) is a research scientist at the Center for Effective Organizations at the University of Southern California Marshall School of Business. Between 1997 and 2005, he served as director of the Master of Science in Organization Development (MSOD) program at Pepperdine University. He was the Luckman Distinguished Teaching Fellow from 1995 to 2000 and continues as a core faculty member in the MSOD program. His publications include more than twenty articles and chapters, as well as two books: *Integrated Strategic Change* (Addison-Wesley, 1996) and *Organization Development and Change* (Southwestern, 2005).

Worley served as chair for the Organization Development and Change Division and as the Interactive Paper Program chair for the Academy of Management. He is on the advisory board of the Wiley Series on Organization Change and Development and on the editorial boards of the *Journal of Strategic Management Education* and the *Journal of Applied Behavioral Science*. His recent consulting clients include Microsoft, Infonet, American Healthways, British Petroleum, and the Canadian Broadcasting Company.

Index

A

Abercrombie & Fitch, 165
Ability, as determinant of performance, 237; to develop skills and knowledge, 164
Accenture, 133
Acquisitions: for developing new businesses, 110–113, 115–116; for obtaining talent, 175–177
Activity-based costing methods, 144–145
Adelphi, 242–243
Advertising job openings, 170–171, 200–201
Aggressiveness, as element of strategic intent, 64
Alliances, 113–116
Allstate Insurance Company, commitment-to-development contract of, 167–169
Amazon, 43
Ambidextrous organizations, 106
AMD, 43
American Airlines, 35, 57
American Healthways (AMHC), 84–86
AOL, 58
Apple, 82, 259
Applied Materials, 157
AT&T, 15, 83, 259, 291

Attitudes, employee, 194
Automobile industry, changing competitive advantage in, 17–18. *See also specific companies*

B

Ballmer, Steve, 34
Bancroft-Whitney (BW), 60–61
Bank of America, 103
Bell Labs, 15
Berkshire Hathaway, 98, 111
Beyond Budgeting (Hope and Fraser), 145–146
Beyond-budgeting movement, 145–146
"Big rocks" exercise, 54
Birkenstocks, 70
BMG Entertainment, 67–68
Bodyworks, 111
Bonuses, 263–267; impact of, 263–265; linked to risk taking, 278; recommendations on designing, 265–267
Bossidy, Larry, 109
Boudreau, John, 198
BP, 10, 103, 200, 300
Brands: company, 7; employer, 164–171; leadership, 220–223
Breadth, of strategy, 64
Brin, Sergey, 278

Budgets: as performance measures, 143–146, 248; supporting innovation, 144, 226

Budweiser, 33, 64

Built-to-change (b2change) logic, 20–21

Built-to-Change (B2Change) Model, 26–28, 284–285; partial implementation of, 286; role of strategy in, 56–58

Built-to-change (b2change) organizations: designing, 21–22; environment as viewed by, 28–32; strategic features of, 86–87; strategizing in, 37; structure of, 105; types of change and, 20–21. *See also* Transition to b2change organization

Business process outsourcing (BPO), 103–105

Business structures. *See* Organizational structures

Business units: as designed for change, 96–99, 305; measuring performance of, 138–140, 248; new, 107–109, 279–280

C

Canadian Broadcasting Company (CBC), 68–69

Capabilities: competencies vs., 43–44; defined, 38–39; importance of, 39–40; measuring, 141–143, 253–254; orchestration as, 65, 66–67, 298–299; relationship between strategic intent and, 57–58, 69–70; rewarding, 254; as source of competitive advantage, 41–42

Capital One, 93, 134, 229, 233, 300

Career development: discussed in individual performance appraisals, 136; individual employees as responsible for, 167, 206–208, 231–232; internal movement in company for,

199–203; person descriptions as basis of, 189–193. *See also* Commitment-to-development employment strategy; Leadership development; Training

CEOs: committed to human capital management, 180; compensation comparisons made by, 183; earnings from stock options of, 271; hero-leaders as, 217. *See also* Senior management

Change: context demanding, by organizations, 4–8; current view of, 3; disruptive, new companies and, 14–16; environmental, 48–51; identity and, 62–63, 68–69; increased rate of, 1–2, 4, 283; leadership's importance to, 16; organization design to stimulate, 17–19, 21–22; promoting, as natural process, 292–293; publications on, 2; resistance to, 12–13, 161–163; selecting talent favorably responding to, 171–175; strategic, 71, 72, 77–86; transformational, 10–11, 20–21, 76–77, 83–86; types of, 9–11, 20–21; willingness to, 160–163

Change capability, 40

Change management: developing skills in, 299–300; traditional approach to, 14, 20

Charan, Ram, 109

Christensen, Clayton, 10

Ciba Vision, 108

Cisco, 112, 113, 115, 176, 206

Commitment-to-development employment strategy: employment contracts stating, 158, 167–169; minimization of losses with, 162; pros and cons of, 154–155; rewards with, 160

Communication: b2change view of, 78–80; of employer brands, 170–171; of information to em-

ployees, 122–125, 139–140; leadership brand committed to, 221
Companies. *See* New companies;
Organizations
Compaq, 77
Compensation: bonus-pay
approach to, 263–267; executive, 182–183; merit-pay
approach to, 260–263;
perquisites as, 249, 250,
276–277; person-based pay
approach to, 274–276; profit-
sharing approach to, 267–269;
stock ownership as, 270–274,
278–279. *See also* Rewards
Competencies: capabilities vs.,
43–44; defined, 38; managing,
187–188; measuring, 135–136,
141–143, 253–254; relationship
between strategic intent and,
57–58, 69–70; rewarding, 254;
as source of competitive advantage, 40–41, 42–43
Competency modeling, 9
Competitive advantages: changing
nature of, 6–7, 17–18, 19; competencies and capabilities as
sources of, 40–44; series of
temporary, 41, 310–311
Competitors, information about
performance of, 122
Connectors, 79
Contract employees, 174–175
Coors, 36
Corning, 32, 109
Costco, 2, 33
Creating value process: in
B2Change Model, 27, 28, 56,
57, 284–285; as contributor to
organizational effectiveness, 27;
as leveraging competencies and
capabilities, 37–44
Creative destruction, 51
Critical configuration: defined, 36,
45; in virtuous spiral organizations, 45–48
Critical work, management of
employees doing, 195–199

Crucible jobs, 196–197, 228–229
Culture: learning, 210–211; organizational, 33, 58–59
Customers, organizational structures focusing on, 89–91, 105,
307–308

D
Dayton Hudson Corporation,
49–50
Decision making, 149–152; in
b2change organizations,
151–152; employee involve-
ment in, 149, 151–152; trans-
parency in, 150, 152
Dell, Michael, 129, 233
Dell (company), 15, 45, 129–130
Delta, 35, 57
Deploy Solutions, 124
Designing process: in B2Change
Model, 27, 28, 285; as contributor to organizational effectiveness, 27; as integrating elements of organization, 44–45.
See also Organization design
Development. *See* Career development; Commitment-to-development employment strategy;
Leadership development
Differentiation, as element of
strategic intent, 64–65
Disruptive technology, 10
Downsizing, managing, 185–186,
196, 203–206
Dynamic alignment: defined,
44–45; requirements for, 306;
in virtuous spiral organizations,
45–48

E
Ebbers, Bernard, 217
Eckert, Bob, 230
EDS, 133
Effectiveness: measuring, of individual performance appraisals,
130; need for dynamic view of,
25. *See also* Organizational
effectiveness

Egan, Al, 23–25, 28, 33
Electronic Arts, 29
Email, resistance to using, 12–13
Employees: communicating information to, 122–124, 139–140; critical, management of, 195–199; involved in decision making, 149, 151–152; measuring attitudes of, 194; measuring performance of, 127–137; moving internally in company, 199–203; person descriptions for, 189–193; recruiting former, 177–178; as responsible for career development, 167, 206–208, 231–232; viewing change as natural, 292–293. See also Human capital; Talent
Employer brands: communicating, 170–171; developing, 165–169
Employment contracts: as basis of employer brands, 165–169; as change enablers for organizations, 169; commitment-to-develop stated in, 158, 167–169; employment strategies stated in, 157–159; rewards and, 159–160, 166–167
Employment strategies, 154–159; commitment-to-development approach to, 154–155, 158, 160, 162, 167–169; in employment contracts, 157–159; travel-light approach to, 155–157, 158–159, 160
Enron, 34, 217, 242–243
Environment: b2change organizations' view of, 28–32; business, leadership behaviors adjusted to, 215–216, 221–222; external, organizational identity focused on, 291–292
Environmental change, virtuous spiral organizations and, 48–51
Environmental scenarios: in B2Change Model, 26–27; as driving strategizing, 28–32; for Internet providers, 29–31; as providing context for strategy,

56–57. See also Scenario planning
Executive compensation, 182–183
Expectancy theory: goals and, 241–242; motivation and, 237–238, 239–240, 243
Exxon, 33, 34
ExxonMobil, 286

F
Failure, rewarding, 280–281
Fairchild Electronics, 43
Federal Express (FedEx), 69, 198
Feedback, customer, 91
Fiat, 191
Ford Motor Company, 39–40, 70
Fortune 1000 companies: changing list of, 1–2; employment contracts of, 166–167; with profit-sharing plans, 267
Fraser, Robin, 145–146
Front-back structures, 100–103, 104–105
Fuji, 114
Future, planning for, 295–297. See also Scenario planning

G
Galbraith, Jay, 90
Gates, Bill, 34, 46, 294
Gateway, 45
General Electric (GE), 15; breadth of strategy of, 64; business unit structuring of, 98, 99; change-management capability of, 299; leadership development at, 180, 224–225, 235, 300; ranking system at, 133, 186; reorientation decisions by, 81; risk taking rewarded at, 278; Six Sigma capability of, 42; as virtuous spiral organization, 48
General Mills, 151
General Motors (GM), 65, 76, 286
Globalization, 4
Goals: impact on motivation, 241–242; setting, performance appraisals and, 130–131, 147–148

Google, 278–279
Google Lab Aptitude Test
    (GLAT), 170–171
Gore, Bill, 227
Gore (company), 227–228, 273
Grove, Andy, 37
GTE, 291

H
Hallmark, 191
Hamel, Gary, 38
Handfield-Jones, Helen, 185
Hasbro, 199
Hay Management Consultants,
    8–9, 10
Hewlett-Packard (HP), 15, 76–77,
    106, 309
Honda, 38
Honeywell, 15–16, 42, 107
Hope, Jeremy, 145–146
Human capital: increasing impor-
    tance of, 5, 6, 7–8, 153, 179;
    need for "mobile," 169. *See also*
    Employees; Talent
Human capital management,
    179–212; by creating career
    opportunities within company,
    199–203; of critical work and
    employees, 195–199; human
    capital measurement and,
    186–195; of layoffs and down-
    sizing, 185–186, 196, 203–206;
    senior management committed
    to, 180; of training, 206–211; of
    turnover, 181–187. *See also*
    Recruitment; Selection process
Human capital measurement,
    186–195; importance of,
    186–187; for managing skills
    and competencies, 187–188;
    person descriptions for,
    189–193; useful metrics in,
    193–195
Human nature, resistance to
    change as, 12–13
Human resources consulting,
    change in product offered by,
    8–9
Hurd, Mark, 217

I
IBM: intranet HR tools of,
    201–202, 233; jam sessions at,
    125; leadership development at,
    235; MS-DOS licensed to, 46;
    outsourcing by, 103; responses
    of, to environmental changes,
    48–49, 51; retirement plans at,
    259
Identity: at center of B2Change
    Model, 27, 284; as central to
    strategizing, 33–34, 57; clarify-
    ing, 58–61; as component of
    strategy, 55, 56; consistency of
    strategic intent with, 68–69;
    creating change-friendly,
    288–293; defined, 33, 55; hon-
    oring, in change efforts, 62–63,
    68–69; importance to perform-
    ance, 34; leadership brand
    reflecting, 220–221; reward
    systems and, 251–253; transfor-
    mation of, 76–77, 83–86,
    252–253
Immelt, Jeff, 224, 278, 294–295
In-N-Out Burger, 165
India, call centers in, 18
Information, 119–126; communi-
    cating, to employees, 122–124,
    139–140; gathering, 119–121;
    transparency of, 121–122
Information systems: characteris-
    tics of good, 125; silo problem
    with, 120–121
Innovation: budgets supporting,
    144, 226; capability for, 39, 41;
    failure of attempts at, 280–281;
    by new companies, 14,
    106–107; rewards for, 277–280.
    See also New businesses, devel-
    oping
Intangibles: increasing importance
    of, 6–7; measuring and report-
    ing, 140–141
Intel: aggressiveness of, 64;
    change-friendly budgeting at,
    144; change-management capa-
    bility of, 299; cross-calibration
    ratings meetings at, 134;

Fairchild Electronics and, 43; new venture business structure used by, 107; strategic shift by, 50; training of existing employees by, 157

InterContinental Hotels, 142, 148

International Paper, 103, 145, 151

International trade, 4

Internet: environmental scenarios for providers of, 29–31; rapid evolution of, 5. *See also* Intranet systems

Interviews, on individuals' response to change, 172–173

Intranet systems: individual performance appraisal information on, 136–137; intangibles measured using, 141; job openings posted on, 200–201; leadership assessment using, 233

J

Japan, automobile industry of, 17–18

JCPenney, 2

Jet Blue, 35, 250

Job descriptions, 92–93, 282

Job evaluation, human resources consulting and, 8–9

Job openings: advertising, 170–171; intranet posting of, 200–201; transparency of, 231

Job satisfaction: relationship between motivation, performance and, 243–245; rewards and, 181–184; turnover and, 184–186

Jobs: crucible, 196–197, 228–229; individuals' history of changing, 174; organizational structures without, 92–94, 305–306; rewards and designing, 245–247; shifting focus from, to individuals, 274–275, 282, 307–308; underestimating skills needed for, 154

Jockey International, 70

Johnson & Johnson (J&J), 98, 108

Joint ventures, 109

Just-in-time training, 208–209

K

Kmart, 2

Knight, Phil, 46

Knowledge: as focus of person descriptions, 190–191; individual ability to develop new, 164; for organizational effectiveness, 5–6

Kodak, 155–156

Kozlowski, Dennis, 217

Krispy Kreme, 7

Kroger, 286

L

L-3 Communications, 98

Lafley, A. G., 226

Lay, Ken, 217

Layoffs, managing, 185–186, 196, 203–206

Leaders, managers vs., 213–215

Leadership, 213–235; assessing performance by, 233–234, 235; behaviors of, adjusted to business environment, 215–216, 221–222; capability of diverse styles of, 223–225; difficulty of managing, 219–220; hero-leader style of, 217, 219; importance to organizational change, 16; organizational performance and, 25; shared, 216–219, 226–228, 235; situational, 221; yellow-light, 222

Leadership brand, 220–223

Leadership development: at all levels of organization, 225–226, 228; selecting candidates for, 228; senior management's role in, 229–230, 234–235; with shared leadership, 226–228; through job experiences, 228–229; transparency of program for, 230–233. *See also* Career development; Commitment-to-development employment strategy; Training

Learning, rewards for, 209–211

Lessons from the Top (Neff and Citrin), 217

The Limited, 111–112

Lincoln Electric, 250

Listening, in performance appraisals, 131

Logic: b2change, 20–21; strategic, 65, 80–81

Loyalty, 166, 167, 208

Lucent, 32

Lufthansa, 114

M

Management. *See* Change management; Human capital management; Senior management

Managers, leaders vs., 213–215

March of Dimes, 83–84

Marriott Corporation, 176–177

Maslow's hierarchy of needs, 159, 160, 238

Matrix structures, 99–100

Mattel, 199

Mavens, 79

McKinsey, 137

Mead Paper, 107

Measurement: of capabilities, 141–143, 253–254; of competencies, 135–136, 141–143, 253–254; of effectiveness of individual appraisals, 130; human capital, 186–195; of intangibles, 140–141. *See also* Performance measurement

Medco, 82

Merck, 82

Mergers, 110

Merit-pay plans, 260–263

Microsoft, 106; change-management capability of, 299; identity of, 33–34, 289; orchestration by, 66; as virtuous spiral organization, 46–47, 51

Miller Beer, 64

Mobility, 169, 208

Montgomery Ward, 2

Motivation: customer feedback as, for change, 91; impact of goals on, 241–243; information on competitors' performance as, 122; relationship between job satisfaction and, 243–244; rewards and, 163, 237–239

Motorola, 39, 42

N

Nabisco, 25–26

Needs, rewards and, 159, 238

New businesses, developing: acquisitions for, 110–113, 115–116; alliances for, 113–116; difficulty of, 105–107; joint ventures for, 109; mergers for, 110; new business units for, 107–109, 279–280; by new companies, 14, 106–107. *See also* Innovation

New companies: disruptive change and, 14–16; increasing number of, 1–2; new businesses developed by, 14, 106–107; strategic logic and, 65

Nike, 46, 56

Nordstrom, 151, 165, 307–308

Nortel, 32

O

Oracle, 188

Orchestration: building capability for, 298–303; as element of strategic intent, 65–67; initiation of strategic change by, 78–80; of reorientation, 81–83

Organization design: with goal of stimulating change, 17–19, 21–22; importance of, 6–8; traditional, stability as goal of, 13–16, 18; view of change and, 3–4. *See also* Designing process

Organizational change. *See* Change

Organizational culture, 33, 58–59

Organizational effectiveness:

creating function in, 300–303; knowledge as central to, 5–6; need for dynamic view of, 25; primary contributors to, 27, 28. *See also* Effectiveness

Organizational structures, 88–117; acquisitions as, 110–113, 115–116; alliances as, 113–116; business process outsourcing (BPO) as, 103–105; business units as, 96–99, 107–109, 279–280; customer focus of, 89–91, 105, 307–308; for developing new businesses, 105–116, 279–280; front-back structures as, 100–103; importance of, 88–89; joint ventures as, 109; linking reward systems and, 245–251; matrix structures as, 99–100; mergers as, 110; teams as, 94–95; virtual work relationships as, 95–97; without jobs, 92–94, 305–306

Organizations: ambidextrous, 106; capabilities of, 38–40; competencies of, 38; context demanding change by, 4–8; measuring performance of, 140–143; traditional, strategizing in, 37. *See also* Built-to-change (b2change) organizations; New companies

Orvis Company, 131

O'Toole, Jim, 222

Outsourcing, 103–105

Owens Corning, 259

Ownership mentality. *See* Stock ownership

P

Palmisano, Samuel J., 125

Pay. *See* Compensation

PECO Energy Corporation, 133

People Express, 57

PepsiCo, 103, 151, 235, 275, 299

Performance (individual): equation on determinants of, 237; job satisfaction and, 243–245; reward systems and, 239–245.

See also Performance appraisals

Performance (organizational): bonus-pay plans based on, 264–265, 266, 267; communicating information about, to employees, 122–125; importance of identity to, 34; leadership and, 25; profit-sharing plans and, 268; transparency of information about, of competitors, 122

Performance appraisals, 127–137; career development discussed in, 136; common problems with, 127; eliminating, 127–128; goal setting and, 130–131, 147–148; intranet systems for information from, 136–137; of leadership behaviors, 233–234, 235; listening in, 131; measuring effectiveness of, 130; objective measures used in, 131–132; ratings in, 132–135; rewards discussed in, 136; of senior management, 128–130; skill and competency assessment in, 135–136

Performance management systems, 187–188

Performance measurement, 126–149; budgets used for, 143–146, 248; of business units, 138–140, 248; coordinated system for, 146–149; issues in developing system for, 126; of organizations, 140–143; reward systems and, 247–248; of teams, 137–138. *See also* Performance appraisals

Performance motivation. *See* Motivation

Perquisites, 249, 250, 276–277

Person descriptions: developing, 189–193; example of, 192

Person-based pay, 274–276

Planar Systems, 124–125

Prahalad, C. K., 38

PricewaterhouseCoopers, 137

Procter & Gamble (P&G): crucible jobs at, 196–197; high-involvement decision making at, 151; leadership development at, 226; new venture business units used by, 107; outsourcing by, 103; person-based pay at, 275; as virtuous spiral organization, 47
Profit sharing, 267–269
Promotion, merit-pay plans and, 262–263
Proximity: defined, 29; importance of, 284; pursuing, to transition to b2change organization, 293–298
Prudential, 145

R
Ratings, in individual performance appraisals, 132–135
Recruitment: ability to develop skills and knowledge as consideration in, 164; of former employees, 177–178; of individuals who respond favorably to change, 171–175; performance motivation and, 163; stock options used in, 272; willingness to change as consideration in, 160–163. See also Selection process; Talent
Reorientation. See Strategic reorientation
Resistance to change, 12–13, 161–163
Retention: bonus-pay plans and, 263–264; creating opportunities within company to promote, 199–203; of critical employees, 196–197; seniority-based rewards and, 258. See also Turnover
Retirement plans, 259
Reward systems: identity and, 251–253; importance of, 254–255; linking organizational structures and, 245–251; motivation and, 237–239; performance and, 239–245; strategic intent and, 253–254; to support change, 281–282
Rewards: discussed in individual performance appraisals, 136; employment contracts and, 159–160, 166–167; hierarchical vs. egalitarian, 249–251, 276–277; job satisfaction and, 181–184; for learning, 209–211; needs and, 159, 238; performance motivation and, 163, 237–239; for risk taking and innovation, 277–281; seniority-based, 167, 257–259; with shared leadership, 226–227. See also Compensation
Risk taking: dealing with failure from, 280–281; rewards for, 277–280
Ritz-Carlton, 151, 176–177
Robustness, of strategic intent, 67–68
Rock, Milton, 8, 10

S
Salespeople, 79
SAP, 188
Sarbanes-Oxley Act, 140
SAS, 137, 189, 211
Satisfaction. See Job satisfaction
Sauer-Danfoss, 96
Scandals, corporate, 217, 242–243
Scenario planning, 293–298. See also Environmental scenarios
Schumpter, Joseph, 51
Sears, 2
SEI Investments, 96
Selection process: importance of, 185; for leadership development opportunities, 228; performance management system and, 188. See also Recruitment
Senior management: committed to human capital management, 180; leadership development

role of, 229–230, 234–235;
leadership modeled by,
229–230; leadership shared by,
216–219, 235; performance
appraisals of, 128–130
Seniority: layoffs based on, 205;
rewards based on, 167,
257–259
Shared leadership, 216–219;
advantages of, 218–219, 235;
leadership development with,
226–228; rewards with,
226–227
Siebel Systems, 147–148
Situational leadership, 221
Six Sigma quality capability,
41–42, 193
Skills: ability to develop new, 164;
assessing, in individual performance appraisals, 135–136;
critical, employees with,
197–198; developing change
management, 299–300; as focus
of person descriptions,
190–191; managing, 187–188;
underestimating, required for
jobs, 154
Smallwood, Norm, 141–142
Sony, 38, 106
Southwest Airlines: advertising by,
170; identity of, 33, 55, 289;
innovation by, 14; performance
of, 35, 57–58; reward system at,
250; strategic intent of, 55;
strategy of, 55, 57–58; as virtuous spiral organization, 49
Stability: as goal of traditional
organization design, 13–16, 18;
individual preference for, 160,
161; reframing identity based
on, 290–293
Staff reductions, managing,
185–186, 196, 203–206
Star alliance, 114
Starbucks, 165
Start-ups. See New companies
Steinway, 297–298
Stock options. See Stock ownership

Stock ownership: impact of, 196,
270–272; linked to innovation,
278–279; as support for change,
272–274
Stock price, intangibles' importance to, 6–7
Strategic adjustments, 9, 20,
75–76, 304–308
Strategic change, as phase of
strategizing process, 71, 72,
77–86
Strategic choice, as phase of
strategizing process, 71, 72,
75–77
Strategic intent: as component of
strategy, 55–56; critical configuration and, 36; defined, 35,
38, 55, 63; determinants of
quality of, 67–70; elements of,
63–67; orchestration as element
of, 298; reformulation of, with
reorientation, 10, 20, 76, 77,
80–83; relationship between
competencies and capabilities
and, 57–58, 69–70; reward system and, 253–254
Strategic logic, 65, 80–81
Strategic reorientation, 10, 20, 76,
77, 80–83
Strategic review, as phase of strategizing process, 71, 72, 73–75
Strategizing process, 71–86; in
B2Change Model, 27, 28,
284–285; in b2change vs. traditional organizations, 37, 70–71;
as contributor to organizational
effectiveness, 27; defined, 35;
diagram of, 72; environmental
scenarios as driving, 28–32; features of b2change organizations
important for, 86–87; identity
as central to, 33–34, 57; as pivotal conversation, 35–37;
strategic change phase of, 71,
77–86; strategic choice phase
of, 71, 75–77; strategic review
phase of, 71, 73–75
Strategy: components of, 55–56;
implementing, 37, 76; role of,

in B2Change Model, 56–58; vs. continuous strategizing, 21. *See also* Strategic intent
Strategy Maps (Kaplan and Norton), 142
Structuring. *See* Organizational structures
Sun Microsystems, 96
Svenska Handelsbanken, 146
SWOT analysis, 28, 31
Sysco, 112–113

T
Talent, 153–178; acquisitions for obtaining, 175–177; attracting, 164–171; employment strategies and, 154–159; leadership, 219–225; reward strategy and, 159–160, 239. *See also* Employees; Human capital
Tangible assets, declining importance of, 7
Target, 50, 199
Teams: decision making in, 151; as designed for change, 94–95; measuring performance of, 137–138; structuring work to motivate, 246–247
Teamwork, rewarding, 252
Technology, disruptive, 10
Teerlink, Rich, 230
Telecommunications, 5
Teleworking, 13
Temporary employment, 174–175
Terminating employees, 185–186, 196, 203–206
Thatcher, Margaret, 83
360-degree appraisals, 129–130, 233–234
3M: budgeting at, 144, 226; competencies and capabilities of, 38, 39, 41; identity of, 289
Toyota, 75–76
Toys "R" Us, 43
Training, 206–211; to develop change management skills, 300; just-in-time, 208–209; measuring investment in, 195; responsibility for decisions about,

206–208; rewarding learning and, 209–211. *See also* Career development; Leadership development
Transformational change, 10–11, 20–21, 76–77, 83–86
Transition to b2change organization, 286–311; adopting strategic adjustment as normal to, 304–308; building orchestration capability to, 298–303; creating change-friendly identity to, 288–293; managing process of, 286–288; pursuing proximity to, 293–298; seeking virtuous spirals to, 308–311
Transparency: of bonus-pay plan, 265, 266–267; in decision making, 150, 152; of individual performance appraisal information, 136–137; of information in organization, 121–122; of leadership development program, 230–233; in reward systems, 240–241
Travel-light employment strategy: employment contracts stating, 158–159; example of company with, 155–156; pros and cons of, 156–157; rewards with, 160
Trust, reward systems and, 240–241
Turnover, 181–187; employer satisfaction and, 184–185; management of, 185–186; measuring, 193–194; reward-satisfaction link and, 181–184
TWA, 82
Tyco, 217

U
Ulrich, Dave, 141–142
Unisys, 11
United Airlines, 35, 58, 114
United Technologies Corporation (UTC), 99, 209–210, 211
University of Southern California (USC), 257
UPS, 69–70

V
Victoria's Secret, 111
Virtual work relationships, 95–97
Virtuous spirals: described,
   45–46, 308; environmental
   change as threat to, 48–51;
   examples of organizations with,
   46–48; model of dynamic,
   51–52; seeking, to transition to
   b2change organization,
   308–311

W
W.L. Gore, 227–228, 273
Wal-Mart: competitor for, 50;
   employee meetings at, 124;
   growth of, 2, 199; structure and
   identity of, 89, 289
The War for Talent (Handfield-
   Jones), 185–186
Washington Mutual, 64
WD-40, 64
Welch, Jack, 81, 133, 186, 278
Whole Foods, 151, 250, 265
Willingness to change, 160–163
WorldCom, 217, 242–243

X
Xerox, 14, 15, 81, 114

Y
Yellow-light leadership, 222